THE JEWISH PEOPLE IN AMERICA

THE JEWISH PEOPLE IN AMERICA

A Series Sponsored by the American Jewish Historical Society

Henry L. Feingold, General Editor

Volume I
A Time for Planting
The First Migration, 1654–1820
Eli Faber

Volume II
A Time for Gathering
The Second Migration, 1820–1880
Hasia R. Diner

Volume III
A Time for Building
The Third Migration, 1880–1920
Gerald Sorin

Volume IV
A Time for Searching
Entering the Mainstream, 1920–1945
Henry L. Feingold

Volume V
A Time for Healing
American Jewry since World War II
Edward S. Shapiro

A Time for Planting
The First Migration

THE JEWISH PEOPLE IN AMERICA

A TIME FOR PLANTING

The First Migration
1654–1820

Eli Faber

The Johns Hopkins University Press

Baltimore and London

Second printing, 1992

The Johns Hopkins University Press
701 West 40th Street
Baltimore, Maryland 21211-2190
The Johns Hopkins Press Ltd., London

Library of Congress Cataloging-in-Publication Data

Faber, Eli, 1943–
A time for planting : the first migration, 1654–1820 /
Eli Faber.
     p.   cm. — (The Jewish People in America ; v. 1)
Includes bibliographical references and index.
ISBN 0-8018-4343-X (alk. paper)
  1. Jews—United States—History—17th century.
2. Jews—United States—History—18th century.
3. Sephardim—United States—History. 4. United States—
Ethnic relations. I. Title. II. Series.
E184.J5F3   1992
973'.04924—dc20   91-45341

In Honor of My Parents
Salamon and Gertrude Faber

CONTENTS

Contents

Illustrations follow page 68.

SERIES EDITOR'S FOREWORD

OVER the generations, there has been much change in the content of Jewish culture. Some writers argue that in the benevolent and absorbent atmosphere of America, Jewish culture has been thinned beyond recognition. But one ingredient of that culture—a deep appreciation of history—continues to receive the highest priority. The motto on the seal of the American Jewish Historical Society enjoins us, "Remember the Days of Old." It is taken from the Pentateuch, itself a historical chronicle.

Indeed, the Jewish community boasts almost one hundred local historical societies and two professional archives for preserving source material. The cherishing of its history goes beyond any biblical or cultural injunction. History is especially important for Diaspora communities because corporate memory rather than territorial space ultimately ensures their survival. That is what Bal Shem Tov, founder of the Hasidic movement, may have meant when centuries ago he counseled his followers that "memory is the key to redemption."

The American Jewish Historical Society offers this history of the Jews in America to both the Jewish community and the general reading public as a repository of memory. For Jewish readers this series provides an opportunity to enrich their self-understanding, quickening Jewry's energies and enhancing its potential for survival. We hope to remind the general reading public that, at a time when the American dream may be found wanting, the American Jewish experience is evidence that the promise of America can still be realized. Without the opportunities, freedom, and openness found in this land, American Jewry would not have been able to realize its energies and talents and become what it is today.

How that has happened over the generations is a story the American

Jewish Historical Society is committed to tell. In fact, the society could think of no better way to honor its historical task and its rich hundred-year history than by recounting that story through this series. No single volume by a single historian can do justice to the multilevel historical experience of American Jewry. Drawing on the talents of five historians with a common vision and purpose, this series offers a historical synthesis at once comprehensible to the intelligent lay reader and useful to the professional historian. Each of these volumes integrates common themes: the origins of Jewish immigrants, their experience of settling in America, their economic and social life, their religious and educational efforts, their political involvement, and the change the American Jewish community experienced over time.

Predictably, the project encountered many conceptual problems. One of the most vexing stemmed from the difficulty of classifying American Jewry. To treat American Jews solely as members of a religious denomination, as was once the practice of the Reform branch, was a distortion, because most American Jews are not religious in the sectarian sense. And though some sociologists have classified Jews as a race, clearly that category does not adequately describe how they differ from other Americans. More than other ethnic communities, American Jewry is influenced by two separate historical streams: the American and the Jewish. To be sure, American Jewry is but one of the many ethnic groups woven into the American national fabric. Yet it is something beyond that as well. It is part of an evolving religious civilization that has persisted for millennia. This persistent tension between assimilation and group survival—the will to remain part of the universal community of Israel—is well evinced in the volumes of this series.

In this first volume, Eli Faber deals directly with how that tension between accommodation and group survival was played out in the setting of colonial America by cosmopolitan Sephardic and Ashkenazic Jews. Confronted by a host society reluctant to fully accept Jews as part of civil society, the Sephardic and Ashkenazic Jews in colonial America were the first to establish a model of how these pulls could be balanced to assure survival.

On behalf of the society, I thank the many participants of this venture, which had its beginnings over fifteen years ago as a way of commemorating the society's 1992 centennial. Dr. Abraham Kanof, Rosemary Krensky, and the late David Lubart provided initial support for the project. Dr. Kanof has been repeatedly generous in his financial contributions over the years, while the Max and Dora L. Starr Foundation has provided additional welcome assistance. The authors, Eli Faber, Hasia R. Diner, Gerald Sorin, and Edward S. Shapiro, deserve special thanks. In addition, we are grateful to Ruth B. Fein and the late Phil Fine for their efforts on behalf of the project. For their technical and legal expertise in making publishing arrangements for the series, Robert L. Weinberg and Franklin Feldman need to be singled out. Words of thanks also go to Henry Y. K. Tom, executive editor of the Johns Hopkins University Press, and to his colleagues for their dedication and professionalism in bringing the society's dream to realization. Last, a special appreciation is in order for the society's untiring staff, particularly Bernard Wax and the late Nathan M. Kaganoff, for their administrative support.

Henry L. Feingold
General Editor

PREFACE AND ACKNOWLEDGMENTS

THAT a series summarizing more than three centuries of the history of the Jewish people in America should appear in 1992 is appropriate for several reasons. It is the centennial year of the American Jewish Historical Society, as well as the quincentennial year of Columbus's discovery of America, an event precipitated by developments during the fifteenth century in the Iberian peninsula that link also to the first settlement by Jews on the North American mainland in 1654. The series appears, moreover, during a period of debate about the extent to which multiculturalism should be acknowledged in the nation's classrooms. Often impassioned, this controversy is the latest phase of a perennial discussion about the role of ethnicity in American life, the preservation of ethnic, racial, and religious identities by each particular group, and the obligation of the general community to acknowledge the experiences and the contributions of each.

The subjects of this volume, the Jews of early America, were among the first Jews in the modern world able to choose among separation from the larger society, acculturation, and assimilation. These have been choices faced by successive waves of immigrants to America, Jews and non-Jews alike, and often by their native-born descendants. The history of early American Jewry is, therefore, an early chapter in the more general history of the many ethnic, racial, and religious groups that, together, have shaped American civilization and produced a complex multicultural society.

Participation in the creation of this series was first suggested to me by the late Richard B. Morris, Gouverneur Morris Professor of History at Columbia University. A scholar of great erudition and insight, Richard

B. Morris is sorely missed by those whom he inspired with his zest for life, for learning, and for the written word. His curiosity about early America knew no bounds and extended to the Jews of colonial and revolutionary America, about whom he wrote several pieces. I am grateful that I was privileged to be his student and to work under his direction on the John Jay Papers Publication Project at Columbia University, one of his many undertakings in his later years. I regret that I cannot present a copy of this work to him as a token of gratitude.

To my colleague Henry L. Feingold, series editor, I extend great appreciation for the opportunity to participate in this series. Professor Feingold conceived of the undertaking and then worked tirelessly to give it life. He shaped and organized it with infinite patience, and, above all, with fidelity to his belief in the independence of each author. To Professor Feingold and to my colleagues Daniel Gasman, John Cammett, Leo Hershkowitz, and Carol Ruth Berkin I extend appreciation for much sound advice and many good suggestions for improving the manuscript. Failures to heed their advice are, of course, my own.

I acknowledge, as well, the assistance of Henry Y. K. Tom, the executive editor of the Johns Hopkins University Press; the skill and perceptiveness of Diane Hammond, copy editor; the helpfulness of the staff of the Jewish Division of the New York Public Library; the aid of Gina Hsin of the American Jewish Historical Society library; and the efforts of Bernard Wax of the society to bring the series to fruition and to further my contribution to it.

I owe the greatest appreciation of all to my wife, Alane Faber, and my daughter, Elizabeth Sara Faber. I thank them for their love and friendship, their tolerance and trust. I hope that the present work proves worthy of their confidence during the days apart as work upon it proceeded.

A Time for Planting
The First Migration

INTRODUCTION

For CENTURIES they had prayed daily to God to gather them from the four corners of the earth and restore them to the ancient homeland from which they had been exiled. Dispersed throughout Europe, North Africa, Asia, and now the Western Hemisphere, the Jewish people yearned for the day when the ingathering of Israel foretold by the prophets of old would lead them back to Zion. And yet in Charleston, South Carolina, in the year 1806, a member of the Jewish community rose to praise America and expressed the hope that the United States might now be the place to which the Jewish people would be gathered. Citing the freedom, civic equality, and dignity his country accorded Jews, describing it as a promised land and a New Jerusalem, Myer Moses called upon God to transport the Jewish people to America. "Collect together thy long scattered people," he exclaimed, "and let their gathering place be in this land of milk and honey."[1]

The Jews who began gathering in America in 1654—few in number, certainly no more than some twenty-five hundred when Myer Moses spoke—were among the first Jews in the modern world to live in a tolerant environment. Though for the most part excluded from voting and officeholding during the colonial and revolutionary eras, they mingled freely with fellow Americans, conducted commercial ventures with them, intermarried in some cases, and in general encountered comparatively little in the way of anti-Semitism. In the aftermath of the American Revolution, American Jews gradually achieved civic equality by acquiring the right to vote, to serve in office, and otherwise to participate in civic affairs as fully empowered citizens. It was no wonder, then, that Myer Moses would call upon God for an even greater gathering of Israel in the United States—or that Sampson Simson, an early Jewish graduate of Columbia College, would, in the commencement oration he delivered in 1800 in Hebrew (in New York's Saint Paul's Chapel, at that), call down God's blessings upon the people of the United States, adding: "Long live the Republic in honor and respectability." So, too, Isaac H. Levy, in 1798—during his commercial voyage from New York to Madras and Calcutta in the company of another American Jew—celebrated the Fourth of July: "This being the anniversary of American independence," he explained, "we kept it as was becoming American citizens."[2]

For the Jews of early America, however, the blessings of toleration, equality, and citizenship brought in their wake important questions regarding the maintenance of Jewish tradition and Jewish distinctiveness. Given the opportunity to participate in the larger society, to what extent would American Jews be able to preserve their ethnic identity and religion? What were to be the limits, if any, of what is today referred to as acculturation? Isaac Levy resolved the problem for himself by observing not only the Fourth of July during his voyage to India but also the festival of Passover, noting that "this being the first day of Pesach, Mr. Moses and myself kept it with strictness, as much so as was possible on board a ship. God send we may spend the next one in New York." Levy and Moses, and others like them, were among the first Jews in the modern world to explore the blending of traditions and cultures, to experiment with voluntary acculturation, and to confront their implications for the maintenance of the group's distinctiveness. Thus the early American Jewish experience constitutes not only a chapter in the history of Jewish ethnicity and religion in the modern world generally but an early case study in the development of the United States as a multiethnic and multiracial society. The tension between loyalty to one's ethnic group and the preservation of that group's distinctiveness, on the one hand, and acculturation, identification with the larger society, and assimilation, on the other, constitutes the underlying theme of the pages that follow.

The Jews who gathered in America between 1654 and 1820—whether Sephardic or Ashkenazic, from Portugal or England, Jamaica or Holland, Curaçao or Poland—did not create a literature in which they explored the meaning of ethnicity, debated the merits of acculturation, or weighed the balance between particularism and affiliation with the greater society. By their actions, however, they demonstrated that they were quite aware of these issues, which have been central to political discourse and social policy throughout the course of American history, and which have come to dominate much of modern Jewish life as well.

CHAPTER ONE

ORIGINS AND ANTECEDENTS

EARLY in the autumn of 1654, early enough to observe the religious new year in their new home, twenty-three Jews aboard the bark *Sainte Catherine* sailed through the lovely, spacious bay that led to Manhattan Island and made landfall there at the town of New Amsterdam. Most of them, perhaps even all, had journeyed earlier in their lives from Europe to the New World, but this particular voyage had begun in northeastern Brazil and had probably taken them to the islands of Jamaica and Cuba on their route northward. Although several Jewish merchants from the Netherlands had preceded them by several months, these twenty-three created the first permanent Jewish settlement in North America, and it is their arrival that began American Jewish history.[1]

During the next century and a half, other Jews from Europe followed the first twenty-three, settling not only in New Amsterdam (renamed New York when the English captured it in 1664) but also in Newport, Charleston, Savannah, and Philadelphia. On the eve of the American Revolution, approximately twenty-five hundred Jews resided in these and such other locations as New Haven, Connecticut, and Easton, Pennsylvania.[2] Although they constituted far less than 1 percent of the American population during the eighteenth century, their presence was noteworthy enough to attract the attention of the author of a significant traveler's account in the 1740s, the frequent interest of a future president of Yale College during the 1760s and 1770s, and the assurances of George Washington when he assumed the presidency that they were welcome as citizens of the fledgling republic.[3]

Many among the original twenty-three could trace their origins to the Iberian peninsula, where Jews in abundant numbers had thrived in earlier centuries. During the Middle Ages, the Jews of Spain had flourished under Moslem rule, participating in the economic and public life of the country and simultaneously creating a rich Hebraic culture of their own. With the resurgence of the Christians in Spain, who gradually reestablished hegemony from their bases in the northern part of the peninsula and ultimately drove out the Moslems, the tide began to turn against the Jews. In 1391, massacres of Jews erupted across Spain, and thousands of them consequently converted to Christianity, accepting baptism in order to preserve their lives.

During the following century, mass conversions recurred, while new economic and social policies promulgated by the civil rulers more and more circumscribed the lives of those who chose not to convert. The final blow came in 1492, with the decree that all Jews must forthwith leave Spain. The expulsion of 1492—a turning point in Jewish history recalled to this day on the annual religious day of mourning— brought to a resounding end the open presence of Jews in that country. Spanish Jews dispersed around the Mediterranean and beyond, seeking to reestablish their lives and careers in southeastern Europe and Turkey, western North Africa, Egypt, or Italy. Significantly for early American Jewish history, thousands sought refuge in the closest haven of all, neighboring Portugal, where their initial welcome would sour in only five years.[4]

Within Spain, the New Christians, the term applied to Jews who had accepted conversion in 1391, often prospered and achieved prominence in public life. By the beginning of the 1430s, however, the Spanish church began to denounce them as heretics and blasphemers, for many of the New Christians secretly practiced Judaism and, in the presumed safety of their homes, transmitted it to their children.[5] Outwardly Christian but often secretly Jewish, New Christians also incurred the wrath of the nobility because of their frequent social prominence as well as their influence upon the governance of the realm. In addition, the general population despised them because of their success as financiers and their service as tax collectors. Had they remained Jews, went the argument, they would have been barred from public life, from financial careers, and from purchasing the right to collect taxes. By masquerading as New Christians, they had fastened themselves upon the backs of true Christians in addition to committing the religious crimes of heresy and blasphemy.[6]

Hatred of New Christians as a class erupted in violence in Toledo in 1449 and, in the succeeding four decades, in other parts of Spain. But it was the church that undertook to extirpate the false Christians in an organized manner, by replacing episodic violence with a permanent institution responsible for identifying and punishing heretics. In 1478, the pope authorized the creation of an Inquisition like that which, in the thirteenth and fourteenth centuries, had suppressed a variety of heresies in southern France and which had functioned during the fourteenth century in Spain. The Spanish Inquisition began to operate in 1483, and—during the succeeding decade and using torture to conduct its investigations—convicted hundreds of New Christians of heresy and delivered them to the civil authorities for execution by burning. Many more were obliged to recant their heresies in humiliating public spectacles and to forfeit their property. Thereafter, the Inquisition continued to operate against New Christians and their descendants for long years to come, not only in Spain but also in Spain's New World possessions. To be sure, the Spanish Inquisition displayed less interest in New Christians after 1550, but it nevertheless periodically conducted campaigns against them.[7]

Developments in Portugal during the 1490s gave rise to a large population of New Christians there, too. In 1492, perhaps as many as a hundred thousand expelled Spanish Jews entered Portugal. Five years later, King Manuel, responding to Spanish pressure, ordered them to leave so that he might wed a princess of Spain. Recognizing, however, that the continued presence of Jews would be beneficial to his realm, Manuel adopted a policy of forced conversion in preference to expulsion. During 1497, Jews, both children and adults, were physically dragged into church and forcibly baptized. Others voluntarily accepted Christianity in order to remain in the country and escape enslavement to the monarch, the penalty for accepting neither expulsion nor conversion. In the end, relatively little emigration under the order occurred, and most Jews became New Christians rather than face enslavement.[8]

Portugal's New Christians were even less likely than those in Spain to sincerely embrace the new faith. After all, they had already resisted conversion in Spain, choosing expulsion instead. Accordingly, many New Christians continued to practice Judaism secretly. The king's policies for some years to come permitted crypto-Judaism to strike deep roots. In 1497, for example, the Crown proclaimed that for twenty years there were to be no prosecutions for religious offenses and that offenders were thereafter to be prosecuted by civil rather than ecclesiastical authorities. During the early 1500s, massacres of New Christians—who were blamed by the general population for plague and famine—were brutally repressed by the Crown. And in 1512, the Crown decreed that there were to be no prosecutions for heresy for the next twenty years. Under these circumstances, secret adherence to Judaism became well entrenched among Portugal's New Christians, in contrast to Spain, where it virtually disappeared during the sixteenth century, until Portuguese New Christians immigrated there after 1580.[9]

The relatively benevolent disposition displayed by the Crown toward Portugal's New Christians following the forced conversions of 1497 did not long outlast King Manuel, who died in 1521. Ten years later, his successor petitioned the pope to establish an Inquisition in Portugal. The New Christian community struggled to prevent this development by offering substantial bribes to ecclesiastical officials in Rome and Lisbon and by maintaining a hired representative in Rome for a decade to intercede on their behalf with the papacy. But in the end, their efforts were to no avail. Through papal proclamations in 1536, 1539, and 1547, an Inquisition modeled after that in Spain was created in Portugal. For the next two centuries, until the regime of the Marquis de Pombal in the 1760s, it conducted a war against heresy by initiating successive, if episodic, campaigns against New Christians, many of whom perished at the stake.[10]

Notwithstanding frequent worldly success in the scholarly and cultural worlds, in medicine, and above all in commerce and finance, where some accumulated great fortunes, Portugal's New Christians found themselves stranded on the margins of Portuguese society. Apart from the danger of denunciation by the Inquisition for practicing Judaism secretly, they endured existence as members of a separate, despised class. Popular prejudices attributed natural disasters, such as Lisbon's earthquake in 1531, to them. Old Christians shunned marriage with them; when they did occur, labels such as *half New Christian* and *quarter New Christian* were applied to the offspring. Legal restrictions on New Christians imposed late in the 1580s precluded ecclesiastical, military, and government careers for almost two centuries thereafter. The very term *New Christian* came to function as an insult when applied to anyone—including Old Christians—whom the speaker wished to vilify.[11]

Branded socially undesirable, vulnerable to a ferocious Inquisition and to capital punishment for the heresy of practicing Judaism, New Christians during the sixteenth, seventeenth, and eighteenth centuries often chose to abandon Portugal. During the sixteenth century, the Crown repeatedly promulgated bans on their emigration, but these proved unenforceable. Portuguese New Christians who immigrated to North Africa and Palestine, to Salonica and Constantinople, and to many of Italy's city-states often reverted quickly to Judaism. Others sought refuge in France, notably in Bordeaux and Bayonne, where they remained outwardly Christian, because of France's prohibition on Jewish settlement, but practiced Judaism with little difficulty in a progressively more open manner during the course of the seventeenth and eighteenth centuries. In all of these locations, they established themselves in commerce and international trade; in France they were referred to interchangeably as *New Christians* and *Portuguese merchants*. And the possibility of careers as merchant traders drew them to northern Europe as well, where they created communities in the important ports of Hamburg and Amsterdam. It was migration to the latter that would in the middle of the seventeenth century propel some among them to Manhattan Island's New Amsterdam.[12]

In addition to a flourishing harbor and expansive Dutch trading networks, international developments involving Spain and Portugal doubtlessly contributed to the attractiveness of settlement in Amsterdam. In 1568 the seven Dutch provinces in the northwestern corner of

Europe rose in rebellion against Spain. Save for a truce that lasted for the twelve years between 1609 and 1621, the struggle against Spanish rule continued for eighty years, until Spain recognized the independence of the United Provinces in 1648. In 1580 Portugal and Spain had joined under the rule of a single monarch. For New Christians, the unification of the two realms presented greater danger than before, for Spain's Holy Office combined its expertise, resources, and sources of information with Portugal's, which in any case was at this juncture even more aggressive than Spain's. In the 1590s, shortly after the unification of the two kingdoms, New Christian immigration began to Amsterdam, a logical destination because of the Dutch struggle against Spanish domination.[13]

Jewish settlement in Holland continued unabatedly during the seventeenth century. Holland offered religious toleration, commercial opportunity, escape from the Inquisition, and an end to the social prejudices and legal prohibitions that afflicted New Christians in Portugal. New Christians in substantial numbers abandoned all pretenses to Christianity, underwent circumcision, often changed their names, and resumed living as Jews. To be sure, even in tolerant Amsterdam, where the majority settled, certain economic and religious restrictions existed, but many of these gradually disappeared. In 1639, for example, public worship, hitherto prohibited, was permitted. Holland's Calvinist ministers would have preferred the establishment of religious uniformity, and they targeted not only Jews but Lutherans, Mennonites, and Remonstrants, but without success. The civil authorities supported neither an enforced orthodoxy nor religious exclusivity, arguing that toleration was more conducive to the commercial and financial development of their cities and provinces. The antagonism of the Calvinist ministry did prove troublesome to the first Jews who settled in North America, but here too the predilection of Holland's governing elite for religious toleration triumphed.[14]

Seventeenth-century Amsterdam's Jewish population enjoyed uninterrupted calm and stability, which permitted the development of a vigorous communal and cultural life. While most made their living as small merchants and craftsmen, a small number achieved significant success as financiers and international traders. Others established a substantial printing industry, contributing to Amsterdam's global leadership in the production of books. Several congregations and synagogues were created, along with a network of charities and a school for advanced religious studies. Various members of the community distinguished themselves in medicine, biblical studies, and letters, generally. Within the short span of a half century, Amsterdam emerged as Europe's leading Jewish community.[15]

Comfortable as they were in their new location, some among Holland's Jewish population elected during the 1630s and early 1640s to try their luck in northeastern Brazil. In doing so, they participated in the daring effort by the inhabitants of the United Provinces during the first half of the seventeenth century to seize Portugal's colonial possessions around the globe. (In 1654, some of them, once again in flight from Portuguese rule, would establish the Jewish settlement at New Amsterdam.)

To the Dutch, the attack upon Portugal's Asian, African, and South American colonies and upon Portuguese shipping was part of the struggle for independence from Spain, inasmuch as the two Iberian nations were united between 1580 and 1640. In addition, control of the seas and acquisition of colonies were viewed as essential to the expansion of Dutch commercial capitalism. The Dutch prescription for empire called for harnessing the capital and skills of financiers and merchants rather than sending government expeditionary forces overseas. Accordingly, the United Provinces chartered two commercial corporations—the Dutch East India Company in 1602 and the Dutch West India Company in 1621—empowering them to monopolize trade in their respective domains, to establish and administer colonies, to maintain armies and navies, and to conduct war. Within five years of its creation, the Dutch West India Company succeeded in establishing the colony of New Netherland in North America, stretching north from the Delaware River to Manhattan Island and then along the Hudson River as far as present-day Albany. On the other hand, the company's contemporaneous expedition to South America to seize the vast Portuguese colony of Brazil, desirable for the sugar and dyewood grown there, failed. In May 1624, the fleet sent from Holland seized Bahia but lost it a year later to a superior force dispatched by Spain and Portugal.[16]

Not to be denied the wealth of Brazil, the West India Company late in 1629 launched another expedition, this time to seize the large captaincy of Pernambuco. Early in 1630 the Dutch conquered its capital, Recife, and gradually thereafter established control over most of northeastern Brazil. During the ensuing twenty-four years of Dutch rule in Brazil, a considerable number of Jews immigrated there from Holland, attracted by a number of considerations. Many Jews had facility with both the Dutch and the Portuguese languages, in contrast with the Dutch and the Portuguese in Brazil, few of whom had mastered each other's tongue. The West India Company's commitment to religious toleration, even for Catholics in Brazil, made Recife as comfortable as Amsterdam. When assailed by the Calvinist clergy in Brazil, the Jewish community could rely upon the Amsterdam Jewish community, which interceded successfully on their behalf with the West India Company. Finally, many New Christians lived in Brazil, providing a community useful to the new immigrants. Amsterdam's Jews had been in contact with them well before the Dutch conquest. Indeed, many of them secretly practiced Judaism and suffered visits from the Portuguese Inquisition in 1591, 1593, and 1618. Many openly resumed the practice of Judaism with the advent of Dutch rule.[17]

Jewish immigrants established a presence in the new Dutch possession as early as 1630 by serving as mercenaries in the West India Company's army of conquest. Thereafter, their numbers grew rapidly: in 1637, other Dutch settlers and Portuguese oldtimers complained to the company that Brazil was being overwhelmed by the influx. By 1645, close to fifteen hundred Jews resided in Dutch Brazil. Two religious congregations were established, one of which (Recife's) employed the first rabbi in the New World. It established a panoply of communal institutions, including a synagogue building and a school for children. Many individuals prospered economically, as well—notably in the slave trade, in tax collecting, and as intermediaries in the sugar trade.[18]

Brazil's Jewish community ceased to exist in 1654, with the collapse of Dutch rule in that year. Nine years of rebellion by the colony's Portuguese inhabitants, devastating sieges, and gradual loss of territory culminated in 1654 with Recife's capture by a Portuguese expeditionary force. The Dutch were unable to hold Brazil, in no small part because of war with England between 1652 and 1654 for control of the seas and for the commercial hegemony that went with it; they were given three months to vacate the colony with their possessions and their ships.[19] With them went the last of the Jewish population, whose numbers had declined steadily through emigration between 1645 and 1654 with the growing prospect of a Portuguese victory. From a high of 1,450 in 1645, approximately 650 Jews remained in 1654. Most returned to the Netherlands, but from their ranks came the twenty-three who made their way to New Amsterdam in North America.

The refugees from Brazil who landed on Manhattan Island included several individuals with names that are discernibly Sephardic, indicating that either they or their ancestors originated in Portugal or Spain. From those two countries, Jews and New Christians—many of whom began to practice Judaism openly once they were safe from the clutches of the Inquisition—fanned out across Europe. Now, via Amsterdam and Brazil, the dispersal of the Sephardim reached North America as well. In addition, however, New Amsterdam's twenty-three newcomers included several individuals with names that are recognizably Ashkenazic, indicating that they or their families originated in central or eastern Europe. The names of two more Jews known to have been present in New Amsterdam when the refugees from Brazil arrived indicate that they too were Ashkenazim.[20]

During the seventeenth and eighteenth centuries, Jews from central and eastern Europe migrated westward in numbers significant enough to establish communities and congregations entirely distinct from those of the Sephardim. In this transformation of the demographic distribution of European Jewry, seventeenth-century Holland served as an entrepôt for Ashkenazic as well as Sephardic Jews. By 1635, an Ashkenazic congregation had been organized in Amsterdam. Jews from Poland and Germany went from there to Brazil; now they went to North America, as well.[21] The embryonic Jewish community on Manhattan Island in 1654 thus brought together representatives of each of the two great subdivisions of the Jewish people, foreshadowing the demographic pattern that would characterize all of American Jewry in the seventeenth and eighteenth centuries. Subsequent Jewish immigration to colonial North America drew upon Europe's Ashkenazic as well as Sephardic populations.

The attempt by the United Provinces of the Netherlands to build a colonial empire at the expense of the Portuguese, the Dutch failure in Brazil, the dispersal of the Sephardim that began at the end of the fifteenth century and continued for the following three centuries, the beginnings of westward migration by Ashkenazim in the first half of the seventeenth century—these provided the background to the establishment of the first North American Jewish community. One other factor, the comparatively benign attitude of the Dutch toward Jews, contributed as well, notwithstanding efforts by the Calvinist ministry in Holland and Brazil to circumscribe the place of Jews in Dutch society. On the contrary, the men and women who journeyed northward from Recife in 1654 in search of a haven knew that, even if they encountered religious prejudice in New Amsterdam (and they did), they would be able to count upon the adherence of the civil authorities of Amsterdam to a policy of toleration and upon access to these authorities through Amsterdam's Jewish community.

During the seventeenth century, Dutch religious toleration continued to attract Jews to Holland. Between 1645 and 1660, for example, hundreds of New Christians fled to Holland from Spain in the wake of a renewed assault by the Inquisition. During the second half of the century, immigration by Ashkenazim helped double the Jewish population of Amsterdam; it stood at about eight thousand in 1700. Furthermore, Sephardim and Ashkenazim also immigrated to Holland's possessions in the Caribbean and to the Dutch colony of Surinam in South America. Only in North America did benevolent Dutch attitudes cease to draw Jewish settlers, but this was not because of a change in policy but, rather, the abrupt termination of the Dutch colonial presence there.[22]

New Amsterdam fell victim to the conflict between England and Holland for maritime supremacy, a struggle for commercial leadership that embroiled the two nations in three wars between 1652 and 1674. The first Anglo-Dutch war, fought in 1652–54, had already affected the

Jews of the New World by contributing to the Dutch defeat in Brazil. Bent upon destroying the hitherto predominant position of the Dutch in world trade—including the control of slave traffic between Africa and the Americas—a cabal of London merchants, abetted by the monarch's younger brother, the Duke of York, schemed successfully during a period of peace to commit the government to the seizure of New Amsterdam by force. In 1664 England dispatched an expedition, which in short order overwhelmed New Amsterdam. Subsequently, the entire colony of New Netherland was seized, from its outposts on the Delaware River in the south to Fort Orange, northward on the Hudson. The victorious English renamed New Amsterdam New York, in honor of the king's brother.[23]

Fortunately, a new toleration for Jews was emerging among the English: the articles of capitulation that ended the brief conflict included a guarantee of freedom of conscience to all the inhabitants of New Netherland. Furthermore, the English government's policy of extending toleration to Jews in its colonial acquisitions had already been made manifest on the island of Jamaica. Captured from the Spanish in 1655, Jamaica was of considerable strategic importance because of its geographic position among Spain's American possessions and athwart Spain's trade routes in the New World. In an effort to increase the size of Jamaica's population, the Crown in 1661 proclaimed that all settlers and their children born on the island were to be "free denizens" of England, with all the rights and privileges of "natural born subjects of England." Jews had been in Jamaica since 1655, the year of the conquest, and therefore were beneficiaries of the Crown's declaration.[24] Moreover, in the Rhode Island charter of 1663, the Crown was precise and explicit regarding liberty of conscience, stating

> that our royall will and pleasure is that noe person within the sayd colonye at any tyme hereafter shall bee in any way molested, punished or called in question for any differences in opinione in matters of religion, and doe not actually disturb the civill peace of our sayd collony; but that all and everye person or persons may from tyme to tyme and at all tymes hereafter freelye and fullye have and enjoye his and theire owne judgements and consciences in matters of religious concernment.[25]

But the most important and most reassuring sign of all was the fact that, nine years prior to the aggression against New Amsterdam, Jews had been permitted to settle in England for the first time in more than three and a half centuries. Their readmission, to be sure, had been opposed by the merchants of the City of London, who attempted for many years thereafter to impose religious and economic restrictions upon them. Despite the hostility of the merchants, and despite a reservoir of anti-Semitic sentiment in English society, Jewish immigrants succeeded in establishing themselves in England and in openly organizing their religious and communal life. Unlike Amsterdam's Jews, who had been forced to wait until 1639—approximately fifty years after Jewish immigration to Holland had begun—for permission to build a synagogue where they could worship publicly, London's Jews were able to worship openly as early as 1657, two years after readmission had been quietly approved by the government.[26]

This approval can be attributed to the influence of the Amsterdam Jewish community, which was coping with a surge in Jewish refugees from Spain, Brazil, Poland, and Germany and which was perhaps eager, as well, to neutralize the effect of recent English legislation curtailing trade with the Dutch. In 1655, the Jews dispatched Rabbi Menashe Ben Israel to London to negotiate with Oliver Cromwell's government for the admission of Jews. Cromwell's government informally responded affirmatively, whether motivated by the prospect of enhancing England's commercial prowess or by the Puritan postulate that the advent of the millennium required first the conversion of the Jews. By 1660, approximately thirty-five Sephardic families had taken up residence in London; during the following twenty-four years, the number rose to ninety households. Thereafter, Sephardim continued to immigrate to England from all parts of Europe, including Spain and Portugal, but by the middle of the eighteenth century, when seven thousand to eight thousand Jews resided in England, the Sephardim were outnumbered three to one by Ashkenazim from Poland, Germany, and Holland.[27]

The readmission of the Jews and the subsequent increase of their numbers through emigration from the Continent did not mean that anti-Semitic ideas were absent in England: on the contrary, religious biases persisted. Many Englishmen assumed that Jews were hostile to

Christians, that they prayed for the demise of Christianity, and that they worked with Satan to overthrow it. Furthermore, Jews were believed to bear physical stigmata attesting to their guilt for the murder of Christ. Anti-Jewish feeling manifested itself in the economic area, as well. In addition to the London merchants and financiers who viewed the Jews as unwelcome competitors, others feared that, because of their wealth, Jews would come to dominate the realm. Moreover, Jews were thought to be inordinately devoted to the acquisition of wealth and, therefore, would take unfair advantage of those they dealt with.[28]

Other forces counterbalanced these animosities. The slow accretion of liberal economic ideas during the eighteenth century was conducive to an egalitarian outlook, one that portrayed Jews as exporters and importers who contributed to the wealth of the nation. In addition, the great landowning families that dominated government looked upon Jews positively and reacted favorably to requests for the elimination of civil disabilities. The disabilities that did exist, those that barred Jews from political participation and the universities, also applied to Catholics and Dissenters (Protestants who drew apart from the official Anglican church). The Anglican ministry did not engage in campaigns against Jews, nor, significantly, did the hierarchy's representatives in the House of Lords oppose the Jewish Naturalization Bill of 1753 (which ultimately failed to pass). Finally, although Jews in eighteenth-century England were, as individuals, occasionally the victims of thugs and bullies, and although Jews were the objects of two small riots in 1763 and 1776, organized violence was more prevalent and devastating against Catholics and dissenting Protestants. Mobs attacked the meetinghouses of Dissenters in London in 1709 and 1715–16, regularly hounded Methodist leaders John Wesley and George Whitefield, erupted in a full week of riot and pillage against Catholics in 1780, and in 1791 destroyed the homes, shops, and meetinghouses of Baptists and Unitarians in Birmingham.[29]

Jews who chose to immigrate to the New World were assured of finding at least the same measure of toleration in most of England's colonies as that prevailing in the mother country. The exceptions were

Massachusetts and Connecticut during the seventeenth century, where anyone who did not subscribe to Puritan orthodoxy was unwelcome (as Sabbath breakers, Baptists, and Quaker intruders learned) and Jamaica, which, despite the Crown's proclamation in 1661, imposed discriminatory taxation upon the island's Jewish inhabitants. Jamaica provides a useful contrast to the climate that existed for Jews in most of the mainland colonies. Like London's merchants and financiers, the island's traders resented the competition of Jewish merchants, accusing them of trespassing where they were not wanted to the detriment of Christian merchants and their families. As the president of the Council of Jamaica wrote in 1692 to the Lords of Trade and Plantations:

> The Jews cut us and our children out of all trade. . . . We did not want them at Port Royal . . . and though told that the whole country lay open to them they have made Port Royal their Goshen and will do nothing but trade. . . . Had we not warning from other Colonies we should see our streets filled and the ships hither crowded with them. This means taking our children's bread and giving it to Jews.[30]

Unlike Jamaica, which maintained higher taxes for Jews until 1740, the mainland colonies adhered to the example of England, where, despite frequent suggestions to the contrary, Parliament never imposed discriminatory taxation. As the Reverend Martin Bolzius, minister of Georgia's Salzburg Lutheran settlers, wrote in 1739, "The Englishmen, nobility and common folks alike treat the Jews as their equal. They drink, gamble and walk together with them; in fact, let them take part in all their fun. Yes, they desecrate Sunday with them, a thing no Jew would do on their Sabbath to please a Christian!"[31]

A year later, Parliament enacted a naturalization law for the American colonies that provided the clearest evidence to eighteenth-century Jews of the scope of English toleration in the New World. Noting in the preamble that the strength and wealth of a nation increased as its population grew, the act offered naturalization to foreign Protestants and Jews who resided for at least seven years in the colonies, without an absence of longer than two months during that period. To qualify, applicants would ordinarily have had to swear allegiance to the Crown, with the oath, "upon the true faith of a Christian." But Parliament decreed that foreign Jews who applied for naturalization could take the oath without the seven words.[32]

The benefits of naturalization were considerable. A naturalized citizen became "a natural born Subject of Great Britain," entitled to all the rights of Englishmen and to relief from the mercantile disabilities imposed upon foreigners. Because of this act, English toleration of Jews was greater in the colonies than it was in England itself, for foreign-born Jews could not secure naturalization in the mother country, where no exemption from the words in question was available. Consequently, Jews born in foreign countries, in common with other aliens, could not hold real property in England, could not own shares in English ships or trade with the colonies, and were required to pay higher customs duties and port fees. Only at great expense could the foreign-born individual in England purchase the right to trade with the colonies, but even this did not carry with it exemption from the customs duties and port fees imposed upon aliens.[33]

Confident of a modicum of toleration among the English, Sephardic immigrants during the late seventeenth and eighteenth centuries journeyed to mainland North America from Holland and England and their Caribbean possessions, settling primarily in Rhode Island, New York, Pennsylvania, South Carolina, and Georgia. Some came as well from Bordeaux, increasingly a source of newcomers late in the eighteenth century.[34] A few of the settlers originated in Spain and Portugal, refugees from resurgent Inquisitions. Louis Moses Gomez, for example, founder of New York's leading Sephardic family, was born in Spain by the year 1660. And by the 1720s, Abraham Rodriguez Rivera had fled Spain, settled in New York, changed his name to a Hebraic one, and undoubtedly submitted to circumcision.[35]

The Inquisition in Portugal reasserted itself with particular forcefulness in 1720, provoking as many as fifteen hundred people to flee directly to London during the following thirteen years, some of whom crossed subsequently to the New World. Dr. Samuel Nunes Ribeiro, for one, persecuted in 1703–4 and required by the Inquisition to testify in 1706, fled from Portugal to London with his family in 1726, when he had again come to the attention of the Holy Office. He emigrated to

Georgia in 1733. Isaac Mendes Seixas, the father of America's first native-born religious functionary, was born in Lisbon. He probably emigrated to London with his parents, who died there in 1738 and 1739; he arrived in New York in 1738. Jose Lopez abandoned Portugal for England in the early 1730s because of the Inquisition, changed his name to Moses, and reached America by 1739. His half-brother Duarte Lopez and brother Gabriel left Portugal in 1752 for Rhode Island, where both changed their names (Duarte to Aaron, and Gabriel to David) and underwent circumcision. Aaron Lopez forged a prominent career as a Rhode Island merchant, and in 1767 spirited another half-brother, Miguel, out of Portugal to America, together with the latter's wife and three sons.[36]

These Sephardim could have chosen, of course, to remain in Amsterdam, London, or Bordeaux, or to settle in any of the other cities in western Europe where their families and compatriots had established a presence. Instead, they elected, as did the hazan (the salaried reader) of the New York synagogue in 1759, to leave; in the hazan's words, to abandon "my native place, the great city of Amsterdam, and come to a very populous city, more highly praised and more glorious than all others, London, where I began to find rest for my feet," only then to "come hither [to New York] across the dangerous seas."[37] The decision to forsake "great" Amsterdam and "glorious" London for the comparatively modest towns of the New World and to brave the rigors of the Atlantic crossing is partly attributable to the gradual decline of eighteenth-century European Sephardic Jewry.[38] In Amsterdam, Sephardic population growth diminished, while in Sephardic centers in southern and southeastern Europe it fell markedly.

More pertinently, many Sephardim were simply poor. In Amsterdam, the number of Sephardic families financially dependent on the organized Jewish community increased fourfold between 1720 and 1740. Between 1725 and 1748, according to a contemporary observer, contributors to the Sephardic congregation declined from 629 to 610, while the number of families requiring poor relief rose from 450 to more than 750. The congregation consequently assisted any who were willing to depart Amsterdam, often for Surinam in South America.

In London, poverty was rampant among the Jewish population throughout the eighteenth century. Repeatedly from 1700 to 1710, and then again during the 1720s and 1730s, the elders of the Sephardic synagogue found that the congregation's capacity to provide poor relief could not keep pace with the need, in part because of the refugees from Spain and Portugal. The drain upon the community's resources led directly to the establishment of a new Jewish community in North America in 1733. London's Sephardic leadership participated in the creation of Georgia, whose founders envisioned it not only as a strategic emplacement against the Spanish in Florida but also as a refuge for the impoverished of England. Despite opposition among the colony's trustees to Jewish settlers, England's Sephardic community sent forty-two Jews to Savannah, of whom thirty-four were Sephardim. Poverty continued to afflict the Jews of England, though London's Sephardic community, except for a brief flurry of interest in the mid-1740s in an abortive scheme to send Jews to South Carolina, did not endeavor again to dispatch settlers in organized groups to North America. In 1767, the elders of the synagogue could send only thirty pounds sterling to Newport's Jews who had requested assistance to complete their new synagogue, explaining that poverty was the reason for the small donation. Near the end of the century, slightly more than half of the Sephardic congregation in London lived in penury, according to its secretary.

Concurrent with the prevalence of poverty, the involvement in the Jewish community by wealthier members of Amsterdam's and London's Jews diminished. In England, where some of the wealthy did provide leadership, this lack of commitment extended to marriage with non-Jews and conversion to Christianity. By distancing themselves from the Jewish community, Jewish economic leaders weakened communal institutions, reducing their ability to provide assistance to those at the lower end of the social and economic spectrum. Moreover, they lost interest in channeling business opportunities to other Jews. In the previous century, by contrast, the practice of establishing and perpetuating trading connections within the Jewish community undoubtedly had assisted those on the lower end of the social and economic hierarchy. In sum, changing attitudes among the Sephardic elite regarding their identity as Jews and their responsibilities to the Jewish community probably contributed to pauperization and to a reduction in economic opportunities for those of middle and lower status. For that matter, signs of economic decline were apparent even among the elite. As Jonathan Israel has suggested, wealthy Sephardic Jews in mideighteenth-century Holland exhibited less economic initiative, vigor, and daring than in previous eras. Though still wealthy, "stagnation and loss of dynamism were unmistakable," and "the picture was one of slow eclipse."[39]

Despite the fact that the Sephardic commercial elite in Europe relied less than it once had upon trading connections with other Jews, the individuals who undertook to try their fortunes in America may well have hoped otherwise. Commerce during the seventeenth and eighteenth centuries depended to a considerable extent upon family connections, maintained at times over several generations.[40] Kinship ties linked merchants in the American colonies with their counterparts in the Caribbean islands and the ports of western Europe, supplying the personal ties that business conventions and trade expositions provide in the modern world. Furthermore, the hazards of shipping on the high seas, together with the absence of international credit-rating institutions, necessitated a means for gauging the reliability of commercial associates in distant harbors: kinship reduced the risks of trading with unknown parties.[41]

Religious and ethnic affiliation supplemented family ties in international trade, operating to the advantage of minority groups. Groupings along such lines functioned as even larger "families," extending the range of reliable suppliers and customers. Eighteenth-century Quakers, for example, made up a circle of traders that encompassed England, the North American colonies, and the Caribbean. Similarly, Huguenots who fled from France in the wake of the revocation of the Edict of Nantes in 1685 built trading networks with relatives and partners who remained behind, thereby contributing to an increase in exports from France.[42] In the instance of the Sephardim, the relation between membership in an ethnic group and success in international trade was apparent throughout the sixteenth, seventeenth, and eighteenth centuries. As Yosef Yerushalmi has noted, Sephardic Jews, together with New Christians, comprised "a huge extended family," whose "common origin, historic fate, and collective identity . . . bound them together." Indeed, "quite often there were real ties of blood and kinship" that crossed international boundaries and contributed to commercial achievement.[43]

During the seventeenth century, Sephardic merchants in Holland established trading relationships with their counterparts all over the Caribbean. Their commerce in textiles, silver, and wool linked Sephardim in Amsterdam with New Christians in France and Spain. Beginning in the middle of the century, trade and banking united Sephardic Jews in the Netherlands and Hamburg with New Christians in Portugal. New Christian financiers in Spain maintained commercial contacts with Sephardim throughout Europe and the Caribbean. During the second half of the century, Dutch Jews traded extensively with Spain's colonies in South America, depending upon Jewish merchants on the Dutch island of Curaçao to function as middlemen. In turn, Curaçao's Sephardim dealt frequently with their New Christian counterparts on the mainland. Sephardic communities on the islands of Jamaica, Martinique, Tobago, Nevis, and Barbados, as well as in Surinam, Holland's colony on the South American mainland, were part of a network that reached through Curaçao back to Amsterdam via the Sephardic trading community.[44]

Sephardic immigrants to North America were entirely aware of these trading possibilities and relied extensively upon commerce with their counterparts in the Caribbean. As early as 1656, the Jews of New Amsterdam established commercial ties with their coreligionists in Curaçao, an island of particular significance to the Jews of the New World. Seized by the Dutch from Spain in 1643, the island attracted Jewish settlers from Holland during the 1650s, and by the end of the century approximately 125 Jewish families resided there, surely surpassing the size of the Jewish population in the English mainland colonies at that juncture. By 1713, 140 Jewish families were present, almost one-third of the total number of white families. The population was augmented in the early part of the century by refugees from the resurgent Inquisitions in Spain and Portugal; in some instances, New Christians went directly to Curaçao from the Iberian peninsula without first going to the Netherlands. In the middle of the eighteenth century, the Jewish population reached its apogee of 250 families, for a total head count between thirteen hundred and fifteen hundred, the second-largest ethnic group on the island. Attracted by its favorable location, one that enabled it to function commercially as a transit point between North America, South America, the Caribbean, and Europe, the Jews of Curaçao established the largest single community of Jews in the New World during the eighteenth century.[45]

The value of family connections to commerce and finance in the seventeenth and eighteenth centuries is amply apparent in the case of Curaçao. Nearly every leading Jewish merchant residing on the island had a relative in Amsterdam. Indeed, as historians of the Jews of Curaçao have written, "Most Jews who traded with the Jews of Curacao were related to one another so that Curaçao was virtually the commercial and religious center of a large family."[46] Thus, Sephardic Jews who chose to chance their fortunes in New York or Newport, in Philadelphia or Charleston, headed not for isolated outposts on the margin of a wilderness continent but, rather, for participation in a far-flung commercial network.

In addition to Curaçao, other islands in the Caribbean, as well as the Dutch colony of Surinam on the mainland of South America, were in the familial mercantile network. In Jamaica, the Jewish population expanded despite the animosity of the island's non-Jewish merchants and the imposition of discriminatory taxes. Jamaica's Jews established three congregations and employed an ordained rabbi by the middle of the eighteenth century, outpacing the North American communities in this regard, where the first rabbi did not settle until 1839. In the aftermath of the collapse of the Dutch regime in Brazil in 1654, most Jews returned to Amsterdam, but some subsequently returned to the Caribbean, establishing a Jewish community in Barbados. There, Sephardim predominated among the Jewish population in 1680, according to a census that year. By 1710, as one contemporary observer reported, about 170 Jewish families resided on the island. Four families were on the small island of Saint Eustatius in 1722; by 1740, the number was large enough to erect a synagogue. Forty years later, 101 Jewish males were enumerated, presumably all of them heads of families. In Surinam, Jewish settlement began probably during the 1660s. In 1694, ninety-two Sephardic families and as many as a dozen Ashkenazic families were to be found there, along with fifty single individuals. The settlers constructed a synagogue in

1685, and by the 1730s there were at least two, one Ashkenazic and one Sephardic.[47]

Ashkenazim immigrated to England's colonies in numbers comparable to the Sephardim, as Jews moved westward from central and eastern Europe. Although few in number when they began emigrating during the first half of the seventeenth century, their numbers grew between 1650 and 1800, eventually spilling over from Europe to the North American mainland. Ashkenazim abandoned their homes in Poland and Lithuania because of war, persecution, the presumption of greater economic opportunity farther west, and the willingness of certain German states, along with Holland and England, to admit them.[48]

During the second half of the seventeenth century, substantial numbers of German Jews, expelled from many of the German states in the aftermath of the Thirty Years' War, immigrated to Holland, attracted by the benign attitudes of the Dutch toward their religion as well as by the possibility of participation in Jewish commercial networks that connected the Netherlands with Germany. Drawn from both eastern and central Europe, Amsterdam's Ashkenazic population grew from approximately five thousand in 1674 to nine thousand in 1720. Similarly, during the eighteenth century, England's Ashkenazic population increased markedly with emigrants from Poland, Germany, and Holland. The majority came from German jurisdictions that limited the size of the Jewish populations within their boundaries and imposed economic restrictions upon them. Overall, German Jews were pushed westward by a general economic decline during the eighteenth century, attributable not only to commercial prohibitions but also to the migration of Polish Jews into Germany, to the detriment of the indigenous Jewish population.[49]

A handful of Europe's Ashkenazic migrants crossed the Atlantic to North America. Some resided first in England or Holland, suggesting that Ashkenazim, like Sephardim, encountered conditions in western Europe that made settlement in the New World preferable.[50] For one, poverty was widespread in the Ashkenazic communities of England and Holland. Thousands of German and Polish Jews were reduced to being itinerant, homeless *Betteljuden* (Beggar Jews) and were frequently unable to improve their condition after settling in England and Holland. In Holland during the seventeenth and eighteenth centuries, a variety of economic restrictions impeded their progress. In England, destitution bulked large among the entire Jewish population, the Sephardim included, and poverty was often a permanent condition, transmitted from one generation to the next. Apart from individual poverty, a general economic and demographic malaise settled upon European Jewry during the eighteenth century. The way out—and up—frequently pointed west.[51]

Not every Jew of central or eastern European origins immigrated to the colonies to escape poverty; some belonged to families of financiers and merchants that had achieved considerable success in England as the eighteenth century progressed. These emigrants functioned as representatives of their families, much as the Sephardic settlers in Curaçao who traded with their relatives in Amsterdam. Indeed, this was one motive for emigration, with Ashkenazic mercantile families in England widening their trading sphere by dispatching a son, brother, or cousin to the New World. Jacob Franks, for example, probably New York's most successful Jewish merchant during the colonial era and a major figure in its synagogue, was the son of a broker in England, who maintained commercial ties with his family in London long after he arrived on Manhattan Island. Similarly, brothers Barnard and Michael Gratz, after leaving their village in Upper Silesia and joining Solomon Henry, their merchant cousin in London, immigrated to Philadelphia, where they believed they would prosper because of their English connection. As Michael Gratz, before he left England for America, wrote to his disapproving brothers who remained behind in their hometown in eastern Europe, "I can inform you of our brother Barnard, that he will establish himself well in Philadelphia, for he is concerned with a great merchant of London." Subsequently, Solomon Henry traded from London with Michael Gratz as well, after the latter also relocated to Philadelphia.[52]

Whether Sephardic or Ashkenazic, the archetypical Jewish emigrant from the Old World who settled in colonial America was part of a general movement of Jews within Europe from the eastern, central, and south-western parts of the continent to its northwestern quadrant. Whether because of war, poverty, expulsion, or the Inquisition, Jews in the seventeenth and eighteenth centuries abandoned Poland and Germany, Portugal and Spain in numbers significant enough to create major new centers in Amsterdam and London. Within a generation or two, they or their descendants departed in small numbers from Holland and England for the New World, thereby conforming to the pattern of the many thousands of emigrants from England, Scotland, Ireland, and Germany who traversed the Atlantic to Britain's colonies during the eighteenth century. Movement within Britain and Germany preceded movement across the Atlantic; as Bernard Bailyn has argued, the settlement of North America by Europeans during the eighteenth century must be viewed in the context of domestic population shifts within Europe.[53] The Jewish pattern differed in that the range of movement inside Europe, involving relocation from one country to another, covered greater distances and began earlier. Seventeenth-century Jews who moved first within Europe and subsequently to America may thus be described as predictive of the migratory patterns of the far more numerous Britons and central Europeans who, during the eighteenth century, populated the English colonies.

The prototypical Jewish newcomer differed in one additional, but important, respect. Non-Jewish immigrants were in the main artisans and farmers,[54] while the Jewish settler, whether as the representative of an Old World or a Caribbean family or merely taking a chance on affiliating with the ethnic and family trading networks that spanned the Atlantic, identified as a merchant and pursued a career in commerce. Some, to be sure, established themselves as skilled artisans, but to judge from the wills of eighteenth-century New York's Jews, the majority of colonial America's Jewish population thought of themselves as merchants.[55] As such, their horizons encompassed not just their immediate surroundings but the entire Atlantic world of the eighteenth century, a subject to which we now turn.

CHAPTER TWO

THE ATLANTIC WORLD OF
COLONIAL JEWRY

ALTHOUGH short in duration and curtailed by untimely death, the career of Jacob Henry in the New World illuminates the ambitions of Jewish emigrés who chose settlement in the colonies over residence in England or Holland. Born in the village of Langendorf in Upper Silesia, Henry left that region in eastern Europe and its restrictions upon Jewish economic activity and made his way west, first to England, to join the brother who had preceded him there and had become a successful merchant. Counting on his brother as his commercial correspondent, Henry immigrated to America and settled in the backcountry of Pennsylvania, in the new town of Lancaster. His business enterprise, however, failed in the mid-1750s, perhaps because of disruptions in the fur trade caused by the outbreak of the French and Indian War.

Returning to eastern Europe, Henry was robbed at Breslau, Silesia's provincial capital, fell ill at Amsterdam, and at length arrived in London in 1757, reduced to poverty. Provided with credit by several non-Jewish merchants who respected his honesty as well as his familiarity with the American market and buttressed by a loan of two hundred ten pounds sterling extended by his brother—which underscores the value of family connections to Jewish settlers who hoped to succeed in the New World—he returned for a second time to Pennsylvania. Without his brother's assistance and the credit extended by the others, Henry probably would not have returned again to the colonies, for, as his brother informed their parents in eastern Europe, "he was ashamed to return to Philadelphia and be a mere employee, and had no money to be a merchant." Unfortunately, he fell ill not long after he returned to launch his second attempt "to be a merchant" and, after seeking a cure in Newport and New York, died in Philadelphia.[1]

Whether Sephardic or Ashkenazic, Jews who settled in colonial America, like the unfortunate Jacob Henry, aspired to become merchants participating in the transatlantic commerce that bound England's ports in North America to western Europe, Africa, and the islands of the Caribbean. Ships, credit, and English manufactured goods interested not only a Jacob Henry but most of the Jewish inhabitants of the colonies as well. Had Jacob Henry lived and succeeded as a man of commerce, he—like his cousins Barnard and Michael Gratz in Philadelphia and like the Lopez family in Newport and Isaac DaCosta in Charleston—might have become involved with the markets in North America for Caribbean sugar and African slaves and the demand abroad for furs from the continent's interior, for wheat from Pennsylvania and New York, for rice and indigo from South Carolina, and for naval stores harvested in New England and North Carolina.

Jacob Henry, according to his brother's account, would have been humiliated to return to America as anything less than a merchant. One might start out in colonial society as a shopkeeper, but the greater horizons and activities of the merchant, and the larger profits to be had in admittedly risky ventures conducted across great distances, bestowed greater prestige—and not just upon Jews. For example, in Lancaster, seventy miles west of Philadelphia, where Indians exchanged furs and German farmers sold wheat for English manufactured goods, Christians and Jews described as shopkeepers in 1759, when the town was still young, graduated to the designation of merchant a mere twenty-one years later, evidently preferring this description. In Charleston, Joseph Tobias called himself a "shopkeeper" when he advertised the sale of bread, flour, milk, and loaf sugar in 1737 and 1739, but by 1743 he had become a "merchant," a case paralleled by another Jewish resident of Charleston, Isaac DaCosta, described as a shopkeeper in 1751 and a merchant eight years later.[2] More tellingly, the Jewish inhabitants of colonial New York made certain to inform posterity that they had been merchants. The authors of nineteen of the twenty-three wills known to have been written by adult Jewish males who died in New York between 1704 and 1774 identified themselves as merchants. (Only one described himself otherwise—as a chandler—and the remaining three did not provide any career identification.) In addition, some among the foregoing, as well as two women, identified their Jewish executors, witnesses, and the like as merchants.[3]

The ambition to succeed in Atlantic commerce dictated residence in a port, so most of colonial America's Jewish population settled in Newport, Philadelphia, Charleston, Savannah, and New Amsterdam, the site of the first Jewish community. Settlement in New Amsterdam did not proceed smoothly, at first. In contrast to the generally benevolent disposition of the Dutch toward the Jews of the Netherlands, an attitude that had attracted Jews to Brazil during its Dutch phase, Governor Peter Stuyvesant of New Netherland, along with his council and the colony's Calvinist clergy, adamantly opposed a permanent Jewish presence. It should be noted, however, that the governor and his associates also discriminated against Christians who belonged to denominations other than their own; they deemed Lutherans and Quakers as repugnant as the Jews.

Within three weeks of the arrival of Jews from northeastern Brazil in September 1654, Stuyvesant informed his employers, the directors of the Dutch West India Company, that—with the support of the clergy, the council, and all others loyal to the company—he had ordered the Jews to depart from the colony. The general good of the colony necessitated this step, Stuyvesant wrote, lest the Jews become public charges during the coming winter. (He did not explain, in justification, that the newcomers had not been able to pay for their passage to New Amsterdam and were being sued by the captain of the vessel that had transported them there.) In addition to their poverty, Stuyvesant argued, the Jews were a "deceitful race,—such hateful enemies and blasphemers of the name of Christ," that they ought to "be not allowed further to infect and trouble this new colony." Clearly, Stuyvesant did not approve of a permanent Jewish presence for reasons rooted, at least in part, in traditional religious antiSemitism.[4]

To counter Stuyvesant's order of expulsion, New Amsterdam's tiny Jewish population appealed over his head to the company in Holland, relying upon their coreligionists in the mother country to lobby in their behalf.[5] Early in 1655, the Jewish community of Amsterdam petitioned the directors of the Dutch West India Company, citing the loyalty of the Jewish population in Brazil, the participation of some of their number as investors in the company, and the history of toleration extended to the Jewish people by the authorities of Amsterdam and the States-General, who for sixty years had treated them as they had all other inhabitants. The petitioners also argued that refusing Jews residence in New Amsterdam would damage the company, for if the Jews were expelled, they would become burdens in other Dutch colonies: they would not return to Holland, owing to lack of opportunities there; nor, because of the Inquisition, would they head for the Iberian peninsula. Moreover, permitting Jews to remain in New Amsterdam would be to the company's advantage, for they would contribute to the growth of trade, taxes, and imports. In addition, it was argued, the French permitted Jews to settle in Martinique and other possessions, and the English allowed Jewish settlement in Barbados. The conclusion was self-evident: How could the company refuse the potential advantage that Jews brought to new territories, especially in a colony that needed more people?[6]

After receiving the petition of Amsterdam's Jewish community, the directors on 15 February 1655 ordered Stuyvesant to permit Jews to reside in the colony, despite indications in the decision they sent to him that they agreed with his assessment of the dangers inherent in a permanent Jewish presence. Hearkening back to Stuyvesant's anti-Jewish sentiments, the directors resolved that "the new territories should no more be allowed to be infected by people of the Jewish nation, for we foresee therefrom the same difficulties which you fear" but instructed, nonetheless, that he must permit them to remain. Reminding Stuyvesant that Jews were company stockholders and that they had shared in the suffering that accompanied the loss of Brazil, they ruled that Jews could enter, trade, and settle permanently in New Netherland, provided that their poor did not become public charges. Thus giving credence to one of Stuyvesant's reasons for ordering them to leave, the directors decreed that the colony's Jewish inhabitants must assume responsibility for supporting their own poor and not rely upon the resources of New Netherland.[7]

Despite the company's decision, Stuyvesant continued at every turn to impede the integration of New Amsterdam's Jews into the colony. The company's directors had, after all, sent contradictory signals. If on the one hand they ordered that Jews could trade and settle, on the other they agreed with Governor Stuyvesant that the presence of the Jews could create many "difficulties." This ambivalence mirrored the slow evolution of toleration even in the Netherlands, where since the beginning of the century Jews could settle and trade freely but could not, until 1639, worship publicly nor even by the mid-1650s work in a variety of trades.[8]

Perhaps hoping to capitalize on the ambivalent attitude of the directors, the governor and his council ruled that Jews could not serve in New Amsterdam's militia, arguing that they did not serve in Amsterdam's or in that of any other city in Holland. Instead of guard duty and general military training, Jewish males between the ages of sixteen and sixty were to pay a monthly tax into the colony's coffers. Challenging this ruling shortly thereafter, Asher Levy and Jacob Barsimon petitioned to serve in the militia or be relieved of paying the tax, pleading in explanation that they earned their living by performing manual labor. The governor and the council refused, informing them that they could not serve, and that if they found the tax onerous, they could leave the colony whenever they chose. Subsequently, however, the colony's Jewish inhabitants began to serve on the watch, if only because of increasing conflict with the region's Indians.[9]

Late in 1655, Stuyvesant and his council decreed that Jews could not trade northward on the Hudson River nor southward on the Delaware, despite the Company's decision earlier that year that Jews could travel to the colony, reside permanently in it, and trade freely within it. As Councilman Cornelius van Tienhoven explained, "it would be injurious to the community and the population of the said places to grant the petition of the Jews," recommending that the company be so informed. In the instance prompting this decision, however, the council, while denying Jews freedom to trade as a matter of right, permitted one or two Jews to travel south to the Delaware River to dispose of their merchandise, inasmuch as the goods had already been shipped there.[10]

The company's directors did indeed learn, as Councilman van Tien-hoven had recommended, that the Stuyvesant regime refused to abide by the order that authorized Jews to trade anywhere in the colony and, further, that New Amsterdam's council had denied them the right to purchase real estate. Again intervening on behalf of the colony's Jewish population, the directors in June 1656 ordered Stuyvesant and his councilors not to disregard their decrees. Jews were to be permitted to trade freely in accordance with the regulation promulgated in February 1655, and they were to be permitted to acquire real estate, a right they possessed in the Netherlands. On the other hand, the directors ruled, Jews could not work as mechanics, open retail stores, or worship publicly—thereby prohibiting the building of a synagogue, though one had been permitted in Amsterdam for almost twenty years. Rather, they must conduct their businesses quietly and practice their religion unobtrusively in the privacy of their homes. To the latter end, the directors recommended that Jews erect their houses close to each other and reside in the same section of town, as the Jews in Amsterdam did.[11]

Rebuked by the company's directors for not permitting the Jews of New Amsterdam to trade freely or to own real estate, Stuyvesant and his council did not object when four Jews petitioned in the spring of 1657 to be granted burgher rights. Pointing out that in the decree of 15 February 1655 the company had ruled that the Jews of New Amsterdam were to have the same freedoms enjoyed by all inhabitants of the place, the petitioners requested that they be recognized as burghers in view of the fact that they paid taxes and shared in all the obligations borne by burghers. Furthermore, they noted, Jews in Amsterdam qualified for burgher rights. Apparently unwilling at this juncture to clash again with the company's directors, Stuyvesant and the council agreed to admit Jews to burgher rights, conferring upon them the freedoms granted to the other inhabitants of New Amsterdam.[12]

The four men were not among those who had arrived in 1654 but, rather, later immigrants, attracted to the colony no doubt by opportunities to trade in the interior along the Hudson and Delaware rivers, as well as across the Atlantic. Manhattan Island was a superb all-weather harbor, and as early as 1656 Jewish merchants there established commercial ties with Jewish traders in Curaçao. During that year, Jeosuah Henriquez of Curaçao received merchandise from New Netherland, perhaps dealing with Jacob Cohen Henricques of New Amsterdam, one of the four individuals who later petitioned for burgher privileges. Whether the two merchants were related is not known, but, if so, theirs would be an example of commerce enhanced not only by membership in a religious or ethnic group but also in a family.[13] In any case, an important pattern was established at the very outset of Jewish settlement in North America. Jews were to settle largely in port towns, from which—relying extensively upon fellow Jews as commercial contacts—they would trade throughout the Atlantic world. Moreover, their most important center in North America during the colonial era would be on Manhattan Island, despite the fact that New Amsterdam, later New York, was not the preeminent port in seventeenth- and eighteenth-century America. (It was surpassed by Boston and then by Philadelphia in population, shipbuilding, and tonnage imported and exported.)

By the spring of 1655, at least thirteen adult Jewish males resided in New Amsterdam, and this small group petitioned shortly thereafter for the right to establish a cemetery, the first step usually taken by Jewish settlers in a new region to develop their own communal institutions. The company's prohibition of public worship would not have precluded permanent settlement, for according to Jewish law, worship by a congregation in a private home is as valid as that in a synagogue. But the absence of their own burial ground would have made the continued presence of the small Jewish settlement impossible. Balked at first by Stuyvesant and his council, the settlers renewed their petition in early 1656, this time successfully. The acquisition of their own cemetery meant that the small Jewish community in New Amsterdam could remain permanently, able to bury their dead in accordance with religious law.[14]

The advent of the English in 1664 made the permanence of New Amsterdam's Jews even more certain, for the articles of capitulation that ended the brief struggle between Holland and England for New Netherland guaranteed freedom of conscience to all inhabitants of the former Dutch colony. A decade later, the English government reaffirmed its policy of guaranteeing religious freedom in the renamed city of New York, when the Duke of York instructed the colony's governor to "permit all persons of what Religion soever, quietly to inhabitt . . . wthout giveing you any disturbance or disquiet whatsoever, for or by reason of their differing opinions in matter of Religion." Sentiments such as these could only reassure new Jewish settlers, whose numbers increased to the point that the small community acquired land for a second cemetery in 1682. Between 1685 and 1695, the Jewish population rose to approximately 100, or about 2.5 percent of the city's population. The small community doubled in size during the next generation, reaching 200 between 1725 and 1730, and grew to an estimated 300 by the middle of the century.[15]

Although offering religious freedom to all inhabitants, the English regime at first did not permit Jews to worship publicly. The colony's Charter of Liberties in 1683 restricted public worship to Christians, and when in 1685 the Jews petitioned the colony's governor for the right to conduct open services, he passed the matter to the mayor and aldermen of New York City, who rejected their request. In practice, however, New York's Jews appear to have worshipped openly by the final decade of the seventeenth century, for a French observer in 1692 reported that Jews, Protestant dissenters, and Catholics each had their "own church and freedom of religion." A map of the city in 1695 identifies the site of a synagogue, while a real estate document in 1700 mentions a house on Mill Street "commonly known by the name of the Jews' synagogue." That house, rented from a Christian, continued to serve as a synagogue until 1728, when the Jewish community decided to build its first permanent synagogue structure.[16]

In 1731, the Jews erected a two-story wooden building to serve as a school, as a meeting hall for the congregation and its officers, and at times as a residence for the schoolmaster. At approximately the same date, the community erected a ritual bath and a booth for use on Sukkot, the autumn Festival of Tabernacles. In 1758, the congregation completed its complex by purchasing a house next to the synagogue to provide housing for the shammash, the salaried employee who cared for its buildings and called the congregation's members to prayer at the appointed hours.[17]

In the main, the Jews of colonial New York pursued careers as merchants, trading with England, Africa, the Caribbean islands, and the other major ports of North America.[18] Between 25 March and 25 June

1701, over half of the shipments of Jewish merchants went from New York to Barbados and consisted primarily of cocoa, rum, wine, fur, and textiles. Between 18 April and 25 December 1705, cargoes dispatched by the city's Jewish merchants went to Jamaica, Barbados, London, Rhode Island, Boston, and Guinea, and included rum, wine, cloth, and cordage. In the year that began on 24 June 1725, shipments that included coconuts, coral, tobacco, turpentine, sturgeon, wine, and rum were sent to Jamaica, Curaçao, Barbados, Martinique, London, and Bristol. A decade later, ships destined for England, Saint Thomas, South Carolina, Curaçao, Holland, Newfoundland, Jamaica, and Saint Christopher cleared New York's harbor with salt, cotton, sugar, slaves, bottles, bricks, coconuts, pork, textiles, tobacco, and onions on board. Throughout the colonial era, Jewish merchants located in New York traded across the length and breadth of the Atlantic and "constituted at one time, at least, a major segment of the mercantile population, and were an important part of colonial trade."

Jewish merchants reached into the interior as well, to judge from a ledger book attributed to Daniel Gomez, who was a member of colonial New York's preeminent Sephardic family. Gomez's commercial ventures reached to England, Ireland, Holland, Madeira, Curaçao, Jamaica, Barbados, the North American ports of Newport, Charleston, New Haven, and Philadelphia, and also, deeper into the interior, to Albany, New Rochelle, Goshen, Kinderhook, and Rhinebeck in New York and Allentown and Lancaster in Pennsylvania. But while these last locations did not front the ocean, they were as much a part of the Atlantic commercial world of the eighteenth century as were the port towns. The furs, grains, meats, tobacco, rice, indigo, lumber, and naval stores harvested in the North American hinterland were exported abroad to purchase the manufactured goods, sugar, and slaves imported from England, the Caribbean, and Africa. Gomez's father exported considerable quantities of wheat to Madeira and probably to Lisbon, while the son maintained a post near Newburgh in upper New York, where he traded with the Indians, undoubtedly procuring furs from them for export. Gomez, and others like him—such as fellow New York Jewish merchants Isaac Adolphus and Hayman Levy—served to link the continent's interior to the greater world of Atlantic commerce.[19]

Successful as merchants, the Jewish inhabitants of New York prospered in the tolerant, pluralistic environment of the city. A visitor to New York City, Peter Kalm, noted the following in the late 1740s: the Jews "possess great privileges. They have a synagogue and great country seats of their own property, and are allowed to keep shops in town. They likewise have several ships which they freight and send out with their own goods. In fine they enjoy all the privileges common to other inhabitants of the town and province."[20] For New York's Jews, however, the pleasantness of the colonial era came to a precipitous close in the autumn of 1776 with the occupation of the city by the British army. Most of the Jewish population fled, many of them to Philadelphia, and did not return until the 1780s. During their absence, the handful of Jews who remained behind, many of them loyal to the Crown, cared for the synagogue complex, where organized communal life resumed in 1783 with the return of those who, choosing the American cause in the Revolution, had gone into exile.

In 1658 or shortly thereafter, a small Jewish community developed in the town of Newport, Rhode Island, several hundred miles northeast of Manhattan Island. These estimated fifteen families, who created the first Jewish settlement in an English colony on the North American mainland, came probably from the English island of Barbados.[21] Interested in settling in a New England port town, they were attracted by Rhode Island's reputation for religious toleration. In contrast to the insistence upon religious uniformity in seventeenth-century Massachusetts and Connecticut, where the courts enforced orthodox Puritanism with fines, flogging, banishment, and capital punishment in severe cases of heterodoxy, Rhode Island offered a haven for dissenters.

Rhode Island's first settlement had been established in 1636 at Providence by the Reverend Roger Williams, who after differing theologically with Massachusetts's clergy had fled southward. He was followed in 1637 by Anne Hutchinson, who, after her trial, in which she was found guilty of heresy, founded Newport with her adherents. As the two towns grew, they attracted other nonconformists: in Providence, Williams preached a gospel of toleration, while nearby Newport, in the words of one contemporary, hostile observer, served as "a receptacle for people of severall Sorts and Opinions." Dissenters made their way to Newport even from Dutch New Amsterdam, finding there the toleration not permitted by Governor Peter Stuyvesant and the Calvinist clergy of New Netherland, one of whom described Rhode Island as "the receptacle of all sorts of riff-raff people, and . . . nothing else than the sewer of New England."[22] The Jews who settled in Newport chose well, therefore, emigrating from one English colony to another rather than to the Dutch colony on Manhattan Island. And in Newport, they found the settlement that afforded the greatest degree of religious freedom anywhere in North America at the middle of the seventeenth century.

Little is known of these Jews, except that they purchased land for a cemetery in 1677 and that they engaged in trade. The latter is apparent because of two suits, in 1684 and 1685, against a number of Jews for alleged violations of the English Navigation Acts. During the 1690s, the small community grew with the arrival of ninety individuals from Cura-çao, refugees from a devastating epidemic in 1693 on that island. By the middle of the eighteenth century, between fifteen and twenty Jewish families lived in Newport, rising to approximately thirty households in 1770.[23]

Like their counterparts in New York, the Jews of eighteenth-century Newport pursued careers as merchants, trading throughout the Atlantic region. The three members of the community who held title to the land on which the community built its synagogue—Jacob Rodriguez Rivera, Moses Levy, and Isaac Hart—were all identified in the deed to the property as merchants, as were Isaac Elizer, Naphtali Hart, Jacob Isaacs, and Myer Polock, who participated in the building's construction. But the most prominent of all was Aaron Lopez, whose vessels called at ports throughout England's mainland colonies, the Caribbean, the coasts of South America, England, Ireland, Holland, Sweden, Spain, Portugal, the Azores, and the Canaries. Lopez traded in most of the goods transported across the Atlantic in the middle of the eighteenth century: rum, hardware, textiles, spermaceti candles and oil, sugar, naval stores, lumber, fish, flour, and meat, among others. A refugee from the Inquisition, Lopez arrived in Newport from Portugal in 1752, and before the middle of the following decade owned and constructed vessels, some of which he exported for sale. Moreover, he participated in the lucrative slave trade, shipping rum and hardware to Africa and returning with slaves for sale in the New World. Other Newport Jewish merchants, such as Jacob Rodriguez Rivera, Isaac Elizer, and Samuel Moses, along with their Christian counterparts, participated as well in the transatlantic shipment of slaves.[24]

In 1754, nearly a century after their first appearance there, the Jews of Newport began to construct a synagogue. In 1759 they broke ground for it, completed most of the building in 1762, and dedicated it late in 1763. Although not entirely finished at the time of its dedication, the Reverend Ezra Stiles of Newport found it to be an "edifice the most perfect of the Temple kind perhaps in America," one that "could not but raise in the Mind a faint Idea of the Majesty & Grandeur of the Ancient Jewish Worship mentioned in Scripture." Unfortunately, the congregation was not to enjoy it for long. As in New York, the occupation of the city by the British in 1776 prompted most of the members to leave, an event from which the community recovered only briefly during the 1780s.[25]

To the south, Philadelphia's Jewish community owed its genesis to emigrants from New York. Founded in 1685 by William Penn as a haven for Quakers and other dissenters, the city surpassed New York's population by 1720, when it numbered 10,000 inhabitants to New York's 7,000. In 1742 the City of Brotherly Love had 13,000 residents, second only to Boston's 16,382, while New York's population stood third in North America at 11,000. Shipbuilding increased rapidly between 1725 and 1750, on the heels of a soaring export trade in foodstuffs, lumber, livestock, and wool. During the second quarter of the eighteenth century, the city served as a principal port of entry for newcomers to America, for Pennsylvania attracted Germans and Scotch-Irish settlers in considerable numbers. With the city's rapid growth, Jewish settlers began to make their way to yet another gateway to the Atlantic, one that functioned as the portal to a significant hinterland as well.[26]

As if to test Philadelphia's viability as a commercial center, individual Jewish merchants visited the city to trade there during the early years of the eighteenth century. Between 1706 and 1709, six Jews from New York and the Caribbean islands are known to have appeared there, while between 1715 and 1720 at least one Jewish New Yorker, Abraham Lucena, apparently had more lasting commercial interests in Philadelphia, for he came to the city on at least eight occasions. The New York Jewish community also knew of Philadelphia's growth and development firsthand from the visit there by Daniel Gomez in 1719. Permanent settlement in Philadelphia by New Yorkers, however, did not begin until 1737, when Nathan and Isaac Levy emigrated from New York to Penn's city on the Delaware, where they quickly entered its commercial life. The Levy brothers imported manufactured goods from England, but they specialized in placing servants from abroad with masters to whom these servants were indentured for seven years in order to pay their fares to the New World. In 1738, two other New York brothers, David and Moses Franks, joined the Levy brothers. David Franks joined Nathan Levy in a partnership that shipped timber, wheat, corn, and meat regularly to London and imported English goods in return, frequently on vessels owned by the two partners.[27]

During the 1740s and 1750s, other Jewish settlers established residence in the city, some coming from New York, others directly from Europe, gathering around the nucleus of the Levys and Franks. Even after he married out of the Jewish faith in 1743 and raised his children as Christians, David Franks continued to serve as an agent of Jewish settlement. During the 1750s he launched Barnard Gratz, a cousin of the unfortunate Jacob Henry described earlier, in his career as a merchant, employing him as a clerk when he arrived from England. In time, Gratz and his brother, Michael, who subsequently joined him in Philadelphia, provided leadership for Philadelphia's organized Jewish community, which by 1765 contained about twenty-five families, at least half of them headed by men identifiable as merchants. Five years later, the city's Jewish families included probably a hundred individuals.[28]

True to the pattern in the settlements to the north, the first step in the development of a communal infrastructure was the acquisition of land for a cemetery. In 1740 Nathan Levy purchased land for a family burial plot; in subsequent years it served the entire community. Prayer was held in private homes, but by 1761, with the number of Jewish inhabitants increasing through immigration and births, talk of constructing a synagogue began. The elements of an organized community began to appear during the 1760s, when the emerging congregation employed a caretaker, acquired additional land for the cemetery, and maintained a fund for those in need. In 1771 worship finally began in rented quarters.[29]

A governing structure was created three years, at the latest, before the outbreak of the Revolution; in February 1773, the board of elders known as the *mahamad* in the Sephardic tradition, with Barnard Gratz as its president, resolved that, "in order to support our holy worship, and establish it on a more solid foundation," money should be collected for the "uses of the Synagogue now established in the city of Philadelphia." Finally, on the eve of the Declaration of Independence, Michael Gratz engaged a hazan, "for and in Behalf of the Jewish Society," who agreed to serve also as a ritual slaughterer and to teach the Hebrew language to children in return for an annual salary, board, and lodging. Little did Gratz and his fellow congregants know that they were about to be engulfed by an influx of Jews from New York, fleeing from the British capture of that port city at the mouth of the Hudson River.[30]

Approximately seventy miles to the west of Philadelphia, a small but significant Jewish presence arose in Lancaster, beginning with the arrival of Joseph Simon in the early 1740s. Simon served as the nucleus around which other Jewish settlers gathered, providing a room in his house for worship, two Torah scrolls, and land for a cemetery. While some, like the luckless Jacob Henry described earlier, came and went, others remained more permanently, until this small gathering of Jews in Philadelphia's hinterland faded away late in the eighteenth century, disappearing altogether at Simon's death in 1804.

Simon and the others who joined him chose Lancaster because of its role as the commercial center of western Pennsylvania, Maryland, and part of Virginia. Lancaster was a vital crossroads to the west and a linchpin in the defense of the interior; it grew to become the largest hinterland settlement in British North America. Its merchants funneled the furs supplied by Indians and white trappers and the wheat raised by the large, local population of German farmers to Philadelphia for export; they returned with all manner of foreign commodities for distribution in the interior. Joseph Simon, for example, in 1760 imported sugar to Lancaster; early in 1762 he advertised the sale of hardware, cooking utensils, farming implements, weapons, tea chests, and toys from England; and later that year, he shipped racoon and beaver furs to Philadelphia, requesting in return a shipment that included textiles, sugar, coffee, and indigo. Simon and his fellow Jews in Lancaster were as dependent upon Atlantic trade as the merchants who resided in the ports.[31]

Far to the south, four Jewish settlers appeared in Charleston, South Carolina, by 1697. Settlement there, however, remained meager during the first half of the eighteenth century, for between 1695 and 1750 only fifteen adult Jewish men are known to have resided there.[32] As in the north, most were identifiable as merchants.[33] With the arrival of several newcomers from London in 1750, the small community organized a congregation and adopted governing regulations in 1756. Thereafter their numbers appear to have increased steadily, for between 1750 and 1783 fifty-one Jewish family names appeared in Charleston, though not all who bore them settled there permanently. By 1775 the community contemplated building a synagogue, and (unsuccessfully) requested funds from New York's congregation for that purpose. The Jews of Charleston, in any case, were unable to begin the construction of a permanent house of worship until 1792; they dedicated it for use in 1794.[34]

The settlement by forty-two Jews in Savannah, Georgia, in 1733, sponsored, as noted previously, by the Sephardic community of London in order to relieve themselves of some of their poor, faltered within eight years. By 1741, most were gone, immigrating to Charleston and New York following the outbreak of war between England and Spain. Only three families remained; in 1750 they numbered sixteen individuals in a population of approximately three thousand. During the 1760s, the arrival of a few more individuals augmented the tiny group, and in 1771 perhaps six families comprised the Jewish population of Savannah. Already, however, they endeavored to function as a congregation, for in 1774 they resolved that, "having a sufficient number of Jews here to make a Congregation," they would meet at the home of one of their members as "a Congregation of Jews." Shortly thereafter, however, the outbreak of the Revolution thoroughly disrupted their lives. As one wrote, "the American Revolution at this time throughout America did ocation many Jews to be continually coming and going." As the colonial era closed, Georgia's Jews were thus thwarted by war for a second time. Significant growth and development would not come until the 1790s.[35]

Seemingly inconsequential because of their tiny numbers, the Jews of colonial Savannah exhibited the orientation to the larger Atlantic world that characterized all of colonial Jewry, and therein lies their significance. For one, like their counterparts in North America's other settlements, they relied upon contacts with other Atlantic Jewish communities for religious purposes. Accordingly, in 1737 they received books, a Torah scroll, and a Hanukkah candelabrum from one of London's Jews. For another, they built relationships with the other Jewish communities through marriage. In 1761, for example, Mordecai Sheftall married the sister of a Charleston resident. Six years later Daniel Nunes wed a woman from New York's Jewish community. In 1768, Levi Sheftall married a fourteen-year-old on the island of Saint Croix and brought her to Savannah, thereby creating a link with the Caribbean. And in 1774, Philip Minis married Judith Polock in Newport and returned with her to Savannah. The practice of marrying around the Atlantic cemented existing mercantile ties, created new ones, and contributed to the perpetuation of the Jewish community in the New World.[36]

America's Jews were members of an ethnic group of traders that reached around the Atlantic and spread as far as India in the eighteenth century.[37] In spite of the wide expanse of the Atlantic trading world, Jewish merchants readily found one another and established ties both personal and professional. To do so, they needed to travel great distances. From the vantage point of the late twentieth century, with its ease and speed of travel over vast distances and under generally safe conditions, the propensity of colonial Jewish merchants to travel widely and frequently by vastly slower means and under far more perilous circumstances seems nothing short of extraordinary. Indeed, their journeys among the ports of North America, the Caribbean, and England were an essential part of their educations, providing knowledge of market conditions abroad, familiarity with the products of a variety of countries, and, perhaps above all else, contacts with their colleagues in commerce and religion.

The voyage of Newport's Moses Lopez to Charleston in 1764 illustrates the advantages bestowed by ethnic and religious ties and by the journeys that brought coreligionists together.[38] Lopez, representing his successful half-brother, Aaron, as well as Jacob Rodriguez Rivera, the latter's father-in-law, traveled to South Carolina to sell a cargo that included spermaceti and tallow candles, soap, biscuits, flour, fish, axes, and desks, and either to sell the vessel on which he had sailed, and which belonged to Aaron, or to procure a cargo for it and dispatch it to London. Lopez, who had last seen Charleston twenty-two years before, was fortunate to have as his contact there Isaac DaCosta, the Jewish community's hazan, who had arrived in Charleston prior to 1750 and had progressed from shopkeeper to merchant during the 1750s. In addition, DaCosta had for several years corresponded with Aaron Lopez, selling merchandise on commission as Aaron's agent in the port of Charleston. Welcoming Moses Lopez, DaCosta insisted that he reside in his home, offering him its best room. Moses could thus observe the Sabbath in a Jewish household, as he indicated in one of his letters to Aaron in Newport. There too he observed firsthand the disruption to the household when his host's father-in-law died somewhere in the interior of the country. The commercial relationship had evolved into a personal one by the time Moses Lopez sailed for home seven weeks later.

In addition to providing comfortable arrangements, DaCosta may have assisted Lopez as the visitor sized up business and commerce in Charleston. During his stay, Moses Lopez discovered that the port was a crossroads for ships from the West Indies, Europe, and such North American ports as Saint Augustine, Pensacola, and Mobile. Merchant importers sold European goods to the colony's planters, who remained loyal to an individual merchant even if other traders extended more favorable terms. Great profits could be earned by selling to the inhabitants of the interior, who, Lopez concluded, apparently drove softer bargains than did New Englanders. Substantial profits were to be had in winter, when the town's merchants sold provisions to the planters, who came to the city to make their purchases. In addition, the planters typically settled their accounts at the New Year, exchanging their produce for merchandise imported from abroad. Though these practices meant that payments were often late and debts were sometimes bad, fortunes could be made quickly in Charleston, commercial information that Moses urged his brother in Newport to convey to another of their contacts, a cousin in Savannah.

Because Moses Lopez visited Charleston in the spring of 1764, his information regarding business conditions in South Carolina during the winter months could have come only from a local informant. Whether it was his host who provided this information is not known, but it is certain that DaCosta assisted Lopez in an immediately practical manner, the procurement of freight for shipment to England. Unable to sell his brother's vessel, Moses Lopez acquired a cargo of pitch, green tar, and rice thanks not only to his host's friendliness but also his credit and reputation among the leading local merchants. Satisfied, Moses Lopez took ship for home, the successful outcome of his mission to South Carolina secured with the help of a coreligionist with whom he and his brother had dealt previously only through correspondence.

The journey by Moses Lopez was typical of those undertaken by the Jewish merchants of colonial North America.[39] Indeed, at times it was an impending voyage that prompted them to compose their last wills and testaments. Isaac Rodriguez Marques, for example, wrote his in 1707 because he contemplated a voyage from New York to Jamaica. So did Abraham de Lucena in 1725, who explained before his trip to Jamaica that "the Dangers of the Sea And the Uncertainty of this Mortal Life" occasioned his will. In similar fashion, Jacob Fonseca in 1729 cited "the danger & hazards unto which I am Likely to be Exposed," as he wrote his will before setting out for the Caribbean; while Samuel Myers-Cohen, "Considering the Dangers of the Seas," drew his in 1743 because he intended to travel to England, a voyage from which he subsequently returned safely to New York.[40]

The letters of the Franks family between 1733 and 1748 are replete with allusions to the comings and goings of the members of that family. David Franks, son of Jacob and Abigail Franks, journeyed in 1735 to

Boston, where he resided briefly, settled eventually in Philadelphia, contemplated voyages to Jamaica and India, and traveled to Georgia. Moses Franks, a younger son, journeyed to England in 1738, returned to New York in 1739, took up residence in Philadelphia, and soon after settled permanently in England. Coleman Solomons, nephew of Jacob Franks, arrived from London in New York by 1729, returned to England in 1734, and later that year traveled to Philadelphia. In 1735 the family considered sending him to Holland, but instead he journeyed to England, went next to South Carolina in 1736, and returned to New York in 1738. He remained in North America thereafter for at least three years and died in England in 1767. Isaac Levy, brother of Abigail Franks, journeyed to London in 1740, while a second brother, Asher, voyaged about between England, New York, and Philadelphia.[41]

In addition to their extensive journeys across the seas, colonial Jewish merchants established family representatives in as many locations as possible around the Atlantic basin. Again the example of the Franks family is instructive. Jacob Franks, the patriarch, arrived in New York from England in 1708 or 1709, undoubtedly encouraged to immigrate to the New World to represent his London commercial family, with whom he maintained contact for years to come. In or about 1712 he married Abigail Levy, the daughter of Moses Levy, one of New York's Jewish merchants and the father of several sons who later dispersed to Philadelphia, London, and Jamaica. In this manner a commercial network linked by family representatives in various ports arose that could benefit not only Moses Levy but also his son-in-law, Jacob Franks.

Subsequently, the three sons of Jacob and Abigail Franks who grew to maturity emigrated from New York to other locations, where they too represented one another's mercantile interests. Naphtali Franks, the oldest, settled in London by the spring of 1733, where he quickly ingratiated himself with his father's brothers and married one of his cousins. He never returned from England to the New World, but from what was in effect his commercial station in London, he maintained trading connections with his father in New York and his brother, David, in Philadelphia. The third brother, Moses, settled for a time in Philadelphia but eventually immigrated to England, joining his older brother and thus rounding out the Franks family network on the two sides of the Atlantic.

Supplementing this network, Moses Solomons, one of Jacob Franks's nephews, resided in Charleston, from where he too traded with other members of the family.[42]

That dispersal of the family was indispensable to commercial success was eminently clear to Abigail Franks, who nonetheless bemoaned it. To her son Naphtali, gone permanently to England, she wrote in 1741:

> I wish but for the happyness of Seeing you wich I begin to fear I never Shall for I dont wish you here And I am Sure there is Little porbability of my Goeing to England. If parents would Give themselves Leave to Consider the many Difficulties that attends the bringing up of Childeren there would not be such Imoderate Joy att there birtth I dont mean the Care of there infancy thats the Least but its affter they are grown Up and behave in Such a maner As to Give Sattisfaction then to be bereaved of them in the Decline of Life when the injoying of them would be Our Greatest happyness for the Cares of giting a Liveing Disperses Them Up and down the world and the Only pleassure wee injoy (and thats intermixt with Anxiety) is to hear they doe well Wich is A pleassure I hope to have.[43]

The proclivity for travel that characterized the colonial Jewish merchant brought in its wake the problem of impoverished Jews who also journeyed from place to place about the Atlantic. The organized Jewish community assisted poor strangers financially and then sent them on their way by paying their transportation charges. New York's congregation, for example, in 1728 decided to care for unmarried transients by providing them with eight shillings a week for as long as three months and to expend up to two pounds for fare to another port. For families, the amounts allocated were to be determined by the community's leaders. Thereafter, the community assisted wandering strangers who turned up in New York before dispatching them to London, Barbados, Saint Croix, Curaçao, Surinam, Philadelphia, and Charleston. Thus, when Jacob Musqueto in 1768 arrived in New York from Saint Eustatius in need of assistance and requested passage to Barbados, the community's elders sent him as far as Philadelphia and wrote to Michael Gratz asking him to collect funds from the Jewish population there to enable the traveler to continue his journey. Similarly, two years later Jacob Rodriguez Rivera of Newport used his connections to find ship passage for an impoverished individual from Saint Eustatius, who, ostensibly seeking to travel to Surinam, had arrived in Rhode Island, though whether Rivera acted on his own or as the agent of the synagogue of Newport is not known.[44]

The importance of personal connections to commerce also encompassed marriage. By joining families residing in distant locations around the Atlantic, marriage solidified commercial networks, rooting them in ties that were deeper than those provided by mere membership in the same religious group, valuable though that alone was. To be sure, the small Jewish population in any one location, the resulting paucity in the number of eligible partners as one neared the age of marriage, and the commitment to marriage within the faith, a fundamental requirement of the Jewish religion, forced families to look beyond the confines of their communities to the larger domain of the Atlantic. Nevertheless, transatlantic marriages also bestowed commercial advantages, supplementing religious reasons for seeking a spouse for oneself or for one's child in a distant port.

The history of the first three generations of the Gomez clan of New York provides perhaps the best example during the colonial era of how a family, through marriage, established ties across many thousands of miles. Louis Moses Gomez, the patriarch of the family, was born in Madrid between 1654 and 1660, moved with his father to France—undoubtedly to escape the resurgent Inquisition of the mid-seventeenth century—and from France eventually immigrated to New York. There he became a man of commerce, played a leading part during the late 1720s in building New York's first permanent synagogue, and died in 1740. Some time after his arrival in New York, Louis Moses Gomez married Esther Marques, a woman whose family had ties to the island of Barbados, for, following the death of her father in New York, her mother married a member of that island's Jewish community, while her brother died there in 1725.[45]

Louis Moses and Esther Gomez gave birth to six sons, one of whom perished in 1722 during a voyage to the Caribbean, murdered probably by Spaniards on the island of Cuba. Of the remaining five sons, at least two married women who came from Caribbean islands, thus extending the family's ties with the Caribbean. Their third son, Daniel, first married Rebecca De Torres, whose father and brother resided in Jamaica, and then Esther Levy of Curaçao, while their sixth son, Benjamin, became the husband of Esther Nunes of Barbados. That these connections bore fruit in commerce is apparent from the ledger that has been ascribed to Daniel Gomez, in which he posted accounts of his dealings in 1745 with Jacob Da Joshua Naar and in 1748 with Aaron Da Chaves, both of whom he identified as his brothers-in-law in Curaçao. In addition, he recorded transactions in 1744 with Isaac and Benjamin Gomez of Barbados; perhaps the latter was the brother who had married Esther Nunes of that island. The Gomez family's ties may have extended even more distantly across the Atlantic, for Daniel Gomez also conducted business in 1751 with a Miguel Gomez, whom he described as a merchant on the island of Madeira.[46]

The third generation of the Gomez family continued the pattern. Mordecai Gomez, the eldest son of Louis and Esther, was the father of seven children, only one of whom, Eve Esther, married a resident of New York, Uriah Hendricks. Two sons died without marrying, while the remaining four children wed individuals from other Atlantic locations. Sons Moses and Isaac married in Jamaica and Curaçao, respectively, while another daughter married in England. She returned with her husband to New York, only to return to England because of his adherence to the Crown during the American Revolution. The seventh child, Moses M. Gomez, married Esther Lopez, a daughter of Newport's Aaron Lopez. This liaison, however, did not provide the only connection between the two families, for another member of the large Gomez clan, Isaac Gomez, Jr., married Abigail Lopez, another of Aaron Lopez's children.[47]

Marriages uniting the Gomez family of New York and the Lopez family of Newport indicate that colonial America's Jewish inhabitants sought to establish family networks in the ports along the coast of North America as well as in the islands of the Caribbean. The webs that they created tied together the Jews of Newport and Savannah, of Charleston and Philadelphia, and all of these to New York, underpinning trade and contributing to the continuity of the Jewish presence in the colonies.[48] Relationships built upon marriages reached inland as well. Joseph Simon in Lancaster wed a woman whose family resided in New York and whose uncle, Samuel Myers-Cohen, identified himself as a merchant in his will. Barnard Gratz in Philadelphia, one of Simon's important commercial correspondents, married a daughter of the same Samuel Myers-Cohen, thus linking himself not only to the New York merchant but to Joseph Simon as well. Simon subsequently married off one of his daughters to Michael Gratz of Philadelphia, who with his brother conducted an extensive trade to the west in conjunction with his father-in-law, eventually becoming his partner in speculation in western lands.[49]

Connections based upon marriage ties of course did not automatically guarantee commercial success, as Aaron Lopez discovered in the late 1760s. Eager to expand and solidify trade with the island of Jamaica, Lopez endeavored to enlist Isaac Pereira Mendes, a Jamaican merchant, to serve as his commercial agent. Isaac Mendes declined, but recommended his brother, Abraham Mendes, in his stead, who happened to be Lopez's son-in-law. Lopez thereupon dispatched his daughter and son-in-law to Jamaica, where, despite the offer of Isaac to assist Abraham "with zeal and brotherly love," Abraham failed dismally as a resident commercial agent, necessitating his recall to Rhode Island.[50]

Though a failure commercially, the union of Abraham Mendes and Sarah Lopez united two individuals who, in the absence of a tradition of Jewish transatlantic marriage, might have abandoned their ethnic group and religion to assimilate and disappear as Jews. Membership in a community that spanned the Atlantic thus contributed to the distinctiveness of the Jewish settlers as a recognizable group within colonial society at the same time that it played a role in forming commercial ties. It did so not only through marriages but also by encouraging the organized Jewish communities of the Atlantic to assist each other in religious matters. The reliance of Savannah's Jews upon a member of the London Jewish community for religious objects in 1737 was not an isolated incident but, rather, a significant feature of religious life in colonial America. Counting similarly upon the network of Jewish communities around the Atlantic, when Charleston's congregation created a board of trustees for its new cemetery in 1764, it appointed representatives of the congregations of New York, Newport, Savannah, and Jamaica to it.[51]

To construct permanent synagogues and other structures, the colonists relied upon the resources of individual contributors and congregations in other localities. When it undertook to build its first permanent structure in 1728, New York's congregation wrote to Jamaica's synagogue to request funds; it also received donations from individuals in Boston, London, Jamaica, and Barbados, as well as a substantial sum from the congregation on Curaçao. Several years later it recorded a contribution from a resident of Barbados, earmarked, as she specified, to build a wall around the community's cemetery. The community also probably benefited from a contribution by one of London's Jews for the construction of its school building in 1731. New York's Jews in turn assisted Newport Jews when they began to build their synagogue in the late 1750s, lending them the Torah scroll that formerly had belonged to the original community in Savannah and donating funds toward the construction of the building. Newport's congregation, in addition, received financial assistance from the Jewish communities of Surinam, Jamaica, Curaçao, and London, as well as Torah scrolls from London's and Amsterdam's congregations. Likewise, Philadelphia's emerging congregation received a Torah scroll from New York in 1761.[52]

The Atlantic congregations also turned to each other for salaried religious functionaries. In 1757, for example, the New York community wrote to London to find a hazan qualified to teach Hebrew, English, and Spanish to its children as well as to lead the synagogue's services. Eight years later, when their hazan informed them of his intention to resign, the congregation resolved that "notices thereof may be given to Foreign Parts," inviting candidates from abroad to travel to New York at their own expense to apply for the position. Similarly, when the community's ritual slaughterer resigned in 1775, the congregation directed its officers to write to Newport and Philadelphia, asking for qualified candidates.[53]

Finally, the Jewish inhabitants of North America were drawn into contact with their religious brethren in the Atlantic region because of their commerce in meat slaughtered according to religious law. Aaron

Lopez of Newport, for example, was well known in Jamaica for his export of kosher meat there, while other Newport Jews exported meat to Surinam, Barbados, and Jamaica. From Philadelphia, Michael Gratz began to export kosher meat to Barbados and probably Curaçao, following his journey to the West Indies in 1765. New York's congregation devised a seal in 1752 to attest to the ritual purity of meat exported from the city under their supervision, and in 1757 responded to charges and rumors in Jamaica and Curaçao that meat exported from New York was not kosher. Denying the allegations, the New Yorkers assured their correspondents that they would do all that was required to protect the regulations of the Jewish faith.[54]

Impelled by religious as well as commercial considerations, the Jews of colonial America participated in a world far more expansive than their small, provincial cities in the New World. Instead of being isolated in their small towns, they had access to the resources of a large community, thereby increasing their chances for successful settlement in the American colonies. Trading, traveling, and marrying widely, their perspective embraced the entire Atlantic region, to the advantage simultaneously of their religious commitments and their worldly interests. And yet, concurrently with their outward, cosmopolitan gaze, they tended as well to their immediate surroundings, diligently working to establish flourishing Jewish communities in the New World. Their efforts, as will be seen, took them into uncharted waters, for the Jewish inhabitants of colonial America were among the first to experiment with a new kind of Jewish community in the emerging modern world.

CHAPTER THREE

COMMUNITY

IN THE autumn of 1757, the officers of New York's Shearith Israel, North America's largest and oldest Jewish congregation, resolved to proceed against several individuals residing outside the city who had come to their attention for continually violating several fundamental precepts of religious law. The elders had received information alleging that these people were guilty of "such as Trading on the Sabath, Eating of forbidden Meats & other Heinous Crimes," and decided that an admonition must be issued against them in the synagogue on Yom Kippur, the most solemn occasion of the Jewish year. Selecting Yom Kippur, a day devoted to fasting, self-examination, and a penitential liturgy, guaranteed that the largest number possible would hear their call for reformation, for this was the day in the year of greatest attendance in the synagogue. Accordingly, citing a passage in Leviticus that instructed the people "to reprove one another," the elders on Yom Kippur proclaimed that those who continued to violate Jewish law would be expelled from the congregation and no longer be counted among its membership, unless they changed their habits. Expulsion would continue after death, for the obstinate would not be buried "according to the manner of our brethren." As the elders warned in their declaration, just as Nehemiah closed the gates against those who transgressed, "so will the Gates of our Community be shut intirely Against such offenders."[1]

Six months later, Shearith Israel's leaders decided that their Yom Kippur proclamation had to some extent succeeded. On a Sabbath late in March 1758, they announced in the synagogue that the time had come to reopen the gates to those who had heeded the Yom Kippur admonition. Any person who believed that he was qualified to be called to the Torah or otherwise to participate in the synagogue's rites because he conformed to religious law was asked to inform the *parnas,* or president, either in person or through a friend, so that none would be excluded wrongfully. Explaining their role, the leaders depicted themselves as "faithful Sheeperds [who] call into the fold the wandring sheep" and pleaded that all understand that they had been motivated by no other consideration than "the establishing & supporting our holy religion," a request that they directed to "every member of this Community."[2]

On these two occasions, the leaders of Shearith Israel eschewed the term they ordinarily used to describe the synagogue—*congregation*—in favor of "our Community" and "this Community." Clearly, however, they distinguished between the two, for the congregation of worshippers was not necessarily coterminous with the community. Thus in 1769 the synagogue's members ruled that any individual who was not a member, "tho Congregating with us," who did not adhere to Shearith Israel's regulations was to have no rights, benefits, or privileges "in our Community."[3] As an abstraction, *community* connotes a fellowship, one whose members share common values and goals, a common history, and common norms of behavior. It affords its members protection and mutual support and provides a sense of belonging that counterbalances the anxieties of anonymity, loneliness, and vulnerability. The synagogue's eighteenth-century leaders are not known to have conducted theoretical discussions about the concept and the virtues of community, but they did what they could to protect the integrity of the fellowship and to insure its continuity. In insisting upon the supremacy of religious law, they threatened to expel from the group those who would not comply with traditional religious regulations, thereby strengthening the community by reaffirming the principles and the boundaries that defined it in the first place.

The notion of community has in recent decades yielded important insights into colonial America, notably colonial New England, where the tale usually is of the decline of cohesiveness and communitarian values over time.[4] Among colonial Jewry, however, consistent commitment to the fellowship's integrity and its continuity can be discerned readily, whether in threats of excommunication like the one proclaimed on Yom Kippur in Shearith Israel, in marriage patterns, or in provisions for education, for the maintenance of dietary regulations at community expense, and for the support of the poor. Moreover, by overcoming traditional hostilities and creating a fellowship that blended Ashkenazim and Sephardim, the Jews of colonial America successfully institutionalized community values where their contemporaries in Europe did not. Not that the colonial congregation was free of strife: often its members labored to preserve the community in the face of considerable internal rancor and dissension. Consistently, however, the community endeavored to assure that cohesion would prevail over centripetal forces that threatened to shatter the group.

Save for the integration of Ashkenazim with Sephardim, certain of the ideas and practices that undergirded efforts to create a tightly organized and harmonious community were not invented in the New World but, rather, were transported by the settlers from Europe. For centuries, the Jewish inhabitants of each town and city in the Old World had governed themselves autonomously, in conformity with the corporate organization of society whose origins lay in the medieval era. Elected councils, composed largely of the well-to-do, negotiated with secular and religious officials on behalf of the Jewish population, collected taxes for the secular authorities, administered the community's religious and welfare institutions, maintained courts to settle disputes, and regulated personal behavior. Denied membership in a guild or a town or a borough, the individual Jew could belong only to the organized Jewish community, which consequently exercised hegemony over all members of the Jewish faith.[5] Thus universal in its scope, the European Jewish community provided a model that informed and guided the Jewish inhabitants of North America, although circumstances in the New World, as will be seen, were to alter certain features of the European precedent, certainly by the middle of the eighteenth century.

The history of eighteenth-century Shearith Israel provides an important example of a congregation whose members persevered in their commitment to the communitarian ideal despite tendencies by midcentury to fly apart. Little is known of the congregation prior to 1728, when, in four short months of whirlwind activity, it purchased land for a new cemetery, bought property to construct its first synagogue building, and revised its rules of government.[6] A new cemetery was clearly required—for, as the congregation explained to the New York City Common Council, no space remained in the one in use since 1682—but the necessity for a new synagogue building may not have been as obvious. The congregation had worshipped in a rented private house since the turn of the century, and it conceivably could have continued to do so, moving to larger rented quarters if expanding numbers made additional space imperative. Erecting and furnishing a permanent structure, which would require repeated financial contributions by the members, undoubtedly provided greater cohesion than renting quarters, for the entire community shared in the creation of the building that was its embodiment. Buildings inspire and ennoble, they awe and intimidate; and they can draw together the community that erects them because of the common purpose, shared tribulations, and triumphant celebrations that accompany their completion. They define a community. Shearith Israel subsequently dedicated its new permanent structure, a small, modest building, on the seventh day of Passover in 1730 and, in acknowledgement of the importance of this achievement, continued to mark the anniversary of this communal enterprise each year thereafter on the same day.[7]

At the same time that the members of Shearith Israel purchased land for a cemetery and for a synagogue to give physical expression to their community, they undertook to formulate rules that would "preserve Peace, tranquility and good Government amongst ym." Regulations had been adopted around 1705, they explained, but these had fallen into disuse. Accordingly, in September 1728 they assembled to subscribe to a new social contract, noting that their compact met "with common consent." To assure "ye good Government of our Holy Congregation," the congregation was to be governed by a parnas and two assistants, who were empowered to appoint their successors. Anyone who declined to serve as parnas or assistant was to be fined, a provision that spoke to the necessity of guaranteeing the continuity of leadership within the community, so that it would not founder for want of public servants ready to attend to its needs.

Along with his other duties, the parnas was to distribute congregational funds to assist the poor, thereby incorporating the less fortunate within the body of the community. Poor strangers, on the other hand, were not to be permitted to attach themselves permanently to the community. Although they could receive assistance for as many as twelve weeks, they were to be transported to another place at the congregation's expense. The community would discipline any of its members who by word or deed offended another within the synagogue, and the parnas and his assistants were to fine these offenders and enlist the aid of the entire group against those who refused to pay. To finance the community's affairs, the three officers were to assess the men's seats in the synagogue, with charges ranging from five to fifteen shillings per year. To remind the community's membership of the regulations that were to govern, the agreements that gave it structure, the parnas was required to read them twice each year in the synagogue in English and Portuguese. Finally, the salaries and responsibilities of the community's religious functionaries were listed, with the comment that these provisions were agreed to "with concorde," echoing the earlier assertion that the congregation's governing articles were drawn up "with common consent." The intention, clearly, was that this was to be a community that could claim that it had been created in harmony and consensus.[8]

Seventeen men affixed their names to the articles of organization on 15 September 1728, and in early 1739 an additional six subscribed. The practice of signing the community's governing rules confirmed membership in the congregation and was apparently a traditional practice in Sephardic synagogues. In Brazil, for example, the regulations adopted in 1648 prescribed that "there will exist a Book which everyone now present and also the newcomers will have to sign." The New York congregation viewed the matter of the signature as significant, since in 1768 and again in 1769 it threatened to expunge the signatures of members who deserved expulsion from the community because of their "Indecent Behavior in Synegouge," and thereby erase any record of their membership even in times of good conduct.[9]

Governance of the community by a small council, the mahamad, that selected its successors was also standard in the Sephardic tradition, as in Curaçao, where on the eve of Rosh Hashanah, the mahamad would meet to select the officers for the coming year. The powers of the parnas and his assistants were virtually total in the life of the community. The regulations of the congregations in Venice, Amsterdam, and Curaçao bestowed supreme power on them in all matters, while in Brazil the regulations stated that it was "the duty of the Gentlemen of the Mahamad to take care of all matters concerning the said Kahal." Any in Brazil who committed an offense against the community's elders was to pay double the fines imposed when the offense was against an ordinary member.[10]

Similarly, the authority of the elders in Shearith Israel was definitive in all matters, save for the employment of religious functionaries and the determination of their salaries. In meetings called for that purpose by the parnas and assistants, the entire membership elected the hazan, the shokhet, and the shammash—the reader who led services and chanted from the Torah, the ritual slaughterer, and the synagogue's caretaker, respectively—and approved their compensation. In all other matters, the parnas and his assistants reigned supreme, complete with provisions—as in Curaçao, Brazil, London, and Amsterdam—for their personal dignity. To affront the members of the mahamad, to insult them, was to risk the community's disciplinary procedures.[11] This accorded well not only with Sephardic governance elsewhere but also with the social values of English colonial society, where a belief in hierarchy as the guarantor of social order prevailed, replete with expectations of deferential behavior to one's superiors.

The Sephardim and Ashkenazim who composed and signed Shearith Israel's regulations in 1728 shared a religious heritage that coincided in all of its essentials, unlike Catholics and the adherents of the various Protestant sects whose differences over basic religious tenets precipitated conflicts that repeatedly ravaged Europe. Ashkenazim and Sephardim adhered to the same theological pinciples and largely to the same religious laws and observances. As the members subscribed to their newly written compact and completed their first permanent synagogue building after three-quarters of a century of a Jewish presence in New York, there was therefore every reason to assume that their commitment to the community was realistic because of these deeply shared religious principles and traditions. A harmonious fellowship was practical as well, for though Jews were the beneficiaries of English toleration in the New World, they were a people minute in numbers who, in religion, existed apart from the majority. The very name of the New York congregation suggests vulnerability and precariousness: they were a Shearith Israel, a remnant of Israel.

Along with the other congregations in eighteenth-century America, Shearith Israel adhered to the Sephardic rite of worship. During his service as hazan between 1759 and 1765, Joseph Pinto compiled a record of the order of the service in Shearith Israel, which indicates that worship in New York conformed with that in the Sephardic synagogues of London and Amsterdam. It did elsewhere in America, as well. Though nearly the entire Jewish population of Philadelphia was Germanic in origin, they too adhered to the Sephardic liturgy. Affirming the practices that prevailed everywhere in North America, the members of Savannah's Mikva Israel in 1791 specified in their regulations "that the mode of worship be according to the Pourtuguese minhauge [rite]." Despite the fact that probably as early as the 1720s the majority of the Jews in America were Ashkenazic in origin, the Sephardic system of worship established in Brazil when Jews first settled in the New World was transported to New York in 1654 and introduced later, as well, in Philadelphia, Newport, Charleston, Savannah, and in the congregations of the Caribbean islands. Throughout the seventeenth and eighteenth centuries the Sephardic rite was the American rite.[12]

In truth, the rites of the Sephardic and Ashkenazic synagogues did not differ in fundamentals. In both, Hebrew was the language of worship, the prayers embodied the same theological principles, and the Torah was of course the same. Moreover, the structure of the service was identical. On Sabbaths and festival mornings, for example, the Morning Service, whose content had been established many centuries before, was followed by a weekly reading from the Torah and the Prophets, which in turn was succeeded by the Additional Service. Both incorporated within their architecture a gallery for women, a podium in the first-floor men's section where the Torah was read, and an ark on the eastern wall to house the Torah. Unlike Christian churches, which after the upheaval of the Reformation differed profoundly in theology, language of worship, structure and content of the service—with some eliminating the Mass and Holy Communion—and architectures rooted in opposing theologies, Ashkenazic and Sephardic communities agreed upon the essentials.[13]

Although they agreed upon the fundamentals of faith, theology, and religious law, the two Jewish rites diverged in many of their details. Among the Sephardim, for example, the hazan officiated standing on the podium in the middle of the synagogue's men's floor, while the Ashkenazim originally reserved the podium for the reading of the Torah. The Sephardim recited the morning blessings of thanksgiving in the synagogue rather than at home; the latter was customary among the Ashkenazim. This was much in keeping with a general tendency among the Sephardim to rely upon the synagogue more than did the Ashkenazim as the locus for the observance of many rituals. Accordingly, Sephardim constructed temporary huts at the synagogue to celebrate the festival of Sukkot, conducted congregational seders on Passover, and permitted mourners to attend services in the synagogue throughout the seven days of ritual mourning following the death of a family member. Among the Ashkenazim, on the other hand, mourners were restricted to their homes except on the Sabbath, when they were permitted to go to the synagogue. Similarly, the Ashkenazim, employing a fowl as scapegoat, conducted the ceremony of symbolically purging themselves of sin on the eve of Yom Kippur in their homes, while the Sephardim did so at the synagogue.[14]

The two communities diverged as well in the details of the liturgy—though, again, similarities in the structure of the service, its meaning, and the underlying theology far outweighed differences in the wording of prayers and the inclusion of various poetic works in the prayer book. Chants and canticles differed, as did the pronunciation of the Hebrew language, prompting Jacob Emden, an eighteenth-century Ashkenazic rabbi, to accuse the Sephardim of "making the holy profane," citing the Sephardic pronunciation of the vowel sign for "aw" as "ah" in evidence. (Others, however, like one eighteenth-century educational reformer in Hamburg, found the Sephardic pronunciation more appealing to the ear, its pleasantness more likely to inspire holiness.) Finally, marriage, mourning, and birth customs differed. The Sephardim, for example, named children after living relatives, something the Ashkenazim would never do, instead naming offspring in memory of deceased relatives. In addition, the two recited different liturgical poems on the Sabbath before a circumcision.[15]

Despite agreement upon the fundamentals of faith, with divergence merely in the details of rite and custom, a great social chasm separated the Ashkenazim and the Sephardim. Jews who originated on the Iberian peninsula looked with contempt upon those who came from central and eastern Europe, regarding them as uncouth, dirty, uneducated, and generally of inferior caste. One tradition in England had it that the Sephardim deodorized rooms with fragrances following visits by the Ashkenazim. Offering an allegedly historical explanation for their superiority, the Sephardim claimed descent from the nobility of ancient Jerusalem and asserted that all non-Iberian Jews were descended from the commoners of ancient Israel. Some Sephardim traced their ancestry to the royal house of David; many claimed they had belonged to the aristocracy during their residence in Spain.[16]

The Ashkenazim, in their turn, accused the Sephardim of an excessively easygoing attitude toward religious observance—of a willingness to compromise in matters of ritual and practice. Indeed, the Ashkenazim did adhere to stricter religious standards in such areas as fasting, Sabbath and festival observances, family purity, and dietary regulations. Echoes of this particular source of tension reached North America, when the Reverend Samuel Quincy, commenting upon the bitter quarrels among the handful of Jews in Georgia during the 1730s, noted that the colony's Portuguese Jews were lax in the observance of Jewish rituals, that some among them attended church services, and that the German Jews were "a great deal more strict in their way, and rigid Observers of their Laws."[17]

Where they came in contact in Europe, the two groups established separate communal organizations. For example, the regulations of the Santa Compenhia de Dotar Orfans e Donzelas Pobres, established in 1613 to assist female orphans and other impoverished women to find husbands, explained that its charity was available "to marry orphans and poor maidens of the Portuguese and Castilian Nation" and called upon the good offices of "all those wishing to support such a pious work who are of our Hebrew nation, whether Portuguese or Castilian." During the eighteenth century, London's Ashkenazic congregations as a matter of course maintained their own school, their own burial society, and their own organizations to assist the poor, to visit the sick, and to ransom captives seized by Mediterranean pirates.[18]

Separate synagogues were the norm. Following the return of Jews to England in the second half of the seventeenth century, the Ashkenazim at first worshipped with the Sephardim, but hardly any were admitted to membership in the Sephardic congregation. In 1679 the Sephardim prohibited Ashkenazim from being called to the Torah, receiving any honors, voting, holding office or even making contributions without express permission. By 1690 the Ashkenazim began to worship separately, and in 1694 the leaders of the Sephardic congregation decreed that "the Synagogue *Saar Asamaim* shall only serve for the Jews of our Portuguese and Spanish nation . . . and the Jews of other nations that may come shall be admitted to say prayers if it seems good to the gentlemen of the Mahamad." This regulation merely reaffirmed one adopted thirty years before, which required the approval of the governing board for non-Sephardim to worship among them. By 1697 London's Ashkenazim and Sephardim were being interred in separate burial grounds, following a demand by the Sephardic leadership four years earlier that the Ashkenazim establish their own cemetery.[19] In Amsterdam, the two groups built grand, but separate, synagogues during the early 1670s. The Sephardim permitted Ashkenazim to attend services in their synagogue but segregated them to the sides. In 1772, when a large throng filled the structure to observe a competition to select a new hazan, the Ashkenazim in attendance broke through wooden barriers meant to restrict them to the sides, trampling six attendants in the process, in order to gain entrance to the central part of the synagogue. The occurrence undoubtedly confirmed Sephardic views of Ashkenazic barbarism.[20]

Perhaps most indicative of all of prevailing attitudes, the Sephardim looked askance upon intermarriage with the Ashkenazim. When the treasurer of the London Sephardic congregation applied for permission in 1744 to marry an Ashkenazic woman, he was forced to resign his position. Though permission for the marriage was granted, the community's rabbis did not attend the ceremony, and the bridegroom was denied all the usual honors accorded by the synagogue. During subsequent decades, the names of Ashkenazic women who wed Sephardic men were not recorded in the congregational records but were listed anonymously as "Tudesca," the generic term applied by the Sephardim to the Ashkenazim.[21]

Not surprisingly, Ashkenazic and Sephardic emigrants from Europe transported their animosities to the New World. In Surinam, separate congregations existed by the 1730s; anger and recriminations thereafter often characterized relations between the two. In 1773 Rabbi Haim Isaac Carigal, a visitor to Surinam from the land of Israel, reported to a Jewish merchant friend in Newport that "in this firm the Portuguese funds are kept separate from those of the Germans, and the boy, whom I brought with me, being German, they do not pay for his maintenance. . . . I warned you of all this before, but you objected that this company had large funds and that they would be sure to pay for the expenses caused by that boy." Conflict in Saint Eustatius proved so frequent that recourse to the civil authorities proved necessary. In 1760 the island's governor finally appointed a special commission to resolve the differences between the two groups and to establish communal regulations for them.[22]

In Georgia, the initial Jewish settlement of thirty-four Sephardim and eight Ashkenazim in 1733 quickly disintegrated in disputes arising from attempts to build a place of worship. The Reverend Bolzius wrote in 1738: "They want to build a Synagogue, but the Spanish and German Jews cannot come to terms. . . . As I mentioned before, the Spanish and Portuguese Jews are against the German Jews and they are going to protest the petition by the German Jews to build a synagogue." In the following year, he wrote to a correspondent in Berlin that, "they still have no synagogue, for which they themselves are to blame, since one party prevents the other from building one. The German Jews feel justified in building a synagogue and want to let the Spanish Jews participate in its use; but the latter will not consent to this but wish to have precedence."[23]

When Shearith Israel in New York began to construct its first permanent synagogue in 1729, the community in Curaçao responded affirmatively to their request for financial assistance but requested assurances that the Ashkenazim would not be permitted to gain the upper hand, despite their preponderance in numbers. As the *haham,* the rabbi, of Curaçao's Sephardic congregation wrote:

> Now I must tell you that the Members of this Holy Congregation Whom devoutly Contributed to Wards this Benefaction, as they know that the (asquenazum) or Germans, are more in Number than Wee there, they desire of you not to Consent, not Withstanding they are the most, to Let them have any More Votes nor Authority then they have had hitherto and for the performance of which you are to get them to Signe and agreement of the Same by all of them, and that one Copy of the Sayd agreement Remain in the Hands of Mr. Luis Gomez as the Eldest Member, and Another to be Sent to me for the Treasurer of this Congregation to Keep in his Books, and as this request is funded in Solesiting the Peace and Unety of that Holy Congregation I hope that you as Well as the Asquinazim, Whom all I wish God may bless, Will Comply With this my Petition.[24]

The Ashkenazim in New York never did comply with the "Petition" of Curaçao's haham, and the Sephardim probably never asked them to do so, for the hostility that characterized relations between the Ashkenazim and Sephardim in Europe and the Caribbean was not permitted to undermine the congregations in the English mainland colonies. With the exception of Georgia in the 1730s, Sephardic pretensions to superiority, Ashkenazic allegations of Sephardic religious laxity, and differences in rites and customs did not fracture and divide North American Jewry during the eighteenth century, and in fact a veritable alliance of Ashkenazim and Sephardim arose within the colonial congregations.

A desire to ally themselves because of the paucity of their numbers cannot account for the absence of conflict between them. Small numbers did not prevent disruption in Surinam, Saint Eustatius, and Savannah nor dissuade the haham of Curaçao from urging New York's Sephardim to take steps to dominate the Ashkenazic majority. Similarly, London's small Jewish population, numbering no more than several hundred at the beginning of the eighteenth century, divided early. Furthermore, the internal history of eighteenth-century Shearith Israel provides ample evidence of contentiousness, despite the community's small size. Whatever persuaded early American Jewry to eschew conflict along ethnic lines, the result was a unity rare among their counterparts elsewhere.

The Ashkenazim in Shearith Israel accepted not only the Sephardic rite but also the use of the Portuguese language for special purposes. The regulations adopted in 1728 were proclaimed twice yearly in English and Portuguese, and recitation of the prayer on behalf of the king of England continued in Portuguese until the American Revolution. Significantly, at least two of the Ashkenazim who served as parnasim kept the synagogue's accounts in Portuguese.[25] More important, the Ashkenazim and Sephardim shared in governance. Of forty-six individuals known to have served as parnasim and assistants between 1728 and 1760, sixteen (35 percent) were Ashkenazim,[26] while fifteen (33 percent) were Sephardim.[27] The remaining fifteen (33 percent) included nine men whose names suggest that they probably were of Ashkenazic origin; if added to the sixteen who definitely were, then the portion of Ashkenazim who led the New York Jewish community in the period indicated was at least 54 percent of the total.[28]

Moreover, at critical junctures in the community's existence, representatives of the leading Ashkenazic and Sephardic families joined forces. Construction of the first permanent synagogue structure in New York brought together Jacob Franks, the community's wealthiest Ashkenazi, with Louis Moses Gomez, Gomez's son, Mordecai, and Benjamin Mendes Pacheco in 1728 as the committee to build the structure. Louis Moses Gomez and Jacob Franks alternated as parnasim in 1729 and 1730, as the plans for the structure proceeded. In the upheaval of 1746, the first great conflict in the community, the congregation directed its Sephardic parnas, Abraham Rodriguez Rivera, and his assistants, Ashkenazic Naphtali Hart Meyers and Sephardic Isaac Mendes Seixas—who had married an Ashkenazic woman—to rewrite the congregation's regulations in order to formulate "good and wholesome Laws" that would restore the polity. Teetering on the edge of communal chaos, the congregation called upon the Ashkenazic Jacob Franks and the Sephardic Mordecai Gomez to assist these officers of the mahamad. Thus the community recruited its two wealthiest members—each of whom had led the congregation in previous years and had helped build the synagogue—to the cause of order and harmony. Shearith Israel in this manner undertook to repair the breaches through a special committee that combined experience, wealth, and shared leadership.[29]

Sephardic taboos against marriage with Ashkenazim waned in the North American colonies, albeit more gradually than attitudes against sharing responsibility in the administration of the community. Shortly after he arrived in New York in 1738, Sephardic Isaac Mendes Seixas, a member of the mahamad during the disruptions of 1746, proposed to wed Rachel Levy, the daughter of Ashkenazic Moses Levy and the sister-in-law of Jacob Franks—only to encounter the disapproval of his fellow Sephardim. As Jacob Franks's wife, Abigail, wrote, "The Portugeuze here are in a great ferment abouth it And think Very Ill of him." Bucking their opposition, as well as that of his family in London, Seixas married Levy in 1740 and retaliated against New York's Sephardim. "The Portugueze here where in A Violent Uproar abouth it," Abigail Franks informed her son in London, "for he Did not invite any of them to ye Wedding." Six years later, the couple bore a son, Gershom Mendes Seixas, who was destined to become America's first native hazan. Appointed to the position in 1768 by Shearith Israel, Gershom Mendes Seixas was the leader of New York Jewry during the period of the early Republic until his death in 1816. The product of a union assailed by Sephardim, the son grew to serve as the public symbol of the country's oldest Sephardic-rite congregation.[30]

The Seixas-Levy marriage, controversial though it was in 1740, may in fact have been a turning point, for in the years that followed, the Sephardim and Ashkenazim increasingly intermarried. Thus, although David Gomez in the end married a Sephardic woman, for several years he expressed interest in wedding Richa Franks—as her mother, Abigail, reported in 1742, dismissing him as "a Stupid wretch" and asserting that her daughter would never deign to marry him. Among the next generation of the Gomez clan, the New York community's leading Sephardic family, Moses M. Gomez married Sephardic Esther Lopez, while his sister, Rachel, in 1770 wed Ashkenazic Abraham Waage. Another sister, Eve Esther, married Uriah Hendricks, whose father, Aaron, had been affiliated with the Ashkenazic Great Synagogue of London. When his first Sephardic wife died, Uriah Hendricks married a second Sephardic woman, Rebecca Lopez.[31] Within the large Hays family, also of New

York, marriages between Ashkenazim and Sephardim abounded. Judah Hays, for example, one of five brothers, married an Ashkenazi. His son followed suit, and while three of his daughters married Sephardim, a fourth wed an Ashkenazi, and a fifth married first a Sephardi and then an Ashkenazi.[32]

Outside of New York, the tendency toward intermarriage proved the rule as well. Of 942 American Jewish marriages in all localities between 1686 and 1840 identified by Malcolm Stern, 16.4 percent were between Sephardim and Ashkenazim, exceeding the 10.7 percent involving exclusively Sephardic individuals. Among forty-seven Sephardic families listed by Stern, only seven individuals married exclusively with Sephardim; fifteen married with Ashkenazim within one generation of arrival in America, twenty within two, and three within three generations. However, in contrast to the pattern on the North American mainland, fewer marriages between Ashkenazim and Sephardim occurred in the Caribbean, underscoring the uniqueness of the amalgamation of the two groups in English North America.[33]

Encouraged by their integration within a Sephardic-rite community, Ashkenazim readily bequeathed legacies to its synagogue. Hayman Levy, for example, born in Germany, left five pounds to Shearith Israel "for the benefit of having an *Escoba* [a memorial prayer] as is usual." Isaac Adolphus, whose father came from Bonn, bequeathed ten pounds to the synagogue in 1774, while Sampson Simson, whose father also came from Germany, left twenty pounds. Uriah Hyam, who according to his will had a brother in Bohemia, stipulated that six pounds was to be used to purchase a "Lining of the place wherein the five books of Moses is kept," referring to the ark in the synagogue. So too, Samuel Myers-Cohen bequeathed twenty-five pounds to the synagogue, and Joshua Isaacs directed that fifty pounds of his estate was to go "to our Congregation of Jews at New York . . . the Yearly Income of the same to be yearly for ever Imployed For the Support of our Hebrew School . . . to teach poor Children the Hebrew tongue."[34]

Successfully united in a single fellowship, the Ashkenazim and Sephardim of eighteenth-century North America regularly imposed disci-

plinary action upon errant members of the community in order to ensure conformity. Discipline enforced the religious laws that defined the
community in the first instance. It clarified the regulations to which the
members affixed their signatures, and it served to control tendencies to
engage in fractious behavior. Each time that it was imposed, synagogue
discipline described the group's norms and thereby defined the boundaries of the community. In short, reliance upon sanctions reinforced the
community's distinctiveness as a fellowship within the larger society.

Discipline within the religious community, familiar in colonial America in the Congregational church and the Quaker meetinghouse, was
practiced by the Jewish community in Europe, too. In eighteenth-
century London, for example, the Great Synagogue of the Ashkenazim
imposed penalties upon men who held private religious services, who
insulted the rabbi or other synagogue officials, or who married women
without the permission of the women's fathers. Throughout Europe,
Jewish congregations regulated dress, morals, reading matter, attendance at plays and operas, and sexual conduct. Sanctions took the form
of fines, nonadmission to the synagogue during services, exclusion of
the children of offenders from the community's school, denial of interment in the community's cemetery, and confession before the entire
congregation, an appropriate penalty in an age that relied upon public
shame and humiliation to discipline offenders and to deter others. London's Ashkenazim required that offenders stand in full view of the congregation, repeat a confession after the synagogue's caretaker, and apol-
ogize to the congregation. Worst of all, however, was the herem, the
complete excommunication of the miscreant, requiring that all members of the community avoid contact of any kind whatsoever with the
convicted. The regulations of Curaçao's Sephardic congregation even
permitted the mahamad to request the island's governor to banish those
who lived immorally, if private efforts by the community's elders to
convince the offender to reform did not succeed.[35]

The leaders of Shearith Israel in New York imposed complete excommunication in only one known instance during the eighteenth century, that of S.H., whose case is described more fully below.[36] Because
of S.H.'s extreme behavior in the synagogue and his public denunciations of the community's members, the mahamad not only excluded him

from membership but, conformable with the procedures of the herem, ordered that no one was to have any contact, conversation, or other forms of communication with him.

In other instances, the community's elders excluded offenders from membership and its privileges but did not order the cessation of all other contacts with the convicted. Thus in 1737 the entire congregation agreed that each individual who resided outside the city must contribute at least forty shillings annually to the community or "be excluded of being a member of [the] Congregation." Anyone convicted under this regulation could "receive no benifit . . . untill he [paid] the above Sum." Ten years later, when the congregation approved a major tax program, it agreed that those who declined to pay were to be erased from the "book of offerings," were not to be called to the Torah nor enjoy any of the other benefits of membership, "nor be Loock't upon as a Member of [the] Congregation."

When the congregation reaffirmed its regulations in 1769, six members who rejected "the good rules & orders instituted by [the] Community" were ordered to accept them within a month. Should they not, their names were to be erased from the list of members and they were to be denied all rights and benefits. Exclusion from the benefits of membership could extend, moreover, to the grave. In 1752 the elders therefore decreed that any individual who during his lifetime absented himself from the congregation and did not contribute to it was to be denied interment within the walls of the community's cemetery, a policy to be extended as well to his wife and any child below the age of thirteen, unless the mahamad ordered to the contrary.

Discipline in Shearith Israel included fines for behavior offensive to the community's officials. In 1756, for example, H.L. was fined the sum of twenty shillings "for the indecent and abusive language he gave the Parnass President in the Synagogue yard." In 1765, H.L. again incurred a fine in the same amount, this time for abusing the hazan. Two years later, Joseph Pinto was fined for abusing the acting parnas in the street leading to the synagogue, while in 1772, B.H., who repeatedly insulted the parnas during services before the entire community, was fined ten pounds on penalty of being excluded from participation in any religious function in the synagogue. The authority to deprive B.H. of such par-

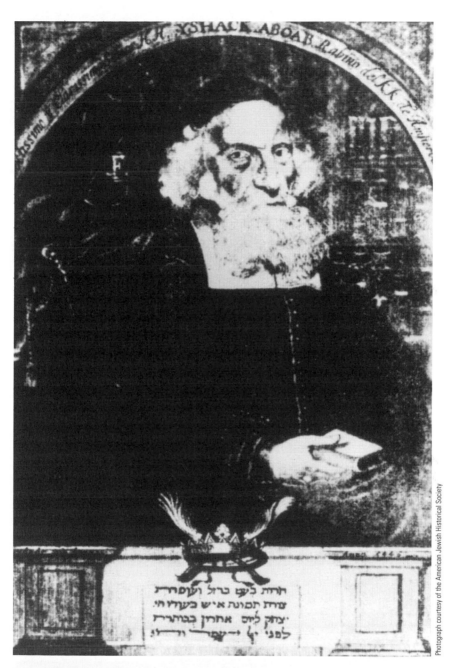

Isaac Aboab da Fonseca, the haham of the Jewish community in Brazil when it was under Dutch occupation. The first rabbi in the New World, he served the congregation where the first Jewish settlers in North America would have worshipped when they lived in Brazil.

Jewish sugar plantation in Brazil during the Dutch occupation.

The oldest extant Jewish cemetery in New York City, established in 1682 after the community outgrew its original burial site. The triangular column marks the grave of Hazan Gershom Mendes Seixas, America's first native-born religious functionary.

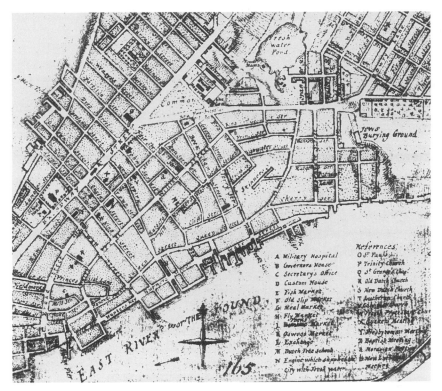

New York City in 1780. *Lower left* (*c*), the synagogue on Mill Street;
upper right, the Jewish community's cemetery.

An *Old Faith in the New World: Shearith Israel, 1654–1954* by David
De Sola Pool (New York: Columbia University Press, 1955). Used by
permission of the publisher

The first two synagogues of Congregation Shearith Israel in New York City.
Left, the synagogue building dedicated in 1730, with high arched windows
for the women's gallery. *Right,* the reconstruction of 1818.

Moses Levy
(1665–1728),
an Ashkenazic
Jew who
emigrated from
England to
New York City
early in the
eighteenth
century. The
vessel in the
background
implies his
career as a
merchant
in Atlantic
commerce.

The apparel of
Grace Mears
(1694–1740),
Moses Levy's
second wife,
attests to the
ease of early
American Jews
in adapting to
the surround-
ing culture.

Phila Franks (1722–1811), granddaughter of Moses Levy, who secretly married Oliver Delancey. Her mother's letter of 7 June 1743 records the acute embarrassment the marriage caused. Abigail Franks wrote to her son in London that she wished she could avoid returning to the family's home in New York City, preferring instead to "leave this part of the world . . . in the first man of war that went to London."

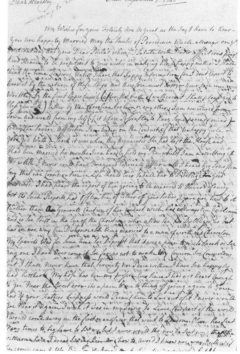

Circumcision implements and trunk. Several of the objects bear the mark of New York's Myer Myers, probably the finest craftsman among early America's Jews.

Etrog (citron) holder, used during the autumn Festival of Tabernacles. Made of silver and blue glass, the holder belonged to the Gomez family, New York City's leading Sephardic family during the eighteenth century.

The first publication in North America related to Jewish communal activity. The author was the hazan of New York's Congregation Shearith Israel.

Certification that a shipment of meat from Philadelphia to Barbados is kosher. The writer, a member of the New York Jewish community, vouched for the character of the merchant handling the meat, attesting that he is "a Jew with all his heart and all his soul."

Michael Gratz
(1740–1811), who
immigrated in 1759
to Philadelphia,
where he became
a merchant.

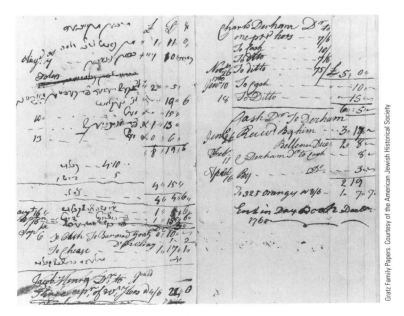

Michael Gratz's Waste Book, with entries posted in 1760 in
Yiddish as well as in English.

Insurance policy for cargoes shipped by Barnard Gratz between Philadelphia and the coast of Africa in 1761.

The 1779 marriage contract of Solomon Myers-Cohen and Belle Simon, witnessed by Michael Gratz and Joseph Simon.

Eighteenth-century Omer calendar, used to count the forty-nine days between the second day of Passover and the Festival of Weeks.

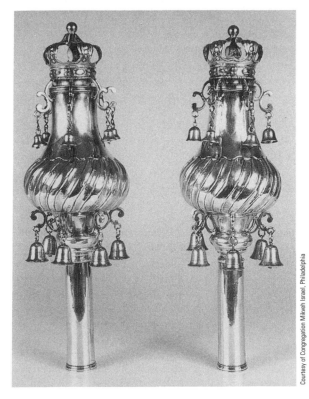

Silver Torah ornaments created by Myer Myers.

The Newport
synagogue,
dedicated in 1763.
The school
building on the
left, added at the
insistence of the
Jewish community,
compromised the
Palladian exterior.

The interior of
the Newport
synagogue.

Rabbi Haim Isaac Carigal (1733–1777), a visitor to North America from Hebron in the land of Israel, who preached in the Newport synagogue in 1773.

Sarah Lopez (1747–1840), second wife of Aaron Lopez, colonial Newport's most prominent Jewish merchant, and their son, Joshua Lopez (1768–1845).

Plan for the 1782 dedication service of Philadelphia's new synagogue building. George Washington and the other individuals listed in lines 7–12 were named in *Hanoten*, the prayer offered on behalf of government officials.

The synagogue in Charleston, dedicated in 1794.

Unlike the building's exterior, the interior of Charleston's synagogue conformed to tradition. On the ground floor were seating for men on both sides, the podium for reading the Torah, and the ark of the Torah scrolls on the eastern wall. Women sat above in the galleries.

Benjamin Nones (1757–1826), an adherent of the American cause during the Revolution who became a major in Pennsylvania's militia. His reply in the Philadelphia press in 1800 to an anti-Semitic denunciation reflected the sense of security Jews enjoyed in the early republic.

Title page of documents in the controversy between 1818 and 1826 over equal rights for the Jewish inhabitants of Maryland.

SKETCH

OF

PROCEEDINGS IN THE

Legislature of Maryland,

DECEMBER SESSION, 1818,

ON WHAT IS COMMONLY CALLED

The Jew Bill;

CONTAINING

THE REPORT OF THE COMMITTEE

APPOINTED BY THE HOUSE OF DELEGATES

" To consider the justice and expediency of extending to those persons professing the Jewish Religion, the same privileges that are enjoyed by Christians:"

TOGETHER WITH

The Bill reported by the Committee,

AND

THE SPEECHES

OF

THOMAS KENNEDY, Esq. OF WASHINGTON COUNTY,

AND

H. M. BRACKENRIDGE, Esq. OF BALTIMORE CITY.

Baltimore:

PRINTED BY JOSEPH ROBINSON,

Circulating Library, corner of Market and Belvidere-streets.

1819.

In his attire—including the absence of the traditional Jewish head covering—Gershom Mendes Seixas (1746–1816), hazan of New York's Congregation Shearith Israel, strongly resembled a Protestant minister.

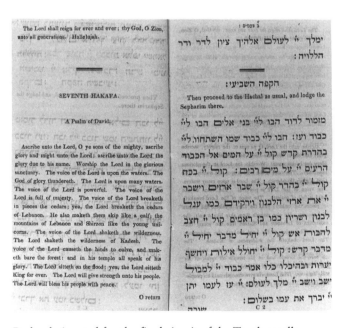

Psalm designated for the final circuit of the Torah scrolls, published in the program of the 1818 service dedicating Congregation Shearith Israel's new synagogue building. Following the last circuit, the scrolls were placed in their new home, the ark on the eastern wall of the synagogue.

ticipation for not paying a fine derived from a proclamation by the mahamad in 1764 that anyone who caused a disturbance "by Quarreling abuse or other indecent behaviour" in the synagogue, its yard, or in the street while going to and from services was to submit to whatever penalty the elders decreed or, if failing to comply, to be excluded from religious activities. This mitigated earlier procedures that called for exclusion from membership upon failure to pay a fine. Thus when Judah Hays refused in 1760 to pay, he was ordered to pay forty shillings for "Contempt" or he would not be "looked upon as Member of [the] Society, but be Excluded from the Rights and Ceremonies of the Synagogue." Hays paid the fine three years later.

Discipline extended beyond the synagogue and its immediate environs to the home. The Yom Kippur declaration of 1757 warned those who resided in the countryside against violations of Judaism's dietary laws. This too was the implication of the case involving the widow Hetty Hays in 1774. Alarmed that she might have served unclean meat in her home, the officers of the community, guided by the advice of a visiting rabbi from London and a former slaughterer in Holland, ordered her to cleanse all of her plates, utensils, and pots according to religious law, or else her home would be labeled "a Treffo [unclean] house."

Guaranteeing the availability of ritually clean meat was not a matter that could be left to private enterprise.[37] Instead, the community expended great energy in supervising the slaughtering, inspection, and certifying of kosher meat. The parnas and his assistants hired a slaughterer and inspector with the approval of the entire congregation in an open meeting, paying him a yearly stipend along with the right to a monopoly in the slaughter of the meat consumed by the members of the congregation. In return for his monopoly, the community expected its slaughterer to provide a sufficient amount of kosher meat, therefore ordering a newly appointed official in 1770 to use "his best endeavors to keep the markets sufficiently furnish'd with meats for supplying of the Congregation." Sufficient stocks, however, required control of the supply, prompting the mahamad in 1752 to limit exports. Responding to complaints that the community did not have enough beef and fat because of exports, the elders ordered the imposition of fines on anyone who purchased these items on the eve of the Sabbath or a holiday with the intention of selling them abroad.

On occasion, the community found itself at odds with its slaughterer and inspector because of insufficient rigor on his part. In 1767, for example, the parnas and his assistants temporarily suspended the slaughterer for leaving his tools where they might become contaminated by contact with nonkosher (ritually unclean) meat. Four years later, the community charged the slaughterer with certifying unclean meat as kosher. The official admitted to error, explaining that he had mistakenly done so, whereupon the community's elders permitted him to continue in office but warned that if there were again mistakes in killing, inspecting, or certifying he would be discharged. In what was the most prolonged such case of all during the colonial period, the slaughterer implicated in supplying nonkosher meat to the widow Hetty Hays refused to submit to an examination by the visiting rabbi from London, inaugurating several months of uncertainty regarding his continued employment by the community.

Supervision of religious dietary regulations by the community thus ranged from cases of individual discipline to a monopoly granted to an official whose appointment had been approved by all of the members of the community, supervision of his conduct in office, and control over supply. By facilitating adherence to the traditional dietary laws of Judaism, the community maintained a critical boundary, one that marked off its members and reinforced the identification of the individual with the group. The community's assiduous attention to the purity and adequacy of its meat supply, as well as to conformity by individual members to the dietary laws, was a central component of its program for perpetuating itself.

The community also provided for the education of its young, thereby assuming yet another responsibility for assuring its continuity. On the first anniversary of the dedication of its synagogue building, the congregation dedicated a school structure for its pupils. Four years later, when a new hazan was engaged, the elders charged him, in addition to his regular duties, "to keep a publick School in due form for teaching the *hebrew* Language, either the whole morning or afternoon as he shall think most proper." In 1755 the community increased the hazan's salary so that he might keep school at his house every weekday during winter and summer, and added Spanish, English, writing, and arithmetic to the curriculum. In the absence of a public system of education in colonial America, religious denominations played an important role in providing general education. While the first prerequisite for Jewish schoolmasters was facility with the Hebrew language, as the community made clear in 1760 when it went in search of a new master, the ability to handle secular subjects was required as well. Thus, two years later a new schoolmaster agreed with the parnas and his assistants to keep "a publick school," where he would teach not only Hebrew, but also translation into English, reading, writing, English, and "Cyphering."[38]

In addition to the instruction provided by religious denominations, colonial Americans depended upon private schools and tutors for their children. But while some of New York's Jewish youths probably studied languages, mathematics, and other subjects privately—as did, for example, the daughter and perhaps the son of Jacob Franks—others could not afford to do so and depended upon Shearith Israel's school. "Any poor that shall be thought unable to pay for their children's Learning they shall be taught gratis," the community noted in 1735. Thereafter, the leadership reaffirmed as necessary the community's commitment to the inclusion of its poorer members, either repeating that their children were not to be charged for schooling or, as in 1759, ordering that several loads of wood were "to be sent for the use of the poor children to School." A year later, when the congregation sought a schoolmaster in Jamaica, it specified that "children whos parents are in needy Circumstances he must Teach Gratis . . . and all other Children he Teaches must and will pay as has been done heretofore."[39]

Care for the poor was provided for adults as well, again serving to incorporate this segment of the population within the fellowship of the community. In the regulations it adopted in 1728, the community agreed to provide as much assistance to impoverished members as the parnas and the assistants believed was necessary. Thereafter, subsidies, yearly allowances, boarding, clothing, and medical care were provided. Often labeled "Obras Pias" in the community's accounts, such expenditures frequently amounted to a substantial portion of the community's annual outlay.[40] In caring for the impoverished, the community was inclined to exclude only the wandering poor, strangers who came from other parts— much in keeping with the policy throughout colonial society against providing assistance to nonresidents to avoid attracting impoverished outsiders. Even so, the community provided temporary care and outward transportation charges for these wanderers, who were a feature, as suggested earlier, of the extensive movement by Jews around the Atlantic world during the colonial era.[41]

The practices in Shearith Israel that imparted cohesion and wedded its individual members to the community were replicated within the other small Jewish communities of North America, to judge from the marriage patterns among Ashkenazim and Sephardim and from a draft of community regulations written in Philadelphia some time between 1750 and 1770. "Concerned about the matter of creating an organized community," the members of the proposed fellowship envisioned procedures for applying disciplinary sanctions to recalcitrant members who violated religious laws, insulted the synagogue, failed to attend services, or refused to support the community financially. In the event that two members quarreled, they were to repair to the parnas and to a board of five elders to settle the disagreement, on pain of losing their seats in the synagogue. Because of this apparent attempt to reconstruct the autonomous courts of the organized Jewish communities of Europe, which went beyond the procedures of the New York community, the members were "warned to be careful to choose people who will dispense justice" and to select a parnas "who is desirous of according justice to everyone." Whether the members of the Philadelphia community ever implemented this system of justice is not known, but their consideration of it suggests that they believed that a well-composed Jewish community in the New World could provide not only fellowship, poor relief, kosher meat, and education, but also the resolution of disagreements and disputes.[42]

As in New York, the Ashkenazim and Sephardim of Newport joined forces to build the synagogue there. The deed to the land on which it was constructed listed one Sephardi and two Ashkenazim, while the structure's six cornerstones were dedicated by two Sephardim and four Ashkenazim. During construction, Sephardic Jacob Rodriguez Rivera served as parnas in 1760 and was succeeded in 1761 by Ashkenazic Naphtali Hart. Reflecting upon the obligations of the community in a letter to Shearith Israel requesting funds, the members spoke of their "Duty to assist the Distressed" as well as their "Duty to Instruct Children in the Path of Vertuous Religion." Indeed, the community added an extension to its house of worship for a school—which in the opinion of a visiting English clergyman in the early 1760s, ruined the appearance of the synagogue's exterior.[43] The Newport community preferred to sacrifice architecture to the community's traditional responsibility to provide education.

Despite the forces and practices within Shearith Israel that were conducive to cohesion, the potential for conflict and disintegration in what was essentially a voluntary association lurked beneath the surface. An early sign of dissension appeared in 1731, not long after the community's approval of its new regulations and the dedication of its synagogue structure. When called to the Torah, some of the members apparently refused to offer prayers for the health of the parnas and the congregation or to pledge donations, traditional accompaniments to such prayers.

In reaction, the community's three elders ruled that anyone honored henceforth with a call to the Torah must offer three blessings on behalf of the parnas and the community or pay a fine of thirty shillings. Pledges offered at places other than the central podium where the Torah was read would not be accepted unless they too named the parnas, and offenders were to pay a fine in the same amount. The parnas and his assistants explained that nothing less than "the peace and harmony of the Kahal [community] and of the holy synagogue were at issue." Whatever the circumstances were that precipitated this incident, the synagogue's elders viewed the implied insult to the parnas and the congregation as threats to the community's stability. Though minor and transitory, with major disruptions not to occur thereafter until midcentury, the episode reveals that disruptive forces did indeed exist within the synagogue.[44]

The immediate sources of conflict in New York's Jewish community are largely unknown, but misunderstandings in commercial ventures may well have been one. In 1734, Jacob Franks and Judah Mears (a merchant like Franks) stopped speaking to each other following an argument related to the loss of a brigantine. Then, too, members of the small, intimate community sometimes rubbed each other the wrong way. Abigail Franks, for one, chose not to socialize with the Jewish women of New York outside the synagogue, for she had come to regard them as "a Stupid Set of people."[45]

In other instances, an angry individual could easily disrupt the synagogue's decorum and undermine the reputation of the entire community, as the case of S.H. suggests, though the basis for his hostility cannot be determined. The elders fined S.H. in September 1755 for creating a disturbance in and around the synagogue but within a month were obliged to take stronger action against him for continuing to create disorders and for filing a suit against the congregation in the courts. The mahamad, noting "the scandalous things he has reported of us about the city," excommunicated him and forbade any member of the congregation to have any form of contact with him, warning that any who communicated with S.H. would in like manner be expelled from the congregation. To reenter the community, S.H. five years later "made proper submission for the Injuries done the congregation," vowed not to behave disruptively again, paid a twenty-pound fine, and gave bond "to deliver up a certain book in his possession wrote against [the] Society." Suitably disciplined, S.H. was thereupon readmitted to membership.[46]

What may be described as "the affair of the benches" provides another example of the personal conflicts that could disrupt the small community. On a Sabbath in 1760, Judah Mears, the same individual who in 1734 had quarrelled with Jacob Franks, entered the women's gallery in the synagogue and ejected the daughter of Judah Hays from the seat claimed by Mears's daughter. The community's elders immediately fined Mears for taking upon himself the authority to determine who should sit where. To placate Judah Hays, the elders decided to lengthen the bench where his wife sat, so that their daughter might also have a place to sit. Because Hays objected subsequently to the new seat, the elders were forced to convene a meeting of the entire congregation to discuss the ensuing controversy. Following a unanimous vote by the members, affirming that the elders had acted correctly, Hays was fined for contempt in not accepting the extension to the bench occupied by his wife, with payment demanded on pain of expulsion from the community and exclusion from the rites and honors of the synagogue. Hays did not pay the fine for three years, evidently preferring the community's discipline to its definition of what constituted orderly behavior.[47]

Tendencies to precipitate conflict evidently ran in families, for six years later a controversy erupted that involved three other members of the Hays family. In 1769 the membership determined in a congregational meeting that six members, three of whom belonged to the Hays family, had acted in ways calculated to upset "the good rules & order instituted by [the] Community." In all likelihood, these were the parties who had been described on an earlier occasion as "some Evil minded persons Members of this Congregation [who] have for Some time past Endeavoured to disturb our Holy Worship, by Indecent Behavior in Synagogue, and making many Scandalous offerings, in Contempt to the Parnas, and to the great disquiet of this Congregation, which Practice if Countenanced we perceive will be great means of destroying the Concord and Unity of the Synagogue." Now, however, after acting leniently for more that a year, the congregation resolved to revoke the membership of these six and to expel them unless they submitted to the congregation's elders within one month. They did not, but again the congregation acted leniently, giving them another month to be reconciled to the leaders.[48]

Three years later, yet another storm involving the Hays family arose. In this instance, Barrak Hays, one of the six who had been disciplined in the previous affair in 1769, after repeatedly insulting the parnas, disrupted services when his brother was called to the Torah to name his daughter. Shouting that his brother was "a rascal," Hays threw the congregation into turmoil, requiring several members to eject him from the synagogue. The congregation subsequently levied a ten-pound fine on Barrak Hays and also restricted the membership rights of his brother.

Barrak Hays, for his part, turned to the civil courts to sue the men who had removed him from the synagogue building.[49]

Far more significant than disputes that arose because of pettiness, misunderstandings between two individuals, or contentious families were those that had their origins in the unwillingness of men to serve on the mahamad, the governing council. Beginning in 1746, the absence of a stable cadre of leaders willing to serve periodically plunged the membership into rancorous disputes. Continuity in the congregations's affairs could not be assured from one year to the next because of the reluctance of many to serve as parnas or assistant. Worse, the community at times hovered on the brink of disorder, when disputes erupted among the members regarding who would serve. These quarrels bespoke problems that ran deeper than individual pettiness or idiosyncratic behavior, and that threatened to tear the community apart.

The regulations approved by the membership in the revitalization of the community in 1728 prescribed that any individual who refused to serve as parnas upon designation by the outgoing governing council was to be fined three pounds, while those who declined service as assistants were to pay two pounds. In September 1746, shortly after the beginning of the Jewish New Year, when a new mahamad customarily took office, Daniel Gomez, a member of the congregation's leading Sephardic family, declined to assume the duties of parnas, choosing instead to pay the required fine. The two members chosen as assistants accepted only upon condition that someone would be found to serve as parnas so that the duties of that office would not devolve upon them. Gomez's refusal to serve inaugurated a period of controversy and disorder that, before it was resolved, required threats of ejection from the synagogue, steps to prop up the congregation's finances, and revision of the regulations in force since 1728. The episode, the first of its kind, revealed that the potential for disruption within the community of Shearith Israel was hardly insignificant.[50]

The disorders accompanying the refusal by Gomez to serve as parnas and the subsequent selection of a replacement apparently bordered on the riotous, and in the aftermath the entire congregation gathered to agree upon procedures to be followed in the event of further misconduct. Explaining that "for the peace of our said Congregation . . .

something must immediately be done," the members instructed the parnas or his assistants to eject individuals who created disturbances during
services in the synagogue and to impose fines on them. Should disruptive persons refuse to leave the premises, then the members would act in
concert to remove them: "Wee all covenant promise and unanimously
agree to turn him or them the aggressors out of the Synagogue without
respect to persons," they vowed. Furthermore, all agreed that the congregation would have recourse to the courts to sue individuals who
created disruptions or misbehaved in the synagogue.[51]

For the long term, however, revision of the community's governing
regulations was required, and the members therefore agreed that the
newly constituted mahamad, together with Jacob Franks and Mordecai
Gomez, were to compose "certain good and wholesome Laws" that
would presumably reconstruct the community. The inclusion of Franks
and Gomez underscored the seriousness of the moment, for they were in
effect the congregation's elder statesmen. Both had played leading roles
in the construction of the synagogue, had served in office, and were the
community's wealthiest members. The fact that Franks was of Ashkenazic origins while Gomez was of Sephardic heritage undoubtedly
dispelled any doubts regarding the community's commitment to reassembling itself after the uproars that had sundered it.

The problem of assuring sufficient voluntary involvement in the
affairs of the community was in fact deeper and more wide ranging than
the refusal by Daniel Gomez to serve as parnas and the disorderly behavior that it engendered. Seven months later, perhaps following a report by
the special committee that had been charged to write "good and wholesome Laws," the congregation adopted regulations designed to force all
members to attend its meetings and to contribute to its upkeep. The first
provision, approved unanimously, authorized a fine of twenty shillings
for any member above the age of eighteen who failed to attend a properly convened meeting of the congregation, except if ill or excused for
other reasons by a majority of the members in attendance. The second,
described by the community as "a Tax" (and approved by a less than
unanimous vote), imposed a sum calculated separately for each individual, to be paid over a period of eighteen months by each person
associated with the community, whether he resided in New York City or

in the country. Those who complied were to be listed in the book of members, be assigned seats in the synagogue by the parnas or his assistants, be given all the rights of membership, and be entitled to serve in office.

As if to remind themselves of the potential for disruption and disorder within their fellowship, the members added that anyone would remain in good standing only if "he behaves with decency quiatly and peasefully and Duly pays what he's taxt with." As for those who refused to pay, they were not to be called to the Torah or receive any other form of honor, their names were to be erased from the "book of offerings," and they were henceforth not to be "Loock't upon as a Member of this Congregation." After sounding that note of warning, the members concluded with the notation, "and Selom all Israell"—Peace upon Israel—as though expressing a hope against all the evidence.

The problem in recruiting leaders for the community in 1746 laid bare a potential for disorder and fragmentation that was not easy to resolve. Two years after the disruptions that ensued when Daniel Gomez refused service as parnas, the congregation increased the penalties in force since 1728, mandating that any person thereafter who declined the office of parnas would be fined ten pounds, while those who refused the position of assistant were to pay five pounds. To enlarge the pool of potential officers, any single man above the age of thirty could be elected parnas; an earlier regulation restricted the position to married men.

Only one month after taking these steps, the congregation was forced yet again to confront the unwillingness of its members to serve. Noting that frequent disruptions had occurred on Rosh Hashanah, the solemn festival marking the start of the new year, when the parnas who was elected refused to serve, eleven members pledged to serve in the position according to the order in which they subscribed their names on a list. The eleven could, with the outgoing parnas, designate someone not among their number to serve, but if that individual declined, then the next among them on their list would do so. Furthermore, the subscribers were empowered to meet with the parnas and his assistants to conduct the business that heretofore necessitated summoning the entire congregation—a measure that provides additional evidence of disengagement and fragmentation within the community. Henceforth, the members at large were to be called into session only in an emergency or to approve the appointment of the community's salaried officers: the hazan, the ritual slaughterer, and the synagogue caretaker.

The commitment by eleven members of the community to take turns yearly serving as parnas lasted for only three years. In September 1751, the elders assembled prior to Rosh Hashanah and agreed that henceforth two men were to be elected parnas, one to serve from Rosh Hashanah to Passover, roughly from September to April, and the other from Passover to Rosh Hashanah. Furthermore, in response to mounting evidence that members of the community now increasingly refused to serve as assistants, arguing that they did not wish to sit on the special bench in the synagogue reserved for the congregation's leaders, the elders resolved that the assistants would no longer be required to sit there and that any who still refused to serve in the office would be fined five pounds. In the event that the two parnasim could not find individuals willing to serve as assistants, then they were to fulfill not only their own functions but those of the secondary office as well.

Although these innovations lasted for twenty years, seemingly resolving the question of how to provide leadership for the community, they too eventually proved inadequate. In 1771 the parnasim and assistants then in office declared that in recent years many difficulties had been encountered because of the practice of designating two parnasim and two assistants each year. Qualified individuals willing to serve were too few in number. "The small number of persons, who are proper, and willing to Accept of the said offices," they explained, made other arrangements necessary. "For the tranquility of our Congregation" (a reference perhaps to the potential for communal disruption that had accompanied the problem of recruiting willing voluntary leaders between 1746 and 1751), the four officials thereupon decided to resurrect regulations that had been adopted as long ago as 1705 and 1728. A single parnas and two assistants were to be selected each year. The assistants were once again to sit "in the Bench" with the parnas and act in his stead during his absence. At the end of the year, one of the assistants would become parnas; the second would continue to serve as an assistant for one more year, together with a new individual selected as an assistant, and then move up to the position of parnas. In this manner, only one new official, instead of four, would have to be recruited in any one year, with each serving a total of three years.

Not surprisingly, this effort failed, necessitating a return only two years later to the practice of selecting two parnasim and two assistants. But, as subsequent events were again to demonstrate, this method was no more workable than it had been in 1771. Thus, in August 1774, "two proper persons" to serve as assistants were not to be found, forcing the outgoing parnasim and assistants to draw lots in order to dragoon two individuals into serving.

The reluctance of the community's members to serve as leaders is attributable in part to the time-consuming nature of the responsibilities that were part of the offices of parnas and assistant. A parnas, after all, met a budget, paid the community's bills, supervised its salaried officials, oversaw repairs to the synagogue and its outer buildings and the cemetery, dispensed assistance to the poor, and presided during Sabbath and festival services. Then, too, sanctions imposed on behalf of the community compelled these officers to discipline their fellow members, an unpleasant feature of their responsibilities, which was undoubtedly made more unpalatable by the community's small size. Indeed, a parnas might be required to impose communal sanctions upon a trading partner, a family member, or a close friend.

While considerations such as these might account for hesitation on the part of particular individuals to serve, the persistence of this problem is traceable to changes in Jewish communal organization everywhere during the eighteenth century, alterations hastened in the case of colonial Jewry by conditions in North America. The members of Shearith Israel approached the administration of their fellowship's life with the model of the European Jewish community before them. In every locality in the Old World, among the Ashkenazim as well as the Sephardim, the kehillah—the organized Jewish community—had served for centuries as the official voice of the Jewish populace. The kehillah collected taxes, administered its own institutions, regulated the behavior of its members, and asserted universal authority over all members of the Jewish faith. The claim to hegemony typically took the form of forbidding the establishment of new congregations without leave. London's Ashkenazic congregation, for example, forbade members to join in worship in any other synagogue within a radius of ten miles,[52] while Brazil's community, relying upon European precedents, in 1648 proclaimed that

> no congregation other than the one existing today, whose numbers God may increase, shall exist. . . . Anyone intending to organize another congregation now or at any other time will be admonished by the Gentlemen of the Mahamad to desist from his plans. And if he will not obey, he shall be chastised with all vigor, and separated from the nation as a disturber of the peace, and of the general welfare. The same applies to all who join together for the same purpose.[53]

Curaçao's regulations decreed that "there shall at no time be erected or procured in this fortress another house as a Synagogue outside of what we now have." Should "an arrogant, bold or headstrong person" endeavor to do so, then the community would impose excommunication.[54]

Doubtlessly recalling the precedent of the Old World, the leaders of Shearith Israel imposed disciplinary sanctions, conducted a school, dispensed poor relief, employed religious functionaries, repaired the synagogue building, and provided for an adequate supply of kosher meat. Most revealing of all, they asserted that the community of Shearith Israel was universal: that it had the right to govern all Jews within its purview. In 1737, for example, the congregation claimed the power to raise funds by taxing "our brethren dwelling in the Country," referring to those who resided outside of New York City. Those who chose not to comply were to be excluded from membership, synagogue honors, and community benefits, an allusion probably to poor relief.[55] Ten years later, in the aftermath of the crisis engendered by the refusal of Daniel Gomez to serve as parnas, the community imposed the general levy of 1747 upon those who resided outside the city as well as upon those within. In 1752, the elders agreed that any party who refused to attend the synagogue or to contribute to the congregation was not to be buried in the community's cemetery, a ban extended to wives and young children, as well. Finally, in the Yom Kippur proclamation described earlier, the officers of the congregation threatened to excommunicate individuals residing outside of the city who violated religious law. Clearly, New York's Jews believed that the authority of the community extended to all Jews in the region.[56]

Conditions in the English colonies, however, made such pretensions to hegemony dubious. The freedom of the Jewish inhabitants of North America to settle where they wished rendered identification with the community and subordination to its rule problematic. The scrutiny of the behavior of those who lived in New Jersey or Connecticut or in New York's Westchester County and the ensuing demand for conformity were not realistic. Nor could the community in New York City expect to easily collect a tax imposed upon a Jewish inhabitant of a remote town on Long Island.[57]

While geographic mobility and unrestricted settlement interfered with efforts to reconstitute the traditional European Jewish community in the English colonies, it was the complete lack of need for such a community that ultimately undermined it. The authority and primacy of the autonomous kehillah of Europe arose from its function as mediator between the Jewish population and the government and from its responsibility to provide for the welfare of a population burdened with civil disabilities and often forced to live apart. In the benign atmosphere of English North America, on the other hand, the Jewish population was not required to provide—and was never directed to provide—an official entity to represent it and to which every Jew was perforce subordinated. The Jewish colonist was free to associate with the Jewish community or not, whatever its claims to universal authority may have been. Furthermore, although the Jewish community provided social services such as poor relief, transportation charges for needy strangers, and schooling, these were available as well from local governments (when they provided them at all), with restrictions based not upon religious identity but upon one's status as an inhabitant of a place. The alternative detracted further from the Jewish community's ability to claim to be the primary public institution in the lives of its members.

In the transition of the Jewish community from an official body to a voluntary association, leadership no longer bestowed the prestige and status, the power and advantage, that it once did. The result was the reluctance among the members of Shearith Israel to serve on the maha-mad, which first disrupted the community in 1746 and continued, there-after, to perplex it. Position and influence—incentives that might have counterbalanced the time-consuming requirements of office and the potential for conflict with other members of the small community—were not to be had to the degree once true in other times and venues.

During the middle and latter parts of the eighteenth century, to be sure, the organized Jewish community that had been in place for cen-turies began to evolve toward dissolution and disappearance in Europe, as well. The autonomous, official community gradually lost its author-ity, declined, and eventually ceased to function. "The collapse of Jewish political and institutional autonomy in eighteenth-century Europe was a virtually universal phenomenon," Jonathan Israel has written, with consequences everywhere for the prestige of traditional leaders.[58] But the comparatively tolerant environment of English America, coupled with geographic mobility, made for an even swifter transition to a new form of Jewish community. Perhaps earlier and more intensively than their con-temporaries elsewhere, the Jews of colonial North America confronted the problems of leadership, participation, and responsibility by forming a new kind of communal organization, one that eventually came to charac-terize organized Jewish life everywhere in the modern world.

It was as innovators and pioneers, therefore, that the Jews of colo-nial America sustained their small communities on the mainland of North America. While they retained important features of the tradi-tional European Jewish community—disciplinary sanctions, the obliga-tion to guarantee an adequate supply of ritually clean meat, responsibility for welfare and education—they also departed from European ways. They united Sephardim and Ashkenazim in governance and marriage, thereby solidifying their small communities. And confronting the conse-quences of the shift to a community built upon voluntary recruitment, contending at times with overt conflict even within the precincts of the synagogue, they accepted and learned, successfully, how to cope with the problem of members who were hesitant to lead and reluctant to serve.

CHAPTER FOUR

FITTING IN

THE ADVENT of the American Revolution brought with it a German mercenary who remarked upon his arrival in New York in 1777 that it was difficult to distinguish between Jews in the New World and their Christian neighbors. The Jews of America, he wrote, "are not like the ones we have in Europe and Germany, who are recognizable by their beards and their clothes, for these are dressed like other citizens, get shaved regularly, and also eat pork. . . . The women also go about with curled hair and in French finery such as is worn by the ladies of other religions." Posted subsequently to Newport, the visiting soldier again noted that the American Jews "are not identifiable because of their beards and clothes as is the case with [the Jews who live among] us [in Germany]."[1]

To all outward appearances, the Jews of eighteenth-century America blended easily with the majority, although the soldier's comment regarding their consumption of pork must be dismissed as an exaggeration.[2] Affiliation with a community that endeavored to preserve its distinctiveness in a traditional manner, like the congregation of Shearith Israel, did not preclude acculturation and integration into the larger society. A religious life in the synagogue and the home, a diet subject to Jewish law, and the use of sanctions to enforce communal norms were counterbalanced by the tolerant atmosphere of English colonial society in the port towns and by the absence of Jewish religious institutions and communal surveillance on the frontier—and on the high seas, for that matter, among the merchants and wandering poor.

For the Jews of the West, the advent of modernity meant not only the dissolution of the autonomous, compulsory community, but also the emergence of the Jew as a citizen of a nation. Until the nineteenth century, the Jewish people defined themselves as a people in exile—strangers in the lands of others, largely unwelcome, and subject to recurrent expulsions—while their host societies agreed for the most part that the Jews were outsiders. The political and social revolutions of the late eighteenth century—coupled with many of the ideas of the Enlightenment, that century's revolution of the mind—produced and institutionalized for the first time the concept of the Jew as citizen. Gradually acquiring political rights and equality under the law, the Jews of Europe moved from marginality to participation, and with their new status as members of society, instead of being intruders, they began to acculturate as well: to enter into, participate in, and adopt elements of the surrounding culture. In its most extreme form, acculturation meant assimilation, or disappearance into the majority, generally through intermarriage and sometimes through conversion.[3]

All this lay beyond the understanding of the German soldier billeted in New York and Newport in 1777. With the exception of the Jews of Holland and England, particularly among the Sephardim there, acculturation lay in the future for most of European Jewry.[4] In colonial America, however, it had been well under way since at least the 1730s, as suggested by the private correspondence of Abigail Franks of New York. Franks read widely in contemporary English literature. She followed local politics, though Jews only modestly participated in public life in New York, and elsewhere not at all. She established close friendships with Christians, spent summers with them, conveyed their regards to her son in London, assured him of the family's fine reputation among New York's Christians, and informed him of invitations to visit with the governor and his wife. She urged her son to establish friendships with various non-Jewish individuals from the colonies who found themselves in London. Perhaps nothing can better convey the ease with which Abigail Franks moved in both the Jewish and Christian worlds of New York than the single sentence in which, simultaneously, she transmitted greetings to her son in London from the members of Shearith Israel and from some of her closest Christian friends: "I Shall goe this Week with fanny riggs to Morrisania all that Family Salute You And Soe doe all the rest of your Acquaintance with our Whole Congregation."5

The ease with which Jews mingled with members of the larger society extended to commerce, where their associations with non-Jews were frequent and maintained over lengthy periods of time. Although the Jewish merchants of colonial America counted heavily upon family members and other coreligionists around the Atlantic, they were not restricted to trading only with them. The ledger ascribed to Daniel Gomez, for example, indicates that about half of his correspondents were Jewish, but it reveals as well that he dealt with Christian traders in various colonies (Maryland, Connecticut, New York, Rhode Island, New Jersey, and Pennsylvania) and in Dublin.6

Formal partnerships between Jews and non-Jews provided even more significant contact. Gomez purchased large tracts of land in partnership with non-Jews. His trade in Charleston brought him into contact with the partnership of Isaac DaCosta, Charleston's hazan, and Thomas Farr, while commerce in Newport brought contact with partners Jacob Rodriguez Rivera and Henry Collins. Joseph Simon of Lancaster maintained a partnership for approximately forty years with Colonel Alexander Lowry in trade with the Indians. Another partnership, with William Henry, under the name of Simon and Henry, sold hardware imported from England and shipped Henry's rifles over extensive distances on the frontier. Simon, in partnership with William Trent, the two Gratz brothers, and David Franks of Philadelphia, supplied goods for the western fur trade after the French and Indian War. During the decade preceding the outbreak of the American Revolution, the four Jews maintained complicated trading arrangements with William Murray and George Croghan, who were leading figures in the western trade in Pennsylvania, and, in partnership with them, speculated boldly in western lands. Finally, Aaron Lopez of Newport established many partnerships with various non-Jews.7

The portraits and miniatures commissioned by these and other colonial Jews indicate the extent to which clothing and hairstyles conformed with those prevalent among Gentile contemporaries. Male Jews appear in these likenesses dressed in the clothing and wigs worn by Englishmen of the era, clean-shaven, and without the head covering traditional among observant Jews. Their wives—among them Abigail Franks—appear in dresses as fashionable as those in the portraits of their female Gentile contemporaries, often with plunging necklines, in defiance of traditional Jewish strictures to dress modestly, and without the wigs that observant married women donned when they appeared in public.[8] The portrait of Rabbi Haim Isaac Carigal, a traveler from the land of Israel who visited Newport in 1773, is especially instructive. Carigal appears wearing a long beard, a high turban, and a caftanlike garment, in marked contrast to the Jews of North America whom he visited in Rhode Island and to whom he preached. His garb differed notably from that of Gershom Mendes Seixas when he officiated as hazan at services in Shearith Israel in 1776: a visiting graduate of Harvard College reports that Seixas was "dressed in a black gown, such as is worn by Bachelors of Arts."[9]

Jewish architecture also displayed inclinations to absorb elements of the surrounding culture. When Jacob Henry, in 1761, wrote from New York to his cousin Barnard Gratz about rumors regarding proposals to build a synagogue in Philadelphia, he requested a sketch of the plans and inquired whether the structure would be in "Hambro [one of the Ashkenazic synagogues of London], Pragg, or Poland fashion." Henry favored the architecture of the New World: "I think it will be best after the old mode of Pennsylvania." Whether he referred to Philadelphia's civic architecture or its Quaker meetinghouse is not known, but in a remarkably short period, this less-than-ten-year-resident of the colonies had absorbed tastes and impressions that led him to reject the synagogue styles he had known in Europe.[10]

Jacob Henry's interest in synagogue architecture may have been piqued by a visit to Newport, where he had gone in a futile search for a cure for his ailments and where he undoubtedly witnessed the construction then under way of the Jewish congregation's first permanent place of worship. The exterior of the Newport synagogue exemplifies how avidly the Jews of colonial America drew from the surrounding culture. Peter Harrison, the gifted amateur architect who had introduced Palladianism to America with Newport's Redwood Library during the late 1740s, was engaged to design the synagogue for the Newport community. The Palladian style, all the rage in England by the 1740s, derived from the classical tradition, employing columns, pediments, entablatures, and cornices and emphasizing symmetry, proportion, and balance. Harrison added to the synagogue what his biographer has called an "exquisite porch." Harrison possibly based its design on an illustration in one of his Palladian handbooks. Framed by columns and surmounted by a pediment, the small Palladian porch announced that Newport's Jews preferred the latest in colonial building to the familiar synagogues of Europe and the New World.[11]

And yet, in the opinion of many colonial Jews, adopting the culture of the majority had its limits. Despite the evident relish with which Abigail Franks participated in New York's culture and society, her commitment to her Jewishness remained paramount. In October 1739, she expressed doubt as to whether she would have time to correspond with members of her family, citing observance of the religious holidays in explanation. In a letter she urged her son in London to exercise restraint in his comments upon religion and more carefully observe such religious regulations as the daily morning prayers and the dietary laws. Indeed, she instructed him to eat only bread and butter in her brother's home, for obviously her own sibling did not observe the dietary regulations.[12]

But if her son in London caused anxiety because of his religious practices, her daughter, Phila, in New York, became the source of outright grief when she secretly married Oliver Delancey, a member of one of New York's leading non-Jewish families; she concealed the marriage for six months, until she left her parents' home to join her husband. Shocked and distraught, Abigail Franks left town, refused to meet her new son-in-law despite his repeated requests, and fell into a depression that for a time made it difficult for her to meet or converse with anyone else. When her husband, Jacob Franks, professed willingness to meet with their daughter, Abigail Franks remained adamantly opposed. (Another of her children, David, who had relocated to Philadelphia, was also to wed a non-Jew, the daughter of the register general of Pennsylvania.)[13] In short, Abigail Franks was delighted to mingle freely in Christian society and occasionally flaunt her familiarity with contemporary English letters, but she drew the line at disregard for religious practices, a point well before marriage outside of the faith. Ready to experiment with acculturation, she nonetheless insisted upon the preservation of Jewish distinctiveness.

Abigail Franks's combination of loyalty to Jewish tradition and participation in the larger culture accurately limn the path carved by America's Jews during the eighteenth century. They wore contemporary dress that made them indistinguishable from their fellow colonials, but they also erected synagogues and schools, provided the supply of kosher meat, and employed the sanctions of the traditional Jewish community that would preserve their distinctiveness. If Manuel Josephson appeared in his portrait without a head covering, he nonetheless decried the fact that North American synagogue services were a hodgepodge, attributable largely to innovations—"new fangled rules & whims"—introduced by each successive hazan. Although willing to abandon the traditional head covering outside the synagogue, Josephson cared deeply about maintaining an orderly, dignified tradition within it and insisted upon the supremacy of traditional practice in synagogue ceremonies as well as in private life. Failure by women, for example, to bathe ritually after menstruation and prior to the resumption of sexual relations with their husbands was, to Josephson, "a transgression . . . highly criminal to both husband and wife," one that could be prevented only by quick construction of a ritual bathhouse by the community.[14]

The most striking effort of all to synthesize contemporary culture with Jewish tradition appeared in the design of the Newport synagogue. The congregation asked architect Peter Harrison to add a school building on one side of the synagogue, an appendage that violated Palladian canons of symmetry. "The outside is totally spoilt by a school, which the Jews insisted on having annexed to it for the education of their children," a visiting contemporary observer, the Reverend Andrew Burnaby, remarked. The one saving grace, as Harrison's biographer observed almost two centuries later, is that the school building cannot be seen when the synagogue is viewed from the street.[15] The building's exterior thus blended the community's traditional obligation to provide for the education of its young with the contemporary interest in the Palladian style, even at the cost of unbalancing the whole. Moreover, the synagogue's graceful interior was based on that of the Sephardic synagogue in London. After entering the building through a classical portal, the worshiper arrived at a room whose proportions, lighting, and wood carving recalled that synagogue, probably familiar from their Atlantic crossings to many members of the congregation.[16] Newport's synagogue, borrowing from both Jewish and Palladian models, exemplified the combination of cultures and traditions that colonial Jewry endeavored to delineate. The public face might reflect contemporary style, taste, and manners, but on the inside tradition would prevail. Adaptation and continuity could indeed combine harmoniously.

As part of the effort to blend tradition with participation in colonial society, colonial Jews endeavored to observe traditional religious law and ritual punctiliously in their private lives. Barnard Gratz, for example, demonstrated that it was possible to form commercial partnerships with non-Jews and leave the Jewish community for travel on the frontier while continuing to observe religious requirements. When Gratz spent Passover in Pittsburgh, where he traveled in the spring of 1775 for business reasons, he refused to violate the festival by writing a letter to his brother in Philadelphia. Instead, he enlisted the assistance of Charles Matheson, one of his non-Jewish associates, who wrote to Michael Gratz that, "as your brother could not write by this opportunity, this being the Holy Days, he desired to let you know that he is well." In the autumn of 1776, unable to return from Pittsburgh to Philadelphia in time to participate in the solemn observance of the Jewish New Year in the synagogue, Gratz requested that his brother send him his prayer books from Philadelphia forthwith, so that he might observe the holiday in the frontier community. Michael Gratz also preferred to adhere to traditional practices rather than conduct business, leading William Murray, one of the Gratz brothers' non-Jewish partners in land speculation, to protest his refusal to engage in commerce on Sabbaths and holidays.[17]

In Lancaster, Joseph Simon employed a slaughterer of kosher meat, at his own expense, for the tiny band of resident Jews and held services in a room in his home, complete with two Torah scrolls and an ark to house them. Others in the Pennsylvania hinterland, like Myer Josephson of Reading, made their way to Simon's home to observe important holidays. As Josephson informed Michael Gratz in 1763, "I am going to Lancaster for minyan [the required quorum of ten men for religious services] for Yom Kippur." Earlier that year he had informed the Gratz brothers that he would soon go to Philadelphia to be naturalized, but only after Passover. Nine years later, a visiting clergyman who passed through Lancaster reported that "the Jews in general are said to be very strict & punctual in the observance of some of the traditionary ceremonies of their law," when Simon refused to cash a money order on the Sabbath, but arranged for a non-Jew to do so in his stead, a procedure in accordance with traditional law.[18]

From Charleston, Moses Lopez, traveling as a commercial representative in 1764, informed his brother Aaron in Newport that he was unable to "write more fully because now it is almost Sabbath" but that he might do so thereafter. Aaron Lopez also refrained from conducting business on Sabbaths and religious festivals and did not permit any of his ships to sail from Newport on the Sabbath. Commerce, all of these merchants agreed, did not preclude the supremacy of the religious tradition, even when non-Jewish partners and associates like William Murray objected.[19]

Other colonial Jews also demonstrated this commitment to religious law. Uriah Hendricks of New York, for example, rejected a man who desired to wed his aunt, explaining that although the suitor had adequate resources he violated religious requirements: "He continually Break Shabbat [the Sabbath] & Eat Trefat [non-kosher meat] & have no Regard to Religion." Every effort was made to bury deceased individuals in Jewish cemeteries. Moses Lopez reported on the "great Consternation" among the members of Charleston's Jewish community in 1764 when their hazan's father-in-law died at a place thirty-six miles outside the city. "It will be necessary to go there and bring him to the City to bury him and they started out immediately on the road, [as the death] took place Tuesday," he wrote. In 1775, Savannah's Jews took note of a woman from a settlement in South Carolina, who, exceedingly ill and obviously wishing to die among Jews so that she might be buried properly, was transported to the city by her husband. Following her death she was interred in the congregation's cemetery.[20] Finally, the degree to which the Jews of Newport observed the Sabbath during the American Revolution impressed an observer in Massachusetts, where some of them had fled even before the British occupation of their city. He wrote,

Though without a place for assemblying for worship here, they
rigidly observed the rites and requirements of their own laws,
keeping Saturday as holy time; but out of regard to the sentiments
of the people among whom they were settled carefully keeping their
stores closed from Friday evening until Monday morning of each
week.[21]

Advocating neither exclusiveness on the one hand nor wholesale
assimilation on the other, the Jews of colonial America were among the
first in the modern world to explore the combination of Jewish tradition
with contemporary culture. Not all colonial Jews, however, were entirely sanguine about acculturation. The effects upon the young were
worrisome, as Peter Kalm heard in the late 1740s during his visit to
America. "They commonly eat no pork; yet I have been told by several
men of credit," he reported, "that many of them (especially among the
young Jews) when travelling did not make the least difficulty about
eating this or any other meat that was put before them."[22] Familiarity
with the synagogue service may also have waned, for New York's Isaac
Pinto published English translations of the prayer book in 1761 and 1765
for use during worship, complete with directions for the user. Key words
in Hebrew were transliterated into English, thereby assisting the attentive
listener to identify the place reached in the service by the praying congregation. In the preface to his second volume, Pinto expressed the hope
that his translation would operate for "the Improvement of many of my
Brethren in their Devotion," because many congregants, he asserted, did
not fully understand the prayers, and some understood none at all.[23]

The community school provided a meager religious education, to
judge from the knowledge acquired by Gershom Mendes Seixas in New
York's school, where he studied only until he was thirteen, the age of
responsibility for males in Jewish law. America's first native hazan possessed little knowledge of Jewish law—none of it learned formally—and
little facility with the Hebrew language.[24] If New York's well-organized
Jewish community felt these effects of rapid acculturation, the plaintive
cry of Levy Andrew Levy in 1784 underscored the dangers in more
remote locations. Reflecting upon a lifetime spent in colonial America
among the minuscule group of Jews in Lancaster, he wrote penitently of
his desire to

remove to a place where a congregation of our society [was] and that I might bring up my children as Jews—this my Dr. Sir is a part of my troubles & which I often consider of, for a family to be Remote from our Society is shocking. The Almighty, I hope will be my guide and Protector, in him I place my trust and hope, forgiveness should I be drawn against my will to a strange Place, that my capacity cannot afford me to keep a Person to kill [meat according to ritual] for me. This place has been my first residence in America for nearly 38 years.[25]

Most troubling of all was intermarriage with non-Jews, and Levy must have had in mind the marriage of Joseph Simon's daughter only two years before. Despite Simon's efforts to maintain a traditional Jewish home in the interior of Pennsylvania, in 1782 his daughter, Shinah, married Dr. Nicholas Schuyler of Albany and converted to Christianity. Like the marriages of the children of Jacob and Abigail Franks forty years before, this marriage indicated that outright assimilation could occur even in the households of the community's leaders. That was also demonstrated by the marriage of Sarah DaCosta, daughter of Charleston's hazan. In all, according to Malcolm Stern, almost 16 percent of marriages by Jews in America during the colonial era and their descendants before 1840 were with Christians. Although some individuals maintained their affiliation with the Jewish community and the spouses of a few converted to Judaism, as many as 87 percent of those who intermarried appear to have assimilated entirely with the non-Jewish population.[26] In its most extreme manifestation, therefore, acculturation led to the disappearance of Jewish distinctiveness.

The ease with which colonial Jews could marry their Christian contemporaries, form personal and commercial ties with them, and adopt elements of their culture had its roots in the benevolent toleration extended to them by eighteenth-century Englishmen. Jews who resided in England enjoyed a remarkable degree of acceptance, according to Moses Cassuto, a Jewish traveler from Florence who visited Britain in 1735 and spoke from the experience of his journeys across much of Europe. English Jews could reside anywhere without restriction, employ Christian servants, and enter the professions. They enjoyed equality under the law with Protestants, paid the same taxes, could serve as constables and soldiers, and shared guard duty in the City of London. "One hears of no mockery or abuse of Jews as in other countries," Cassuto wrote, "where there is a certain vulgar weakness for persecuting and regarding Hebrews as something abominable."[27] Supported generally by the Crown, the great landowners, and liberal economic thinkers who believed that a Jewish presence contributed to the nation's wealth, the Jews of England also benefited from the Christian theory that their conversion, supposedly a prelude to the millennium, could best be effected by welcoming them and integrating them into society. Though at its root an idea that foretold the demise of Judaism, this notion nonetheless predicated conversion upon toleration.[28]

Echoes of this prescription for conversion were heard in the colonies, in a Philadelphia edition of a sermon by Berlin Rabbi David Hirschel Franckel praising Frederick the Great, England's ally during the Seven Years' War. In the introduction he wrote for the Christian reader, the publisher argued that Jews were patriotic despite the persecution they endured under Christian regimes. Rather than mistreat them, he concluded, "all Christian people [ought] to pray yet more earnestly for the conversion and Restoration of this once happy nation, and treat them with kindness in all their Dispersion."[29] Hope for the conversion of the Jews underlay the friendship between the Reverend Ezra Stiles and Aaron Lopez. As Stiles wrote in his diary after Lopez's death, "He was my intimate friend and acquaintance! Oh! how often have I wished that sincere, pious, candid mind could have perceived the evidences of Christianity, perceived the truth as it is in Jesus Christ, known that Jesus was the Messiah predicted by Moses and the prophets!" Stiles could only hope that decent people of all religions and nations "notwithstanding their delusions, may be brought together in Paradise on the Christian system." Advocating civil equality for the Jewish population of Pennsylvania, the Reverend Charles Crawford in 1784 argued that "the drawing of a political line between us and them has a tendency to prevent their conversion . . . [while] the unlimited toleration of them has a tendency to bring them over to the gospel. . . . The unlimited toleration of them is the cause of God." Conversionist sentiments such as these may well have contributed on the Christian side to friendship and intermarriage with colonial Jews, thereby hastening the complete absorption of some within the larger community.[30]

Defying traditional negative images of Jewish traders and brokers, colonial Americans spoke favorably of the Jewish merchants they knew. When Nathan Levy died in 1753, Benjamin Franklin's *Pennsylvania Gazette* eulogized him as a merchant who behaved with probity and praised "the fair Character he maintain'd in all his Transactions." In 1767, the Reverend Thomas Barton in Lancaster described Joseph Simon as "a worthy, honest Jew and the principal merchant of this place" and recommended that Sir William Johnson, the famous Indian agent, establish commercial ties with him. Several months later, the Reverend Barton again described Simon as reputedly "a man fair in his dealing and honest from Principle." At Aaron Lopez's death in 1782, a Massachusetts newspaper writer characterized him as "a good citizen and an honest man," while his friend, the Reverend Ezra Stiles, extolled his generosity not only to his family and fellow Jews but to all people and included the following in the epitaph he composed for his tombstone: "His knowledge in commerce was unbounded and his integrity irreproachable."[31]

Some colonial Americans, however, harbored quite contrary attitudes toward Jews generally and Jewish merchants in particular, for, despite the tolerance accorded Jews in English society, traditional stereotypes persisted. The charges of deicide and of implacable hostility to Christianity remained current, though they tended to wane during the eighteenth century. According to England's anticlerical Deists in the first half of the century, the ancient Jews had introduced such evils as superstition, bloodshed, intolerance, and theocracy to the world, bequeathing them to posterity through Christianity. To other Englishmen, Jews were guilty of an insatiable appetite for wealth, of taking advantage of others in the conduct of business, and, as stockbrokers, of exerting undue influence upon government ministers, thereby corrupting English society. Physically, they were portrayed as disheveled peddlers and filthy hawkers of old clothing.[32]

The stereotype of the rapacious, dishonest Jewish merchant was transported to the New World, offsetting benign depictions such as those offered by the *Pennsylvania Gazette* and Ezra Stiles. If the Reverend Barton could describe Joseph Simon as fair, honest, and principled, the Reverend David McClure, witnessing Simon's strict adherence to Sabbath regulations, characterized Jews as dishonest people, more concerned with the minutiae of ritual than the greater moral values. They "hesitate not to defraud, when opportunity present," he charged, and "like their predecessors . . . they neglect the weightier matters of the Law, as Judgment, mercy, and faith." The Reverend McClure concluded that "they strain at a gnat and swallow a Camel." William Murray's jibe at his partner, Michael Gratz, in 1773 also indirectly called to mind the sharp Jewish trader: "You see, Michael, that a Scotch Irishman can get the better in a bargain of a Jew."33

Allegations that Jewish merchants were disloyal and took advantage of the misfortunes of others and of hard times surfaced in Charleston in 1778. Following the arrival of a group of Jewish women and children in flight from a British advance into Georgia, an item appeared in the *Charleston Gazette* asserting that the refugees were

> of the *Tribe of Israel* who, after taking every advantage in trade the
> times admitted of in the State of Georgia, as soon as it was attacked
> by an enemy, fled here for an asylum with their ill-got wealth,
> dastardly turning their backs upon the country, when in danger,
> which gave them bread and protection.

The writer, who signed himself "An American," proclaimed assuredly that the same would occur in South Carolina.34

Hostility to Jewish merchants, however, did not lead to the sustained, organized opposition to them in colonial America that it did in England and its Caribbean colonies. Fearful of their competition, the merchants of the City of London limited the number of Jewish brokers to a maximum of twelve, excluded them from the Levant and the Russia trading companies, helped defeat the Jewish Naturalization Bill of 1753, and prevented them from opening retail shops in the City by requiring a Christian oath for admission to freemanship. The Christian merchants in England's Caribbean islands were particularly fearful of the threat posed by Jewish merchants to their prosperity and social mobility. In Jamaica, the trading community denounced Jewish competition as ruinous and alleged that it meant depriving Christian children of food. Similarly, a report from Nevis in 1724 indicated that settlers in the countryside had nothing against the Jews but that the inhabitants of the town "charged [them] with taking the Bread out of the Christians' mouths." This, in the opinion of many (together with the presence of "transient traders"), had precipitated the island's decline. Hostility in Barbados compelled Jews to live close together for safety, while legislatures throughout the islands enacted provisions to restrict their right to own slaves, give evidence in court, obtain licenses to trade, hold office, and perform military service. Worse, from time to time the merchants advocated expulsion of the Jews, arguing that they were disloyal and plotted with slaves and foreigners against the English regimes of the various islands.[35]

In contrast, the legislatures of the more tolerant mainland colonies did not impose restrictions upon Jewish merchants, some of whom instead enjoyed privileges that bestowed commercial advantage. In 1753, Moses Lopez petitioned Rhode Island's legislature for the right to produce potash using a secret process. Responding favorably, the legislature granted him a ten-year monopoly. In Charleston, Moses Lindo became inspector general of indigo in 1762, a post that he held for ten years, sorting and certifying the quality of indigo harvested for export. Clearly, the position gave him a vantage point for his own export trade in that product.[36]

In only one known instance in the American colonies in the eighteenth century—the attempt by Aaron Lopez and Isaac Elizer to become naturalized in Rhode Island—did agencies of government endeavor to impede Jewish merchants. Lopez and Elizer applied for naturalization in the autumn of 1761 under the terms of England's Naturalization Act of 1740, that touchstone of English toleration in the colonies that permitted foreign-born colonial Jews to obtain naturalization without taking the Christian oath required of foreign-born Protestants. The Rhode Island Assembly dismissed their petition, explaining that Jews could not be admitted to freemanship in the colony, and referred them to the Rhode Island Superior Court. In March 1762, the latter concurred with the legislature, citing the inadmissibility of Jews to freemanship in Rhode Island because of the colony's origins as a settlement for "the free and quiet enjoyment of the Christian religion and a desire of propagating the same." Their petition rejected, Elizer subsequently applied successfully for naturalization in New York, while Lopez crossed into Massachusetts, met a brief residency requirement there, and became naturalized under the authority of the Superior Court of Judicature for Bristol County in the autumn of 1762.[37]

Freemanship in Rhode Island, which bestowed the right to vote and to serve in office, provided lame justification for the hostile decisions of the legislature and the court, for Parliament had not made freemanship a requirement for naturalization. Moreover, the Superior Court's interpretation of Rhode Island's history, emphasizing the colony's Christian origins and purposes, is to be dismissed in the face of the naturalization secured by Lopez in Massachusetts, a colony established by militant seventeenth-century Puritans who were dedicated to the restoration of original Christianity to the world, shaping their colony to serve as an example of a truly Christian commonwealth.

The Rhode Island Superior Court's reliance upon religious reasons suggests, instead, that relations between the Jewish merchants of Newport and others in the general community may not have been entirely friendly. One month after the Rhode Island Assembly rejected the petition submitted by the two merchants, nine of Newport's Jews established their own social club, where members played cards and dined on Wednesday evenings during the winter season.[38] Clubs were an important feature of urban life in colonial America, at times bringing together individuals of diverse religious and ethnic backgrounds who shared common interests. Christians and Jews, for example, mingled in Masonic lodges in America during the eighteenth century.[39] Newport's club for Jews is the only known instance during the colonial era of a separate Jewish social organization (other than the organized Jewish community), suggesting that Newport's Jewish merchants in late 1761 may have felt the sting of anti-Semitism, prompting them to withdraw in this fashion, contrary to the general pattern of reasonably pleasant interaction between Jews and Christians in colonial America.[40] Lopez—one of the city's most enterprising men of commerce—along with Elizer may have been denied naturalization for reasons akin to those that prompted English merchants in London and the Caribbean to be hostile toward Jews in commerce.[41]

This was not the only anti-Semitic incident in the mainland colonies. In 1737, the New York Assembly, in a hearing regarding the disputed election of Adolph Philipse, learned that several Jews in New York City had voted for Philipse, a revelation that elicited an attack by Philipse's challenger. Jews had no right to vote in the colony, it was claimed, since they were disenfranchised in England (and, furthermore, guilty of deicide). In 1746 and 1751, desecrations of Jewish cemeteries occurred in New York and Philadelphia. In Georgia in 1773, when Savannah's Jews petitioned the legislature to enlarge their cemetery, a successful counter-petition asserted that the value of adjacent land would be depressed, for "no Person would choose to buy or rent an House whose Windows looked into a Burial Ground of any kind, particularly one belonging to a People who might be presumed, from Prejudice of Education to have imbibed Principles entirely repugnant to those of our most holy religion."[42]

Sectarian and ethnic animosities, however, afflicted others in early America as well, for in a similar request in 1770 to the Georgia legislature for authorization to expand their burial ground, Savannah's Presbyterians endured an attack by the Anglican church, and the legislature decided against expansion. In Charleston, Anglicans and Huguenots quarreled during the early years of the eighteenth century. And the English regarded the Germans in the hinterland of Pennsylvania as obtuse and dull, comical and ridiculous; conflict between the two groups at times exploded overtly. Appraising the German settlers in 1764, Benjamin Franklin wondered, "Should the Palatine Boors be suffered to swarm into our settlements, and by herding together establish their language and manners, to the exclusion of ours?" Prejudices against Catholics abounded, including the fear of plots masterminded by the pope. In 1729, a mob in Boston attempted to prevent the landing of newcomers from Ireland, while Philadelphians during the 1760s looked with scorn upon their city's Irish immigrants.[43] A catalogue of anti-Jewish incidents and remarks verifies the presence of anti-Semitism in eighteenth-century America and the inheritance from England of hostile views, rooted in economics and religion, regarding Jews.[44] The tolerant environment of the colonies, on the other hand, amply counterbalanced this hostility, while the fact that the Jews were only one among many groups interacting with the English may well have softened their distinctiveness and mitigated their condition as aliens in what was a nascent multiethnic and multireligious society.

The toleration and inclusiveness enjoyed by the Jews of colonial America did not extend to political life except in New York, for eighteenth-century Englishmen restricted the franchise and public office to males, property owners, and Protestants. Royal charters and locally enacted legislation in the colonies proscribed the participation of Jews as well as Catholics in public life. Rhode Island, for example, guided at first by Roger Williams's belief that religion ought not to disqualify from civil rights, enacted legislation in 1665 that permitted Jews and Catholics to vote and hold office, superseding an act passed in 1662 that barred them from participation in public affairs. In 1719, however, codification of the colony's laws made no reference to the liberal law of 1665 and printed instead the exclusionary one of 1662. In 1729, the legislature approved the codification of 1719 as the law of the colony, thereby confirming the exclusion of Catholic and Jewish residents and bringing Rhode Island firmly into line with prevailing political attitudes and practices.[45]

Pennsylvania, despite its founder's commitment to religious toleration, originally required officeholders to be Christians and later excluded even Catholics from serving as representatives in its legislature. In South Carolina, Jews at first could participate in public life, for under the terms of an act adopted in 1697 they could become naturalized and vote. The few Jews then residing in the colony are known to have participated in the election of 1703, for according to a subsequent protest, "Jews, Strangers, Sailors, Servants, Negroes, & almost every *French* man in Craven & Berkly County came down to elect, & their Votes were taken." In 1721, however, the colony restricted the franchise to white, propertied Christians.[46]

Save for a few cases in Georgia and South Carolina, the colony of New York provided the only significant departure from the otherwise prevalent disbarment of Jews from public life and civic equality.[47] Well in advance of England's Naturalization Act, the New York Assembly approved legislation in 1715 offering naturalization to any foreigner in the colony who possessed real estate or who had been present in New York prior to 1 November 1683. Thirteen Jews were naturalized under the terms of this measure before Parliament passed its own naturalization law in 1740. Moreover, between 1688 and 1770, fifty-seven Jewish inhabitants of New York City were admitted to freemanship, thereby obtaining the right to vote in municipal and colonial elections and to stand for election to municipal office.[48] They are known to have exercised both rights. The disputed election of 1737 revealed to their contemporaries that Jews in fact exercised the franchise. Their right to vote was attacked on that occasion: the legislature unanimously approved a resolution asserting that Jews could not vote for representatives to that body, inasmuch as they could not vote for members of Parliament in England.[49]

The Jews of New York continued nevertheless to exercise the franchise, as indicated by a list of voters in the election of 1761 that includes several Jewish names and by the presence of fourteen Jews on poll lists for the years 1766–1769.[50] Moreover, they were elected to the office of constable in New York City, perhaps in part because its burdensome and sometimes dangerous responsibilities reduced the number of aspirants to it. Still, service in this office placed New York's Jews in positions of authority over fellow New Yorkers of the Christian faith, since constables served warrants, kept the peace, walked the night watch, and endeavored to control vice, profanation of the Sabbath, and excessive drinking in taverns.[51]

Barred from public life except in New York, Jews do not appear to have even informally participated in political affairs. There is no evidence to suggest that they served as advisors to members of the rough-and-tumble political factions that spiced public life during the colonial era, or marched in the raucous crowds that sometimes formed for political action, or participated in public debate regarding policy.[52] Not yet citizens empowered to participate in public affairs, regarded as extraneous to the body politic, colonial Jews sat on the sidelines and did not express political opinions or take public stands. Public policy, office in government, and political activity constituted the one sector in which colonial Jews did not mix with other colonial Americans, save for the exceptions noted.

A decisive turning point came with the American Revolution, when the Jewish inhabitants of the colonies took public political stands for the first time, declaring either for England or America. They need not have done so. In John Adams's well-known formulation, one-third of the population in the colonies supported the American side during the struggle with Great Britain, one-third remained loyal to the Crown, and the remaining third elected to sit on the fence. Without penalty, recriminations, or untoward consequences, America's Jews could easily have chosen neutrality in the conflict between the colonies and the mother county, a choice that would have accorded well with their political nonexistence. The fact that nearly all chose one side or the other, often quite visibly, indicates the degree to which colonial Jews felt that they belonged to early American society, in dramatic contrast to their centuries of exclusion in Europe. The Revolution, therefore, represents a watershed in the history of the Jewish people in America and for western Jewry everywhere; it was a milestone in the emergence of the Jew as a citizen participating in the political life of his nation.

During the Stamp Act crisis of 1765—when England attempted for the first time to impose an internal tax upon the colonists and Americans boycotted English goods in an effort to hobble the mother country and force Parliament to rescind the act—Jewish merchants in Philadelphia signed the nonimportation agreement pledging to stop English imports. Five years later, six Jewish merchants in New York protested the levy on tea.[53] By the middle of the 1770s, as tensions grew because of England's efforts to impose taxes, quarter troops, and punish Boston for the wholesale destruction of a shipment of East India Company tea (the Boston Tea Party), Jews in the southern colonies also played roles in local resistance to British policy.

In Savannah, for example, the committee that enforced the decisions of the American patriots included Philip Minis and Mordecai Sheftall, who served as its chairman. "The conduct of the people here [in Savannah] is most infamous," wrote the governor of Georgia to his superiors in 1775, adding that Sheftall, "a Jew," ordered captains to leave port without unloading their cargoes. The owner of one such vessel deposed that, when examined by the rebel committee, he confronted a group of more than five men, among whom "sitting in the chair [were] one Mordecai Sheftal, of Savannah, [and Philip] Minis, of Savannah, both of which persons profess the Jewish religion." In later years Georgia's governor forbade Savannah's Whiggish Jews to return to the colony, suggesting in explanation that they were extremists. "I judged it also necessary," he wrote, "to prevent the Jews who formerly reside[d] here from returning, or others from coming to settle here. For these people, my Lord, were found to a man to have been violent rebels and persecutors of the King's loyal subjects."[54]

In neighboring South Carolina, Francis Salvador, a recent emigrant from England, was elected to the first and second provincial congresses between 1773 and 1776, convened—like provincial congresses in the other colonies and the Continental Congress in Philadelphia—in reaction to Britain's attempts after the Boston Tea Party to establish control over the fractious Americans. Salvador played an active part, serving on several of the Provincial Congress's committees, helping to draft South Carolina's state constitution, and sitting in the new state legislature. He subsequently volunteered for service in one of the South Carolina militia companies assigned to repel attacks by Tories and their Indian allies on the frontier. He died gruesomely in battle: trapped in an ambush, Salvador sustained three wounds and was then scalped. He remained conscious for forty-five minutes; after asking whether his unit had achieved victory, he shook hands with his commander, bade him farewell, predicted his death within a few minutes—and died soon after.[55]

Like Salvador, other Jews throughout the country volunteered for military service in state militias and in the Continental Army. Between twenty-five and thirty-five of them, including the hazan of Charleston's congregation, served in South Carolina, participating in the Battle of Beaufort in 1779 and in the defense of Charleston when it was besieged by the British for two months in 1780. Jewish soldiers enlisted as well in the militias of Virginia, New Jersey, and Maryland—though these states contained only a handful of Jewish residents—and joined state forces in Pennsylvania and New York. Although an exact number cannot be established, perhaps as many as one hundred Jewish men served in some military capacity on the American side. Their numbers include twenty-two of the members of New York's Shearith Israel, most of whom had left New York to take refuge in Pennsylvania and Connecticut when the British occupied their city.[56]

Many early American Jews, in fact, chose exile rather than remain in cities occupied by British armies. In addition to those who enlisted in military units, more declared where they stood by abandoning their homes and crossing over into areas under American control. They did not do so because of threats to their safety, for those who remained behind were not molested by the British; choosing a self-imposed exile was, instead, an act of political affiliation. New York's Jews led the way: as a community, they had demonstrated their preference for the American side in May 1776, when, assembled in the synagogue on a day of fasting proclaimed by the Continental Congress, they had prayed,

> O Lord: the God of our Fathers Abraham, Isaac and Jacob, may it please thee, to put it in the heart of our Sovereign Lord, George the third, and in the hearts of his Councellors, Princes and Servants, to turn away their fierce Wrath from against North America. And to destroy the wicked devices of our enemies, that it may fall on their own heads.[57]

Four months later, the city fell to the British, and most of the members of Shearith Israel trekked southward to Philadelphia or northward to Connecticut, where they remained for the duration of the war. A similar exodus from Newport began even before the British seized it late in 1776. Only seven Jews remained in the city, while the rest dispersed to Massachusetts and Connecticut. Following the fall of Savannah in 1778 and Charleston in 1780, many more Jews made their way to Philadelphia. During the British occupation of that city, many again moved on, this time to Lancaster and York in the interior of Pennsylvania; only eight or nine Jewish families remained behind.[58]

Following the evacuation of Philadelphia by the British, many of those who had fled returned, and the city continued to serve as a gathering place for the Jews of the United States for the duration of the Revolution; approximately a thousand, perhaps 40 percent of the Jewish population of the thirteen original states, assembled in Philadelphia during these years of war and rebellion. The sudden influx made it possible for Philadelphia's original Jewish population, with the refugees' help, to reorganize their congregation and to construct a permanent synagogue for the first time. In March 1782, for example, Mordecai Sheftall and Cushman Pollack of Savannah, Gershom Mendes Seixas, hazan of New York's Shearith Israel, and Isaac DaCosta, hazan of Charleston's congregation, helped write the regulations for conducting meetings and for governing the congregation. DaCosta of Charleston even served as chairman.[59]

The exiles in Philadelphia included Hyam Salomon, acclaimed by later generations of American Jews as the foremost Jewish patriot of the revolutionary era. Born in Poland, Salomon arrived in New York by the middle of the 1770s and at first remained in the city after it fell to the British. According to legend, he spied for the Americans, assisted imprisoned patriots to escape, was himself arrested, escaped, and fled to Philadelphia, leaving a young wife and an infant behind. Salomon has been hailed by ethnopietists as the financier of the Revolution because of his work between 1781 and 1784 marketing U.S. notes in Philadelphia for Robert Morris, superintendent of the Office of Finance. In addition, he sold Dutch and French bills of exchange, which in effect underwrote loans by those countries to the United States. The importance of Salomon's activities to the war effort as a broker may have been exaggerated by his later admirers, but his is an important example of the way Jews asserted themselves politically during the Revolution, casting their lot with the American side.[60]

Not all did so. Some colonial Jews chose instead to support England, aggressively so in Newport, in the opinion of the Reverend Ezra Stiles. In his account, the few Jews who remained after the British occupation of the city were "very officious as Informing against the Inhabitants—who are one & another frequently taken up & put in Goal [sic]." Stiles had reported eight months earlier that the community's hazan, Isaac Touro, with whom he had spent many hours in more peaceful times discussing religious matters, was excused from taking an oath of allegiance to the American side because he was a foreigner, but Touro was in reality loyal to the Crown. In 1779 he relocated to New York, which was still under British occupation, and toward the end of the conflict chose to leave the United States to live in British Jamaica.[61]

Loyalists like Touro were to be found in all of the Jewish communities, although they appear to have been fewer than those who supported the American cause. Families were divided in a number of instances, some members supporting England, others the patriots. In the Gomez family, for example, aged Daniel Gomez chose to leave New York for exile in Philadelphia, while other members of his family stayed behind because of their adherence to the Crown. The Hays family in New York split similarly, with Barrak Hays switching from early support of America to service with armed loyalists, while two of his brothers in Westchester County suffered for their affiliation with the patriots.[62]

The Revolution added a new dimension to Jewish incorporation within the larger American society and marked the beginning of the political existence of Jews in this country. No longer did Jews regard themselves as merely residents, outsiders in a land that belonged to others; they behaved as citizens. Yet with the termination of hostilities in 1783, the question that loomed before early American Jews was whether their fellow Americans would grant them civic equality. Save for New York, which had already been an exception during the colonial era, the constitutions adopted during the Revolution by the newly independent states did not permit Jews to vote or serve in office. In an earlier day, the Reverend Ezra Stiles had wondered whether Jews would ever gain acceptance as citizens in American society. Reflecting in 1762 upon the rebuff dealt Aaron Lopez and Isaac Elizer when they applied for naturalization in Rhode Island, Stiles wrote,

> Providence seems to make every thing to work for mortification to
> the Jews, and to prevent their incorporating into any nation; that
> thus they may continue a distinct people. . . . The opposition it
> has met with in Rhode Island, forebodes that the Jews will never
> become incorporated with the people of America any more than in
> Europe, Asia, and Africa.[63]

Twenty years after Stiles wrote these words, Jews who had fought on the side of the patriots and had abandoned their homes for exile rather than reside under British control had good reason to question whether their civic position would ever improve. As peace descended upon the new nation, an answer in the affirmative was by no means apparent.

CHAPTER FIVE

THE JEWISH COMMUNITIES OF
THE EARLY REPUBLIC

IN THE spring of 1783, Mordecai Sheftall—after capture and incarceration on a British prison ship, exile in Antigua and Philadelphia, and separation from his wife for several years—delightedly informed his son of the cessation of hostilities between England and the United States. Rather than succumb to tyranny, Sheftall mused, America had secured its independence, and an entirely new future would assuredly unfold. He instructed his son to return home to Savannah as quickly as possible after the festival of Passover, for he planned a voyage for him to undertake at the earliest opportunity. "We have the world to begin againe," he wrote, brimming with an optimism and energy typical of the Jewish population as they began to return to their homes after the British occupation of their cities. The period between the end of the war and 1820 would prove to be one of reconstruction, expansion, and revitalization, as the Jews of America reestablished their prewar congregations, created new ones, and erected new synagogues, fulfilling Sheftall's prediction to his son that "an intier new scene will open itself."[1]

Vigor did not derive from population growth, for, as in the substantially longer colonial era, the Jewish population of the early Republic comprised less than 1 percent of the population of the United States. Between 1780 and 1820, it did not increase significantly. Estimates range from a low of 1,300 to a high of 3,000 in 1790.[2] Thirty years later, the Jews of America still constituted only a minute segment of the entire population. The census of 1820 enumerated between 2,650 and 2,750

Jews, amounting to approximately .03 of 1 percent of the overall population. They lived primarily in New York, Philadelphia, Charleston, Savannah, Richmond, and Baltimore; between 500 and 600 lived elsewhere in Virginia and South Carolina, and in Louisiana and a scattering of other places throughout the nation.[3] Gone, however, were the Jewish communities in Newport and Lancaster, which disappeared late in the eighteenth century as the economic fortunes of those two cities declined.

Newcomers augmented the original Jewish population only slightly before 1820. Approximately fifteen heads of families and their dependents left Bordeaux for Jewish communities in the United States during the decade of the French Revolution, some of them having been refugees from slave revolts in the Caribbean region. Sixteen more are known to have arrived from Bordeaux between 1800 and 1823.[4] Jews from northern and central Europe also arrived but only in small numbers. Between 1804 and 1816, Gershom Mendes Seixas in New York married three American Jews to three Jews from Amsterdam, and one Jew from Berlin to a newcomer from London. New immigrants appeared also in Baltimore; they came primarily from Holland but, in a few instances, from England and Germany as well. The great surge of immigration from central Europe, however, would not begin until the 1820s.[5] The Jewish population also increased slightly with the arrival of immigrants from the Caribbean, though again in limited numbers. In 1784, for example, a party of ten Jews arrived in Savannah from Jamaica, moving soon afterward to Charleston. Other Jews arrived subsequently in these two southern ports from Jamaica and Curaçao, although some later returned to the Caribbean. Several appeared also in New York, where Hazan Seixas married a couple from Jamaica and a New Yorker with a Jamaican.[6]

A considerable degree of geographic mobility characterized this small population, with frequent movement from one location to another within the United States. Movement began immediately after the Revolution, with most Jews leaving their places of exile to return to their original residences. Philadelphia's congregation, which had constructed its first permanent synagogue in 1782 because of the presence and assistance of the many refugees from New York, Charleston, and Savannah, felt the consequences of these journeys of return almost immediately. As the size of their congregation subsided to its prewar level, Philadelphia's Jews discovered that they were unable to meet the community's financial obligations; the cost of maintaining the new synagogue building and employing a hazan and a caretaker were beyond their means. The congregation faced one financial crisis after another throughout the 1780s, at length taking the extraordinary step in 1788 of appealing to leading non-Jews in the city to contribute to the synagogue's maintenance. Two years later, the congregation was compelled to turn to the state legislature for authorization to run a public lottery to raise funds for the building.[7]

The decline of both Newport and Lancaster after the war convinced the Jews who lived there to relocate. At first, the Jewish population began to filter back to Newport in the aftermath of the British evacuation in 1779, but ten years later only about seventy-five individuals in approximately ten families could be found there, down from twenty-five to thirty families before the war. During the 1780s, Newport's Jewish merchants tried to reestablish their commercial enterprises, sending ships to the West Indies and attempting to enter the shipbuilding industry, but with the dim economic prospects in Newport, these merchants began to disperse to New York, Virginia, and South Carolina. Services in the Newport synagogue ceased in 1792, and by 1820 only two Jewish men remained in Newport. Following the death of one of them in 1822, the last survivor of the original Jewish community of Newport moved to New York.[8]

The Jews of Lancaster appear to have contemplated establishing a congregation for the first time in 1781, but shortly after the Revolution they too began to disperse. Lancaster remained an important trading center, but in the aftermath of the war its merchants suffered in the general economic downturn that afflicted the nation during the 1780s. Moreover, with the rise of other towns farther west, Lancaster was no longer the preeminent center for trade in the hinterland that it had been formerly. Non-Jewish and Jewish merchants alike left Lancaster for more promising opportunities. With the death of Joseph Simon early in the nineteenth century, the Jewish presence there ceased, not to reappear until the extensive migration by German Jews to the United States after 1820.[9]

Many of Lancaster's Jews relocated to Baltimore, a rising center of commerce that competed with Philadelphia for dominance in Maryland and Pennsylvania. Baltimore also attracted Jewish settlers from Philadelphia and some of the Jewish newcomers to America. In all, Baltimore's Jewish population grew from five families in the 1770s to thirteen by 1800 and fifteen in 1810; between 1790 and 1810, the number of Jews more than tripled, rising from 29 to 98. The Jewish population continued to grow during the second decade of the new century, rising to 125 by 1820. Newcomers now came primarily from Philadelphia and New York. As before, small numbers of new Jewish immigrants from Europe appeared in the city. Baltimore's Jewish population, however, gave evidence of considerable movement rather than permanent, stable settlement, and this may account for their failure to organize a congregation or construct a synagogue. Many came and went throughout the period between 1789 and 1820, circulating among Baltimore, New York, Philadelphia, and Richmond, this last being the second new Jewish center to develop in the early Republic.[10]

Only one Jew is known to have lived in Richmond before the Revolution, but by the middle of the 1780s six lived there. During that decade, the Jews there increased to almost thirty families and established a congregation in 1789 by formally adopting a set of regulations. By 1820 Richmond's Jewish population rose to thirty-two families, with an aggregate of 191 individuals, but by then many of the founders of the city's congregation had departed, some to Baltimore, others to Philadelphia and New York, much in keeping with the migratory pattern of many American Jews during the era.[11]

The proclivity to move about, evidently in search of the location with the best prospects, also appeared in Savannah. Levi Sheftall, one of the city's oldest Jewish residents, remarked in his journal that the disruptions of the American Revolution caused many Jews to float in and out of Savannah, *"continually going & coming."* But the same could easily have been said of the years following the war's conclusion. In 1783, for example, he noted the arrival of a family from Rhode Island and then added the names of eleven more new individuals, noting, however, that three of these later moved on. Thereafter, until his death in 1808, Sheftall recorded the arrivals and departures of Jews in Savannah, many of whom left for Charleston.[12]

Despite the evidence from Levi Sheftall's records of considerable flux in Savannah's Jewish population, the small prewar congregation reestablished itself in 1786, rented quarters for a synagogue, and elected officers. Four years later, the community, numbering about twelve families, received a charter of incorporation from the state of Georgia and, in 1791, adopted regulations to govern itself. The group planned for the construction of a permanent synagogue in 1791 but abandoned the effort amid recriminations regarding purchases of substandard building materials. A decline in the economy shortly after, followed by a fire in 1796 that destroyed most of Savannah and financially hobbled the community's members, made for further deferral, and it was not until 1820 that the congregation built and dedicated a synagogue. The city's Jewish population at that juncture comprised ninety-four individuals in twenty-one families.[13]

Savannah's Jewish population might have grown more between 1790 and 1820 were it not for the attractions of Charleston; Levi Sheftall often noted in his journal that newcomers to Savannah departed soon after for the South Carolina port city. Two hundred Jews resided in Charleston in 1790, second only to New York's 242, but during the course of the next thirty years, Charleston surged ahead, drawing not only Jews already settled in America but new immigrants as well. By 1820, Charleston's Jewish population stood at approximately 700, a full 5 percent of the entire white population, while New York's crested at about 550, or one-half of 1 percent of the white residents of the city.[14]

At the outset of this thirty-year period of expansion, Charleston's Jews erected their first permanent synagogue in 1794, a symbol of the community's success in reassembling itself in the aftermath of a war that had ended only ten years before and that had been followed by a period of economic contraction throughout the nation. Charleston's Jewish community might well have been scarred irrevocably by the Revolution, for while many in the Jewish community had helped defend the city during its two-month siege by the British and were imprisoned or expelled after it fell, others stayed behind and pledged loyalty to the British general who captured the city. An examining board exonerated them after the war, perhaps thereby stifling any animosities that may have arisen within the Jewish community concerning the loyalists, but the decision ten years later to build a synagogue undoubtedly served to unite them even more strongly.[15]

Little is known regarding the economic base of the Jewish communities of the United States between 1780 and 1820, but in all likelihood the emphasis on careers as merchants trading around the Atlantic declined. Among ninety-seven Jewish businessmen, artisans, and wage earners who lived in New York City between 1816 and 1819, thirty-seven were identified at the time as merchants, but almost none of them were engaged in shipping. In contrast to only one New Yorker during the colonial era who did not call himself a merchant in his will, many among the ninety-seven earned livings in other occupations, suggesting considerably greater diversification than existed before the Revolution. Two to four Jews worked in each of the following callings: physician, attorney, auctioneer, tobacconist, grocer, tailor, and store owner or keeper (clothing and hardware). There were one each of the following: watchmaker, printer, accountant, jeweler, shoemaker, peddler, distiller, mason, milkman, butcher, paper carrier, and brass founder.[16] In Baltimore, the ten heads of households listed in the census of 1800 include three merchants, a blackball maker, an ironmonger, a distillery owner, a grocer, a tobacconist, a boardinghouse keeper, and a captain of the watch. Ten years later, Baltimore's Jewish inhabitants included two merchants, four peddlers, a broker, a blackball manufacturer, a clothing store owner or keeper, and the owners of an iron store, a grocery, and a boardinghouse.[17]

The apparent drift away from Atlantic commerce to more modest activities as local shopkeepers and artisans is attributable to the disruption of trading networks with England as a result of the American Revolution, the general economic downturn of the 1780s, and the risks of travel on the high seas thereafter. The conflict that erupted between England and France in the aftermath of the French Revolution disrupted ocean transport during the 1790s and continued to do so thereafter during the long Napoleonic Wars. America's own undeclared naval war with France during the late 1790s and the American government's restrictions on the nation's merchants for several years before the War of

1812 further hampered Atlantic commerce.[18] In addition, changes in the Caribbean probably disrupted the established ethnic trading networks which the Jews of North America had relied on during the colonial era. Most Jews left Saint Eustatius in 1795 because it had been occupied by the French and the English; by 1818 only five Jewish inhabitants remained on the island. Curaçao's economy was severely disrupted between 1790 and 1816 by the wars involving England, France, and the United States, as well as by several epidemics and a devastating hurricane in 1807. The island's Jewish population declined sharply as a result of all of these causes, with so many men departing from the island to seek their fortunes elsewhere that by 1816 women outnumbered men by four to three.[19]

The risks to Atlantic commerce caused both by years of warfare and the economic vicissitudes of the period between 1783 and 1812—followed by yet another downturn after the War of 1812 and the harsh depression of 1819—account for the apparent reluctance among Jews to pursue careers as Atlantic merchants. Their movement among cities occurred in conjunction with their transition to more diverse occupations, as they endeavored to find new niches in the economy. Whatever the uncertainties of the era, they did not undermine efforts by the Jews of the United States to reestablish their congregations after the Revolution, nor did they impede the Jewish commitment to construct the synagogues that gave concrete form to their communities. Richmond's new community quickly established a congregation, Savannah's created a governing structure in 1791 and built a synagogue in 1820, and Charleston's Jews erected their first permanent house of worship in 1794. Philadelphia's Jews began the era with the construction of their first permanent synagogue in 1782 and the adoption of governing regulations and, despite the community's financial hardships during the 1780s, erected a ritual bathhouse in 1786. Continuing to refine its organization, the community adopted a revised set of regulations in 1798.[20]

In New York, the Jewish community reassembled in 1783 after a hiatus of seven years, adopted new regulations in 1790, revised them in 1805, and under the leadership of Gershom Mendes Seixas established several voluntary organizations within the synagogue for charitable work. In 1817, the community undertook to rebuild its synagogue and, following eight months of construction, dedicated and occupied it on the Sabbath that preceded the festival of Passover in 1818.[21] With the sole exception of the Jews of Baltimore, therefore, the Jewish communities of the early United States, despite changes in their economic underpinnings, exhibited a commitment to expansion and development that transcended their minute numbers.

The institution of the synagogue exhibited greater tendencies to absorb elements of the dominant culture in the post-revolutionary generation than it had at any time during the colonial era. Evidence of acculturation now included not only clothing, hairstyles, and comfortable association with non-Jews, but changes in congregational governance, the role of the hazan, and the construction of synagogue buildings. To be sure, Palladian architecture had influenced colonial synagogue design, and a member of New York's Shearith Israel had published English translations of the prayers to assist members of the community who could not understand Hebrew or follow the service easily, but in the forty-year period following the Revolution a host of innovations suggest the power of the general culture to influence—and the willingness of the Jewish population to alter—even the synagogue. As early as 1790, a practice as fundamental as the use of Hebrew as the language of prayer appears to have been questioned, for a draft of Shearith Israel's regulations affirmed not only the congregation's adherence to the Sephardic rite but also "that no language [was] to be made use of in synagogue but Hebrew, except the offerings."[22]

The dedication of a new synagogue building is a milestone in the life of any Jewish community and centers on the Torah, the scroll of the law of Moses, which is read aloud in the synagogue on Sabbaths, on festivals, and twice each week during morning services. To guard its sanctity, various rituals and precautions against mistakes in transcription govern the writing of each new scroll by specially trained scribes. Guidelines for repairing or retiring a Torah that begins to fade or tear are enforced, and turning one's back upon it as it is carried in procession around the synagogue is prohibited. The transfer of the Torah scroll from the old ark in which it resided to the new one that will house it is the heart of the dedication ceremony of a new synagogue structure, mirroring the centrality of the scroll of the law in the community's life. At the beginning of the postcolonial era, the dedication of Philadelphia's first permanent synagogue in 1782 adhered strictly to tradition. Assembling at its old place of worship for the last time, the congregation recited the traditional afternoon prayers and then carried its Torah scrolls in procession through the streets of the city to the new synagogue. The throng halted at the door to await its opening and then marched into the building and paused at the platform in the middle of the synagogue, where the Torah is read during services. The Torah scrolls were then carried seven times around the reading platform and finally placed in the ark on the east wall of the synagogue.[23]

In contrast, the dedication service of Savannah's synagogue in 1820 included the playing of an organ. The inclusion of musical instruments in synagogue rituals is foreign to traditional Judaism, but the Savannah ceremony featured such music—played, at that, by the music director of the city's Independent Presbyterian Church. The transfer of the Torah scrolls to the new building at first seemingly conformed to traditional practice, with a procession through the streets of Savannah to the new building and the opening of its doors, but during the seven circuits of the Torah scrolls around the reading platform, a choir sang psalms while the organ accompanied them.[24]

Savannah Jewry's proclivity for blending Jewish practices with those of others had been evident even before the consecration of the completed synagogue structure. The dedication of its cornerstone several months before had been conducted as an elaborate Masonic ritual, with a procession through the streets led by Masonic officials, the participation of several lodges, the carrying of a square and compass, and the inclusion of the Masonic sign during the ceremony. The only recognizably Jewish element in the entire rite appears to have been a prayer offered first in Hebrew and then in English and, at the repetition of the Masonic sign, the recitation of the statement, "Blessed ye the Lord Who is every Blessing" in Hebrew, spoken by the Jewish Masons in attendance. That this was a Masonic rather than a synagogue ceremony was apparent from the participation of non-Jewish Masons as well, who recited the same blessing in English.[25]

Charleston's synagogue borrowed even more dramatically from non-

Jewish sources; the building constructed by the South Carolina Jewish community looked like a church. Dedication of the cornerstone in 1792 had also been a Masonic rite, one "conducted by the rules and regulations of the ancient and honorable fraternity of Freemasons." Those who attended the building's dedication two years later saw what appeared to be "a typical Georgian church." Within the structure, a traditional synagogue interior unfolded, with a reading platform in the center of the building, seating for men on the ground floor, and a gallery above for women. Outside, however, the building, with its spire, could easily have been mistaken for a small parish church in an English village.[26] Charleston's new synagogue reflected not only reconciliation within the Jewish community after the Revolution and the vigorous growth that before long would make the community there larger than New York's, but also a readiness to experiment with acculturation in ways that were novel—and undoubtedly provocative to traditionalists.

If the synagogue buildings of Savannah and Charleston borrowed from Christianity and Masonry, the new congregational regulations adopted during the late eighteenth and early nineteenth centuries reflected the impact of the revolutionary era's political ideas.[27] In Philadelphia, the members as early as 1782 began to refer to their rules as a *constitution.* Written constitutions were a product of the Revolutionary era, intended to prevent a recurrence of the tyranny that had been possible under Great Britain, ostensibly because it lacked a document that defined and limited the powers of the Crown. In 1798 the Philadelphians, again in this spirit, adopted a revised "written constitution for the good government of the said congregation."[28]

In New York, Shearith Israel's members met in 1790 to establish a government for the synagogue. In language that echoed the theoretical discussions of the 1770s and 1780s throughout America, they explained that,

> in a state happily constituted upon the principles of equal liberty, civil and religious, the several societies, as members of that government, partaking of that blessing, being free to adopt the best means for preserving their privileges, and for entering into such compact

for regulating and well ordering the internal institutions for the administration of the affairs of their several communities as may be most likely to attain that end . . . declare [that] the following rules shall serve for and be considered as a constitution.

The congregation also contemplated a bill of rights for members that declared in its preamble that "in free states all power originates and is derived from the people" and that, to clarify their rights, the people "frequently from [form?] a declaration or bill of those rights." It is not known whether the subsequent "declaration of our rights and previleges" was in fact adopted by Shearith Israel, but it is clear that New York's Jews endeavored to infuse the synagogue with fundamental elements of contemporary American political ideas.[29]

A democratic wind also coursed through the congregations. Perhaps to acknowledge the dawn of a more egalitarian day, the New York congregation in 1786 removed the special bench in the gallery reserved for the women of the Gomez clan. The Gomez family, successful merchants and the congregation's leading Sephardic family during the colonial era, may have fallen on hard times in the aftermath of the Revolution, judging from a request by Moses Gomez in 1796 for a less expensive seat in the synagogue. If this was the reason for the elimination of their bench in the women's section, the congregation chose not to assign it to another prosperous family but to use the vacated space to extend nearby benches in order to provide adequate seating for married women.[30]

More important, congregations everywhere began to provide for the annual election of their officers by all members. The traditional Sephardic congregation was governed and administered by a small body, the mahamad, whose powers were supreme and whose members appointed their own successors. Richmond's congregation in 1789 resolved, on the contrary, that all members were to meet on the Sunday prior to Rosh Hashanah to elect a parnas and two assistants. In Savannah, the members decided in 1791 to meet annually on the third Monday in August to elect a parnas and six assistants. Philadelphia's 1798 constitution prescribed a meeting approximately three to four weeks before Rosh Hashanah, at which all members were to elect a parnas, three assistants, and a treasurer.[31]

Shearith Israel in New York appears at first to have favored a more conservative tack, prescribing an indirect election reminiscent of the electoral college under the federal Constitution. The members at large were to choose three associate elders, who in turn would meet with the outgoing parnasim and, with them, designate two new parnasim for the ensuing year. If adopted, this procedure would have combined the traditional power of the parnasim to choose their own successors with a measure of participation by the entire membership. In June 1790, however, the congregation decided upon an annual meeting several weeks before Rosh Hashanah, at which all members were empowered to vote for new officers for the coming year, with any member eligible to stand for office.[32]

The democratization of the synagogue included provisions for the amendment of congregational constitutions and the approval of bylaws by the general membership. Savannah's constitution of 1791 could be amended by a vote of three-fourths of the members attending a meeting for that purpose, while Philadelphia's of 1798 could be changed by a vote of two-thirds of all the members. In the Richmond congregation, all regulations had to be proclaimed aloud in the synagogue on two Sabbaths or holidays before they could go into effect, but any member could challenge a new rule within twenty-four hours of its second reading. The parnas was required thereupon to convene a meeting of the entire membership to approve or reject the new regulation. New York's Shearith Israel permitted its leaders to enact new regulations, subject to publication in the synagogue on two successive Sabbaths. Members had a week thereafter to object, and only in the absence of opposition to a proposed regulation could it become the law of the congregation.[33] All these innovations dramatically reduced the traditional supreme authority of the mahamad in Sephardic congregations.

The office of the hazan also changed between 1783 and 1820, taking on certain features of the Protestant ministry. The hazan, rather than the parnas (in the absence of an ordained rabbi anywhere in America until the 1840s), began to represent the Jewish population outside the synagogue, much as Protestant ministers represented their churches. The hazan was an officer of the community who possessed a good voice and knowledge of the liturgy but who was not trained in Jewish law or invested with rabbinic authority. The hazan's new role was apparent as early as 1788, when, in the great parade held on the Fourth of July in Philadelphia to celebrate Pennsylvania's ratification of the Constitution of the United States, Philadelphia's hazan marched arm in arm with two clergymen. As Dr. Benjamin Rush reported, "Pains were taken to connect ministers of the most dissimilar religious principles together, to shew the influence of a free government in promoting christian charity. The Rabbi [sic] of the Jews, locked in the arms of two ministers of the gospel was a most delightful sight."[34]

In New York, Gershom Mendes Seixas, the first hazan born in America, served as a member of the boards of trustees of the Humane Society and of Columbia College, positions of status as well as responsibility that were often held during this era by Protestant clergymen. His membership on Columbia's board of trustees, beginning in 1784 and lasting until 1815, embraced almost the entire period of the early Republic. Seixas, moreover, met frequently with New York City's ministers to plan citywide prayer days of thanksgiving and fasting, in effect appearing as the spiritual leader of the Jewish community.[35] In essence, Seixas moved about the city of New York as the minister of the Jews and, in fact, was addressed as Reverend, though he had not been trained as a rabbi and did not possess anything remotely approaching rabbinic authority.[36]

In part, the change in the role of hazan was thrust upon the Jewish community of New York City by New York State. Its legislature in 1784 enacted a law providing for the incorporation of religious societies, permitting many Christian denominations as well as the Jewish community to acquire the benefits bestowed by charters of incorporation for the first time. The law decreed that the minister of any society planning to incorporate under its terms must announce meetings for the election of trustees. Shearith Israel therefore required a "minister" in order to become a corporation.[37]

Simultaneously, however, Seixas chose to present himself to the world as a minister. He preached sermons, an activity beyond the scope of the traditional responsibilities of the hazan—or of the eighteenth-century rabbi, for that matter. For models, he relied upon Protestant sermons, infusing his own not only with their tone and style but even their language. "We are 'stewards in the house of God,'" he preached. "What avails our earthly possessions . . . if we neglect laying up a treasure for the everlasting happiness . . . in the world to come," he asked. More startling, he employed Christian theological terms foreign to Judaism, referring to original sin, salvation, regeneration, and grace.[38] In part, therefore, the evolution of the office of hazan between 1783 and 1820, another instance of the synagogue's adaptation to the general culture, was related to Seixas's own self-willed acculturation.

As the Jewish congregations reestablished themselves in the aftermath of the Revolution and adopted new constitutions, they implicitly assumed, as before, that common religious observances and commonly shared religious values would bind them together as a community and a fellowship within the larger society, and they took steps to revive the communal institutions of the colonial era. For example, to ensure the supply of kosher food, the New York and Philadelphia congregations employed ritual slaughterers, who were paid by the community and whose compliance with religious law could therefore be monitored.[39] The New York congregation reestablished its school by 1792, though now its instructor taught only Hebrew, translation into English, and the fundamentals of religion. Hazan Seixas contracted to keep the school in 1793, and during the following two years it enrolled thirty boys and five girls. In 1801, the congregation received a bequest to maintain the school, which in 1802 reopened under the name of its deceased benefactor to teach the Hebrew language each day for three hours.[40]

All of the congregations, moreover, reestablished the principle of imposing sanctions in order to enforce religious laws and rituals and thereby define the limits of permissible behavior within the community. Philadelphia's officers, for example, in 1782 debated at length whether a member of the congregation could marry a convert in violation of the law prohibiting a descendant of the priestly caste, to which he belonged, from doing so. Finding that he could not, the elders ordered that no member could attend the couple's wedding, nor could their names be mentioned henceforth in the synagogue. Shortly thereafter, the leaders considered the case of an individual who had shaved during Sabbath while away from Philadelphia in Baltimore, an indication that the congregation intended to monitor private behavior in order to enforce religious law.[41]

In 1790, New York's congregation approved a bylaw stating that anyone who ate nonkosher food or violated the Sabbath or any holiday would not be called to the Torah, receive any other religious honor in the synagogue, or be eligible for any congregational office. Savannah's constitution in 1791 included a provision excluding from all synagogue honors anyone who violated the Sabbath or a holiday. That Savannah's congregation indeed intended to invoke congregational discipline became apparent almost immediately, when the officers summoned an individual who had opened his store on the Sabbath to appear before them (though after hearing his confession and explanation, the officers absolved him of culpability). In Charleston, the constitution adopted in 1820 not only deprived of religious privileges in the synagogue those who violated the Sabbath and other holidays, but also permitted the congregation's officers to fine and punish them in any manner judged appropriate.[42]

Above all, the congregations mandated sanctions for individuals who married out of the faith. To judge from the records of New York's Shearith Israel, there had been no necessity during the colonial era to allude in the community's fundamental regulations to congregational discipline for intermarriage: the laws organizing the congregation in 1728 made no mention of it.[43] In 1790, however, the constitution excluded anyone who married contrary to religious law from the rights and privileges of the congregation. The bylaws subsequently adopted specified that the hazan could not officiate at any such marriage and that any man who married a non-Jewish woman would forfeit his membership or, if not yet a member, be barred forever from obtaining it. The constitution adopted by Philadelphia's congregation in 1798 prescribed the excision of the name of anyone who married a non-Jew from the congregation's books, expulsion from membership, and denial of all religious privileges. Charleston's constitution of 1820 proclaimed that any person who married contrary to religious law would be excluded from membership and denied burial in the congregation's cemetery.[44] Intermarriage had clearly become a problem that attracted considerable attention by the end of the eighteenth century.

In spite of these signs of commitment to the maintenance of a distinctive community, the concern was no longer as acute as it once had been. The increase in marriage out of the community was only one symptom. Another was insufficient interest in a Jewish education. The congregational school in New York, for example, suffered from lack of interest among the members of Shearith Israel. In 1804, only three years after being endowed by its benefactor, it closed for lack of funds to pay Hazan Seixas to teach. The congregation's leaders convened a meeting of the members to address the problem, explaining, in a remarkable statement regarding the importance of education to the Jewish community, that

> in order to make your Children truly Virtuous You must rear them in the strict principles of our Holy religion, and this cannot be efficiently done without they understand what they are saying when addressing the deity. . . . Education generally speaking, is the first thing which ought to be pursued in life, in order to constitute us rational, how much then is to be expected from having in addition thereto, a compleat and full knowledge of the Hebrew Language, being that in which all our prayers are read. Yet notwithstanding this, it is with regret that it is perceived, few, very few indeed, are concern'd with it.

The school did reopen in the autumn of 1804 but disbanded again in the spring of 1805. It resumed again in 1808, staying open for approximately three years. It opened again in 1812, closed in 1816, reopened in 1818, but three years later closed once more because only six students attended (four of whom had been admitted without the permission of the congregation's officers) and because parents were not inclined to send their children to it.[45] In Charleston, site of the largest Jewish community in the early nineteenth century, the congregation did not provide for schooling among its expenditures. Whatever Jewish education was to be had in South Carolina was provided only by private tutors.[46]

Despite the references to communal sanctions in the constitutions of the period, these too declined in significance as a means of perpetuating the community. Excommunication, always a possibility during the colonial period even if it was rarely invoked, ceased to be a factor entirely. The New York congregation's bylaws, as noted previously, prescribed sanctions in 1790 for violating the Sabbath and holidays and for eating nonkosher food, but the constitution adopted in 1805 said nothing regarding communal discipline or infractions of religious law. Philadelphia's constitution of 1798 originally contained a provision punishing Sabbath violators with exclusion from the congregation's privileges and honors, the removal of their names from the records, and exclusion from the congregation's cemetery after death, but the entire section was later crossed out. In subsequent years, the individual who belonged to the priestly caste but married a convert was nonetheless admitted to membership and later served as president. And in a case that underscores the declining importance ascribed to communal supervision and discipline, Shearith Israel's teacher was accused in 1809 of eating nonkosher food in the home of another member of the congregation, but only he, and not the host who had served him, was examined.[47]

Finally, the Jews of America in the late eighteenth and early nineteenth centuries ceased to regard care of the poor as part of the organized community's obligations. Shearith Israel's colonial regulations had provided for the financial support of needy members and impoverished strangers and had included poor families in the community by assisting them to send their children to its school. The constitutions and bylaws of 1790 and 1805, in contrast, did not mention the poor. Furthermore, all parents were to pay "for each Child that we shall send to the Public School of the Congregation," as the contract between Shearith Israel and Hazan Seixas stated in 1793 (again, without reference to congregational assistance for the children of the poor). Like Shearith Israel's constitutions, Philadelphia's in 1798 did not assume any obligation for the poor on the part of the community. Only Savannah's did, in 1791, empowering the parnas to expend twenty shillings in charity and larger amounts after consultation with his fellow officers, while applicants for membership were required to contribute to the charity fund.[48]

Because the community downplayed the obligations it had accepted during the colonial era on behalf of the destitute, which had assured the poor a place within its ranks before the Revolution, individuals acting on their own stepped forward to organize private groups within the synagogue to provide assistance. In New York between 1784 and 1790, a society operated that cared for the sick and buried the dead. Later, Hazan Seixas created an organization during the yellow fever epidemic of 1798 to distribute charity secretly to the needy; this organization appears to have continued to function at least until 1816, the year of his death. In 1802, he established a burial society, which also provided assistance to the impoverished. In Charleston, a Jewish society to care for orphans appeared early in the nineteenth century, independent of the synagogue, with its own charter of incorporation.[49]

The development of such voluntary societies became necessary as the Jewish community, itself a voluntary association, gradually reduced its efforts to maintain a cohesive fellowship. Declining interest in the community's school, in sanctions that reinforced religious practices and laws that originally defined the community, and in including the poor as part of the community characterized the Jewish community between 1783 and 1820. The diminishing commitment to a distinctive fellowship of coreligionists, one that could perpetuate itself from one generation to the next, signaled important changes in Jewish attitudes and self-definition. This first generation of Jews in the American Republic modified the concept of the voluntary Jewish community in a tolerant society that had been formulated and bequeathed to them by their predecessors of the colonial era. The vigor they exhibited in the aftermath of the Revolution as they undertook to reconstruct their communities and to build new synagogues was offset by a tendency to undermine the community by slighting many of the practices and institutional arrangements that could sustain it, particularly at a time when their numbers were small and they confronted losses through intermarriage.

Worse, the community contended with fissures in its midst that had been absent or carefully controlled during the preceding era. The animosities that divided Ashkenazim and Sephardim, neutralized successfully by the Jews of the colonial era, surfaced during the final two decades of the eighteenth century. In Charleston, separate Sephardic and Ashkenazic congregations functioned during the 1780s. A cemetery for

Sephardim opened in 1783. In 1786, Joseph Salvador bequeathed one hundred pounds "to the Portuguese Congregation in the City of Charleston" and twenty pounds "to the German Jewish Congregation." A public advertisement for a Portuguese congregation appeared in the same year, but the two camps thereafter seem to have been reconciled.[50]

Not so in Philadelphia, where a permanent division took place shortly before 1800. In 1801, an Ashkenazic group calling itself the Hebrew German Society Rodeph Shalom purchased ground for a cemetery. In 1812, its members formulated regulations stating that their rite was to be "according to the German and Dutch rules." The new congregation thereafter went its own way, establishing congregational sanctions for absence from the synagogue on Sabbaths and holidays, and mandating that anyone who attended another synagogue—a swipe clearly at Philadelphia's original, Sephardic congregation—was to be punished by expulsion.[51]

In New York, a significant division between the Ashkenazim and the Sephardim did not occur until 1825, when the two groups formed separate congregations. But the issues that provoked the Ashkenazim to spurn Shearith Israel—ranging from the congregation's inadequate school to requirements regarding donations and to the expanded role of the hazan—most likely rankled them earlier.[52]

These conflicts were probably not between ethnic Sephardim and Ashkenazim, inasmuch as the majority of America's Jews were of central and eastern European origins well before the American Revolution. In all likelihood, instead, the split was between older American Jews and newer immigrants, a cleavage evident in Baltimore, where the two groups lived in different sections of the city because of their quite different economic standings.[53]

These divisions reflect a waning commitment to an inclusive community in an era marked also by the power of the general culture to affect the synagogue and by the need the Jewish community felt to address the fact of intermarriage in its congregational constitutions. America's Jews do not appear, however, to have been perturbed by these changes, many of which suggest an inclination to draw gradually closer to the larger community. Perhaps their intention was to do just that, to imply that in America the Jew and the Jewish community need not be too different from the mainstream. Although early American Jews did not leave behind theoretical discussions regarding the place of a distinctive Jewish community in American society, their actions suggest that they did not favor standing too far apart. This, after all, was the era in which they aspired to win recognition as citizens of the Republic and to achieve civic equality—matters that preoccupied American Jews after the Revolution more than did changes in the internal contours of their communities.

CHAPTER SIX

A SECOND JERUSALEM?

ENSCONCED comfortably in a land where they could reside in safety and worship without fear, the Jews of the early Republic described the United States with an enthusiasm that bordered on fervor. In 1798, Hazan Seixas preached in Shearith Israel that God had "established us in this country where we possess every advantage that other citizens of these states enjoy" and urged his fellow congregants to offer "thanks for his manifold mercy" for doing so.[1] "To us, my brethren, should particularly belong a sacred love to this our country," exclaimed Myer Moses of Charleston in 1806, citing liberty, religious toleration, equality of rank, and the possibility that Jews might one day achieve high national and military office. America was a "blessed country," and Moses warmly thanked God that he had been born a citizen of the United States. "At best I am poor in language," he commented at one point during his address to Charleston's Hebrew Orphan Society, yet the wonders of America provoked him to flights of rhetoric:

> I am so proud of being a sojourner in this promised land, that, had I to subsist on the spontaneous production of the earth, and each day to search a running stream to quench my thirst at, I should prefer it to all the luxuries and superfluities which ill fated Europe can boast of. . . . Who is there that has glided thro' this calm and pleasant current of Liberty, that would ever wish to sail through the boisterous sea of Despotism and Slavery."[2]

Similarly, Jacob De La Motta, a physician who spoke at the dedication of Savannah's synagogue in 1820, listed religious freedom, equality under the law for all faiths, and the spread of education among the virtues of the Republic. "On what spot in this habitable Globe," he asked, "does an Israelite enjoy more blessings, more privileges, or is more elevated in the sphere of preferment, and more conspicuously dignified in respectable stations?"[3] Perhaps the clearest explication of all was that of Charleston's congregation, when in 1806 it wrote to London's Sephardic community to request recommendations for a hazan. They described the United States and the dignity that it accorded them in glowing terms:

> In a free and independent country like America, where civil and religious freedom go hand in hand, where no distinctions exist between the clergy of different denominations, where we are incorporated and known in law; freely tolerated; where in short we enjoy all the blessings of freedom in common with our fellow citizens, you may readily conceive we pride ourselves under the happy situation which makes us feel we are men, susceptible of that dignity which belongs to human nature, by participating in all the rights and blessings of this happy country.[4]

Formal commitments in law to religious toleration provided the basis for such confidence. As Mordecai Noah, one of the most visible Jews in the United States during the first half of the nineteenth century, explained in 1818 at the dedication of Shearith Israel's new synagogue, "In the formation and arrangement of our civil code, the sages and patriots whose collected wisdom adopted them, closed the doors upon that great evil which has shaken the old world to its centre. They proclaimed freedom of conscience."[5] New York had led the way in 1777, when it declared in the thirty-eighth article of its new constitution that, without qualification or reservation, all within its borders were to enjoy freedom of conscience. Moreover, the state's constitution stipulated that voters for the legislature and governor were required only to be freeholders, or if they resided in Albany or New York City, freemen. "We look forward, with Pleasure," wrote the members of Shearith Israel in 1783 to the state's governor, as they reassembled in the city and reestablished their congregation, "to the happy days we expect to enjoy under a Constitution, Wisely framed to reserve the inestimable Blessings of Civil, and Religious Liberty."[6]

In the other states of the young Republic, constitutions adopted during the revolutionary war in Virginia, New Jersey, Pennsylvania, North Carolina, and South Carolina likewise guaranteed religious freedom, although they restricted the franchise and officeholding to Protestants and in South Carolina declared Protestantism the state's established religion. Constitutions approved in Massachusetts, New Hampshire, and Georgia during the 1780s established religious freedom, while the Northwest Ordinance in 1787, which extended freedom of conscience to the territories north and west of the Ohio River, revealed that religious liberty was national policy even before the adoption of the federal Constitution. Subsequently, the Constitution of the United States prohibited religious qualifications for officeholding in the federal government, while the Bill of Rights barred the federal Congress from enacting laws to prohibit freedom of religion or to create an established one. Save for Maryland, Rhode Island, and Connecticut, therefore, all of the original states of the Republic, as well as the national government, had by 1790 officially embraced the principle of religious freedom.[7]

Equally reassuring was George Washington's unequivocal commitment, as president of the Republic, to the principle of toleration. Following his inauguration, Washington warmly responded to the greetings and congratulations of the Jewish congregations of Savannah, Charleston, Richmond, Philadelphia, and New York, which hailed him for his heroism during the Revolution, his leadership in creating the new Constitution, and his opposition to religious bigotry. In response to a similar letter of welcome from the Jews of Newport, Washington issued the stirring assurance that "the government of the United States . . . gives to bigotry no sanction, to persecution no assistance." These words had first appeared in the Newport congregation's letter to Washington upon his arrival in the city in August 1790, during his grand tour of New England, and the president, incorporating them in his reply to the congregation, added that the government asked only that "they who live under its protection should demean themselves as good citizens." In one fell swoop, therefore, Washington, who symbolized the nation, acknowledged not only the principle of religious freedom, but also that Jews were citizens—the first time anywhere for a head of state to do so.[8]

Their inclusion in major American institutions served also to reassure the nation's Jews. Some received federal appointments, like Reuben Etting, who became the U.S. marshal for Maryland during the administration of Thomas Jefferson; Levi Sheftall of Savannah, who served in a commissary's capacity as U.S. military agent; Mordecai Manuel Noah, appointed consul to Riga in 1811 and to Tunis in 1813; Joel Hart, consul to Scotland in 1816; and Nathan Levy, consul to Saint Thomas in 1818.[9] Others served in local government, particularly in Georgia, where Moses Sheftall became a justice of the inferior court in 1817, and where many more served in offices in Savannah, including clerk of the city council, clerk of the mayor's court, sheriff, port warden, fire chief, and commissioner of the market. Moreover, three Jewish men sat in the state's legislature between 1808 and 1821.[10] Jewish citizens affiliated with—and participated actively in—the two parties that emerged during the 1790s and around which political life was organized thereafter until 1820. In several instances they worked as newspaper writers and editors, adding to the heated political commentary that in this period enlivened public life.[11] Finally, New York's hazan, as noted previously, served as a trustee of Columbia between 1784 and 1815.

In addition to guaranteeing religious freedom in their constitutions, at least three states with Jewish congregations permitted them to incorporate, thereby bestowing upon them the benefits accruing from a legal identity as corporations. New York's legislature enacted a general incorporation law for religious societies in 1784, and the Jewish community in New York City took advantage of it immediately. When the state revised its regulations in 1801, Shearith Israel again incorporated, this time under the new law. In Georgia, the legislature authorized incorporation in 1790; Savannah's congregation forthwith secured its charter. And in 1806, in their request to London's Sephardic community for a hazan, Charleston's congregation cited the right to incorporate as among the civil privileges enjoyed by Jewish organizations in America.[12]

The unprecedented acceptance and recognition enjoyed by the Jews of the United States conjured up visions of ancient glories and prosperity. America, they proclaimed, was a promised land. Like ancient Israel, it flowed with milk and honey.[13] Modifying the hope of almost two millennia that they be gathered by God from the lands of their exile and restored to the land of Israel, Myer Moses prayed that God might bring them all to America. "Collect together thy long scattered people of Israel," he proclaimed, "and let their gathering place be in this land of milk and honey." Indeed, according to Moses, from the day that it broke loose from the tyranny of England and declared its independence, America was nothing less than a New Jerusalem: "From that period must be dated that the Almighty gave to the Jews what had long been promised them, namely, a second Jerusalem!"[14]

Others too employed the metaphor of Jerusalem: an essay in the *Albany Gazette* in 1820, republished for a national readership in *Niles' Weekly Register,* claimed, "This is the most preferable country for the Jews; here they can have their Jerusalem. . . . Here they can build their temple. . . . Here they can lay their heads on their pillow at night without fear of mobs, of bigotry, of persecution."[15] And Mordecai Noah referred to "a New Jerusalem" in his scheme for a Jewish colony on Grand Island in the Niagara River.[16]

The Jewish population benefited not only from the rule of religious toleration in postrevolutionary America but also from the theological proposition that accepting Jews in society would hasten their conversion. Although this premise implied that Judaism was a transitory phenomenon, the doctrine did benefit Jews by justifying a benevolent attitude toward them among the Christian majority. Accordingly, advocating that Jews in Pennsylvania ought to be enfranchised and permitted to serve in public office, a newspaper correspondent early in 1784 explained that "It would tend to the propagation of Christianity, by impressing the minds of the Jews, from this generous treatment; with sentiments in favour of the gospel."[17]

Dr. Benjamin Rush, one of Philadelphia's leading figures during the last quarter of the eighteenth century, who worked avidly to replace monarchical institutions with republican ones (advocating, for example, reform of the criminal law, abolition of the death penalty, principles of education suitable to a republican social order, and an end to slavery), preferred conversionist sentiments to the idea that religious toleration meant a permanent place for the Jewish religion in the Republic. Attending the wedding of a Jewish couple in Philadelphia in 1787, Rush looked "into futurity and anticipated the time foretold by the prophets when this once-beloved race of men shall again be restored to the divine favor and when they shall unite with Christians with one heart and one voice in celebrating the praise of a common and universal Saviour."[18] Similarly, Abiel Holmes wrote in 1798 in his biography of his father-in-law, the Reverend Ezra Stiles, that

> civility and catholicism towards the Jews is worthy of imitation. It is to be feared that Christians do not what ought to be done towards the conversion of this devoted people. While admitted into most countries for the purpose of trade and commerce, instead of being treated with that humanity and tenderness which christianity should inspire, they are often persecuted and condemned as unworthy of notice or regard. Such treatment tends to prejudice them against our holy religion, and to establish them in their infidelity.[19]

Hope for the conversion of the Jews remained strong during the next twenty years. Benevolence, however, was judged inadequate to attract Jews to Christianity, prompting the formation of two organizations in 1816 to hasten their conversion: the Female Society of Boston and Vicinity for Promoting Christianity among the Jews, and the American Society for Evangelizing the Jews. A third organization, the American Society for Meliorating the Condition of the Jews, appeared in 1820. Founded by a German Jewish convert, this undertaking attracted the support of Protestants such as the Reverend Alexander McLeod of New York City.[20]

Other Americans regarded Jews as meritorious in their own right, rather than as people worthy of toleration and benevolence merely to convert them. By eliminating religious requirements for the franchise and for service in office, counseled one Pennsylvanian in 1784, Jews would settle in the state and prove of benefit to it because of "their wealth, their information, and their attachment to the cause of liberty." And two Philadelphia newspaper publishers argued in the same year for civic equality on behalf of the Jews because they comported themselves as good citizens everywhere and firmly supported the American cause during the Revolution.[21]

Ten years later, the churchlike architecture of the Charleston synagogue won accolades in that city's newspaper because it demonstrated that the Jews, for their part, were free of religious prejudice. John Adams found them to be "men of as liberal minds, as much honor, probity, generosity, and good breeding, as any I have known in any sect of religion or philosophy." Rejecting the anti-Semitic allegation that Jews were disloyal, James Madison suggested that equality under the law, which Jews enjoyed in America, was "the best guarantee of loyalty and love of country." And in 1819, in a pamphlet by one W. D. Robinson, who advocated that downtrodden and persecuted Jews in Europe immigrate to the United States and settle in a midcontinent agricultural colony, Jews were praised as "an industrious, abstemious, and persevering race of people . . . capable of making the same exertions as any other part of mankind."[22]

Secure in their position within American society, committed to it because of the liberty and recognition they enjoyed as citizens, the Jews of the early Republic invited contemporary civic leaders to join them in dedicating their synagogues. In 1782, Philadelphia's Jewish congregation extended such an invitation to Pennsylvania's governor, lieutenant governor, and Supreme Executive Council for the consecration of the city's first permanent synagogue. Twelve years later, Charleston's newspaper reported that "a numerous concourse of ladies and gentlemen" attended the dedication of the new synagogue there, and praised this as evidence that in America religious animosities had been stilled. "That injured people," wrote the newspaper, "in the blessed climes of America . . . have realized their promised land. The shackles of religious distinctions are now no more . . . they are here admitted to the full privileges of citizenship, and bid fair to flourish and be happy."[23]

Shearith Israel prepared in 1818 for the dedication of its new house of worship by sending invitations to the president, the governor, the mayor, the recorder, and other notable non-Jews. Mordecai Noah sent John Adams a copy of his address on that occasion, and in 1820 Jacob De La Motta sent copies of his speech at the dedication of Savannah's synagogue to Thomas Jefferson and James Madison, both living in retirement. Two years later, at the dedication of Richmond's first synagogue building, "the ceremony was witnessed by a large assemblage of Christians," as a local newspaper reported.[24] The synagogue was as much a civic institution in America as any other, these actions seemed to imply.

The New Jerusalem, however, had its flaws. Despite their comfortable position between 1783 and 1820, Jews were very much aware of the presence of anti-Semitism, however mild its manifestations might be when compared with those prevalent in Europe. In 1787, for example, Charleston's synagogue was broken into, a silver ritual spice box was stolen, and "the five books of Moses which contain the law and commandments of Almighty God, were wantonly thrown about the floor," according to a newspaper account. The fact that all this occurred during the ten-day solemn period of penitence that begins on Rosh Hashanah and ends on Yom Kippur suggests that the burglary might have had overtones of anti-Semitism. Some who opposed adoption of the federal Constitution believed that religious uniformity was necessary to prevent the disintegration of the Republic; religious pluralism was an evil to be avoided, for it would provoke conflict. The prohibition of a religious test in the Constitution for holding office was, according to one Anti-Federalist, "an invitation for Jews and pagans of every kind to come against us." Indeed, continued the writer, Christianity was necessary for producing "good members of society . . . [and] those gentlemen who formed this Constitution should not have given this invitation to Jews and heathens."[25]

In later years, the walls and gate of the Jewish cemetery in Savannah were vandalized (in 1800 and 1812), and in 1807 the exclusion of Moses Sheftall from membership in one of the city's social organizations, a dancing assembly, seemed to him to be attributable to his religion. In 1818, Uriah Levy encountered hostility among his fellow officers in the United States Navy, who abhorred the idea that a Jew would dine with them as a member of their mess, though subsequently they overcame their objections and included him.[26]

More vivid than these, however, was the attack upon "Jew Brokers" in the Pennsylvania legislature in 1784. The attack was occasioned by efforts to obtain a charter for a new bank, which would compete with the existing Bank of North America; Hyam Salomon and several Jewish merchants owned shares in the latter. When Miles Fisher, a Quaker lawyer, rose in the legislature to attack the Jewish brokers, he invoked traditional anti-Semitic views regarding Jewish financiers, calling them, for example, "the authors of high and unusual interest." The ensuing controversy over the issue of a charter for a second bank continued for more than half a year, with one anti-Jewish commentator writing that he "could discover worse than a Shylock's temper remaining in the hearts of those despisers of Christianity," alluding to the allegation of unyielding animosity among Jews to the Christian religion, one of the staples of anti-Semitism. Four years later, Fisher influenced the visiting Frenchman, Brissot de Warville, to write that "usurious Jews can never live among economical men, who have no need of borrowing at enormous interest; for a similar reason a seller of pork cannot live among Jews."[27]

In addition to the familiar economic reasons for hostility, claims that Jews did not contribute to the community, were parasites, despised physical labor, and refused to become loyal, permanent members of the societies in which they resided could also be heard. Accordingly, in 1820, an item in *Niles' Weekly Register* asserted that,

> in general their interests do not appear identified with those of the communities in which they live, though there are honorable exceptions among them. They will not sit down and labor like other people. They create nothing and are mere consumers. They will not cultivate the earth, nor work at mechanical trades, preferring to live by their wit in dealing and acting as if they had a home nowhere. It is this cause, no doubt, that an hostility to them exists so extensively.[28]

The author of this statement concluded, however, that "all this has nothing to do with their rights of men." This observation, remarkable in that it followed immediately upon the list of unwholesome characteristics attributed to Jews, indicates that anti-Semitism in the America of the early Republic was milder by far than the virulent hostility of many centuries' duration in Europe. Indeed, Jewish citizens in the United States could, without fear, answer their detractors publicly. In 1784, an item signed by "A Jew Broker" appeared in one of Philadelphia's newspapers in response to Miles Fisher's attack in the Pennsylvania legislature. Written probably by Hyam Salomon with the assistance of the newspaper's editor, the author proclaimed, "I am a Jew; it is my own nation and profession. I also subscribe myself a Broker. . . . I exult and glory in reflecting that we have the honour to reside in a *free* country where, as a people, we have met with the most generous countenance and protection." Moreover, asserted the proud writer, America's Jews from the start of the conflict with Britain had been supporters of the American cause, in contrast to Fisher, who had been exiled from Pennsylvania for Toryism.[29]

Reacting similarly in employing the public press in the face of an anti-Semitic attack, Benjamin Nones of Philadelphia in 1800 noted that he had been accused of being a Jew, a Republican, and impoverished. To the first he replied, "I *am a Jew*. I glory in belonging to that persuasion . . . whose votaries have never murdered each other in religious wars, or cherished the theological hatred so general, so unextinguishable among those who revile them. A persuasion, whose patient followers, have endured for ages the pious cruelties of Pagans, and of christians." As for his poverty, Nones answered that his family was "large, but soberly and decently brought up. They have not been taught to revile a christian, because his religion is not *so old* as theirs." Indeed, commented Nones, even impoverished Jews can be honest.[30]

The attack upon Nones as a Republican referred to his membership in the Democratic Society of Philadelphia, part of the political party apparatus that supported Thomas Jefferson. During the early part of the 1790s, two distinct national parties began to form, largely because of Alexander Hamilton's economic program, the contrasting visions that Hamilton and Jefferson had of the future shape of American society and government, and the attitudes of each toward the French Revolution. Party organizations crystallized in the middle of the decade in the wake of the Jay Treaty with Great Britain. Federalists, the party of Hamilton, supported the treaty, and Democratic Republicans, the party of Jefferson, bitterly opposed it because it tilted the United States toward England at a time when Britain was fighting against France to suppress the revolution there. The venomous rhetoric that characterized political debate during this decade included Federalist denunciations of the Jeffersonians that drew upon anti-Semitic sentiment. In 1795, for example,

James Rivington, New York's prominent Federalist editor, crudely characterized Jeffersonian clubs as filled with French agents bent upon fomenting sedition in the United States. These harbingers of disorder, wrote Rivington, were recognizable "by their physiognomy; they all seem to be, like their Vice-President, of the tribe of Shylock; they have that leering underlook, and malicious grin, that seem to say to the honest man—*approach me* not." The vice president to whom Rivington referred was Solomon Simpson, a leading member of Shearith Israel in New York and the first vice president of the city's Democratic Society.[31]

The denunciation of Benjamin Nones as a Jew and a Republican five years later was again an attempt by a Federalist newspaper to enlist anti-Semitic feeling to assail the Jeffersonians. In his response, Nones firmly agreed that he was a Republican—since Jews, he said, could be none else. Kings, he explained, had afflicted the Jews in ancient times in their own land. "In republics we have *rights,*" he maintained, while "in monarchies we live but to experience *wrongs.*" Monarchy, he did not have to emphasize in his rebuttal, had been eliminated in France but continued to exist in the England supported by the Federalist party.[32]

One of the most thoughtful responses to an anti-Jewish statement was that written to Secretary of State James Monroe by Isaac Harby of Charleston, a newspaper editor who, according to contemporary opinion, exercised a measure of political influence in South Carolina.[33] Harby's letter is important because of its inclusive vision of citizenship in the Republic, one that advocated religious pluralism and recognition on the basis of merit rather than sectarian affiliation. Monroe had written to Mordecai Noah early in 1815 recalling him as consul to Tunis, and in his opening sentence explained that, "at the time of your appointment . . . it was not known that the Religion which you profess would form any obstacle to the exercise of your Consular function." Noah's most recent biographer has suggested that Monroe's anti-Semitic statement was merely a cover for more complex reasons of state, but Harby, of course, could have not been aware of that possibility. Writing to Monroe in 1816, Harby expressed "astonishment" that Noah's religion allegedly made him unfit for his post and reminded the secretary of state of his own role in an earlier period to incorporate the principle of religious freedom in the constitution of Virginia. Harby eloquently presented his view of citizenship.

> It is upon the principle, not of *toleration* (for man has no *power* to tolerate Religion, that is a concern between Man and his maker) but upon the principle of equal inalienable, *constitutional Rights,* that we see Jews appointed to offices, that we see them elected in our State Representation, & that, in proportion as their talents and their influence can bear them through, we see their mingling in the honours of their country. They are by no means to be considered as a *Religious sect,* tolerated by the government; they constitute a portion of *the People.* They are, in every respect, woven in and compacted with the citizens of the Republic. Quakers and Catholics; Episcopalians and Presbyterians, Baptists and Jews, all constitute one great political family.

Harby thereupon pleaded with Monroe to erase the offending sentence from his letter of recall to Noah, for it violated "the liberal character" of American institutions and must not be permitted to stand as a precedent that established a religious test for public office. If it did, he feared, if ever "*Religious distinctions*" came to govern, then the Jews of America would be overwhelmed and would again face the necessity of searching for a haven in the world.

Noah's case, however, evoked more than the issue of a religious test for the consular service in one of North Africa's Barbary states. Harby's preoccupation with the meaning of citizenship, his assertion that Catholics, Jews, and Protestants of all denominations belonged alike to "one great political family," his conviction that Jews belonged wholly to the body of the people and were not merely an extraneous sect to be tolerated mirrored the fact that civic equality for Jews had not yet been achieved in all jurisdictions. Despite the commitment to religious freedom in America, the forthrightness with which Jews could respond to anti-Semitic attacks, and Jewish participation in public life, the Jews of the United States could not yet vote or serve in public office in all states. During the Revolution, New York had granted them the right to vote and to serve in office, but constitutions adopted by ten other states had not.[34] Throughout the period between 1783 and 1820, obtaining the rights that should belong to all citizens was therefore a matter of concern to the Jewish population. Notable victories had been secured almost everywhere when Harby wrote to the secretary of state in 1816, but in a few remaining states Jews were as yet not enfranchised or permitted to serve in public office.

Jews insisted that civic equality was the right of all citizens. "I am an Israelite and am not allowed the liberty of a vote or voice in common with the rest of the voters. . . . I ask of your Honors the rights and privildges due other free citizens," Moses Hays had written as early as 1776 to the legislature of Rhode Island. A decade later, Jonas Phillips of Philadelphia urged the Constitutional Convention to eschew religious tests for officeholding, arguing that no person who acknowledged the existence of God should be "deprived of any Civil Right as a Citizen." In their letter to George Washington in 1790, the congregation of Newport referred to "the invaluable rights of free citizens" formerly denied them but now available under the federal Constitution. And in 1809, when challenged regarding his right to sit in the North Carolina legislature because of his religion, Jacob Henry asserted that his faith did not make him any less a citizen. As he explained, "in all things that relate to the State, and to the duties of civil life, I am bound by the same obligations, with my fellow citizens." The state's House of Commons concurred, permitting him to take the seat to which he had been elected.[35]

Above all, America's Jews, when arguing for their right to vote and to serve in office, pointed to their service on the side of the patriots during the Revolution. In 1784, for example, the Jewish congregation in Philadelphia wrote to Pennsylvania's Council of Censors, protesting the requirement in the state's constitution that representatives in the legislature take an oath affirming that the New Testament was divinely inspired—a religious test that obviously excluded Jews. As they argued,

> the conduct and behaviour of the Jews in this and the neighbouring
> states, has always tallied with the great design of the revolution; that
> the Jews of Charlestown, New-York, New-Port, and other posts,
> occupied by the British troops, have distinguishedly suffered for
> their attachment to the revolution principles. . . . The Jews of
> Pennsylvania in proportion to the number of their members, can
> count with any religious society whatsoever, the whigs among

either of them; they have served some of them in the continental army; some went out in the militia to fight the common enemy.³⁶

Similarly, Jonas Phillips informed the Constitutional Convention in 1787 that the Jews "during the late Contest with England [were] . . . foremost in aiding and assisting the states with their lifes & fortunes, [and] they . . . supported the cause . . . bravely fought and bled for liberty," which now, Phillips argued, "they can not Enjoy."³⁷

Phillips was correct, for civil disabilities existed everywhere but in New York. In Rhode Island and Connecticut, the charters and legislation of the colonial era remained in force. The constitutions adopted during the Revolution in New Hampshire, South Carolina, Virginia, New Jersey, Delaware, Pennsylvania, Maryland, North Carolina, Georgia, and Massachusetts without exception excluded Jews from civic equality. Some explicitly restricted the franchise and officeholding to Protestants or to Christians generally, while others, along with Pennsylvania, required an oath of belief in Christian principles.³⁸ When the Revolution ended in 1783, therefore, the Jews of the United States still faced the possibility that, despite the commitment of many among them to the American side in the struggle with England, they would not be recognized as full citizens of the states where they lived, whose liberty they had fought to secure.

The tide began to turn late in 1785, when Virginia approved an act, written originally by Thomas Jefferson, establishing religious freedom in the state. The act proclaimed that religious affiliation "shall in no wise diminish, enlarge or affect . . . civil capacities." New state constitutions adopted by South Carolina and Pennsylvania in 1790, by Delaware in 1792, and by Georgia in 1798 eliminated the religious qualifications that hitherto had kept Jews from fully participating in public affairs. Among the remaining original states of the Republic, civil disabilities remained in force as the nineteenth century began, but in Connecticut they were eliminated in 1818 and in Massachusetts in 1821. In Maryland, a bitter struggle to admit the Jewish population to civic equality began in 1818 in the state's legislature and lasted until 1826, when Jews in that state were finally granted the same rights as all other citizens. In Rhode Island, New Hampshire, and North Carolina, on the other hand, full inclusion did not occur until later in the century.³⁹

Hailed by its Jewish inhabitants as a New Jerusalem, the young American Republic gradually extended to them the rights of all citizens. Only one of the American states counted Jews fully within the body politic at the time of the Revolution, but by the middle of the 1820s nearly all did, rewarding the assertiveness and confidence of such men as Jonas Phillips and Isaac Harby, who had argued for civic equality. As the third decade of the nineteenth century began, the thousands of Jews who were about to emigrate from central Europe to America would come to a nation in which Jewish predecessors had helped to prepare the way for them by championing the right of all citizens to participate equally in the public affairs and common enterprises of society. The American Republic would be a community composed of citizens of all faiths, fulfilling the aspirations of its Jewish inhabitants in the years that followed the American Revolution.

CONCLUSION: THE SIGNIFICANCE OF
EARLY AMERICAN JEWRY

ALTHOUGH they were few in number, economically unimportant on a global or even regional scale, and not a decisive political force in their new homeland, the Jews of America between 1654 and 1820 were pioneers, exploring the implications of living where Jews were not the objects of debilitating hostility. They were among the first Jews in the modern world to experiment with acculturation and to contend with one of its most extreme forms, assimilation through intermarriage. Engagement with the general culture led them, during the colonial era, to envision a synthesis in which Jewish tradition could combine with elements of the surrounding culture without being undermined. The synagogue they built in Newport, today a national landmark, gracefully preserves in stone, wood, and glass their belief that the combination was possible.

In the years following the Revolution, the Jews of the early Republic took even bolder steps. As they examined how interaction with the religious and secular traditions of their non-Jewish neighbors might proceed, they reshaped both the synagogue and the Jewish community. Political ideas current in the early Republic altered the community's principles of governance. The office of the hazan began to resemble the Protestant ministry, while synagogue dedications borrowed from Masonry and, in one instance, included organ music. Traditionalists in our own era would oppose building a synagogue like the one in Charleston, whose exterior was indistinguishable from a church's, but this innovation, too, attests to the willingness with which Jews in the aftermath of the Revolution continued to explore the blending of Jewish tradition with the general culture that they had first explored during the colonial era.

America's Jews in the eighteenth century also pioneered in the development of a Jewish community based upon voluntary affiliation. The effort demanded resourcefulness and inventiveness, for highly developed models of such a community did not exist elsewhere. It required patience because of members who refused to serve in office, arguments erupting during services in the synagogue, and, in the absence of the universal hegemony enjoyed by the traditional European Jewish community, an inability to command automatic financial support. To encourage adherence to the voluntary community, the Jews of colonial America relied upon, among other traditional means, disciplinary sanctions, support for the poor, and a community school; they also eliminated the long-standing hostility between Ashkenazim and Sephardim. In the period of the early Republic, to be sure, support for communal discipline, the school, and assistance for the poor declined, while Ashkenazim and Sephardim (or more likely, older Americans and newer ones) began to pull apart. The notion of a voluntary community, however, had by now become familiar and could serve as an example for the Jews of central Europe who began to immigrate to the United States in the 1820s.

Early American Jewry was also among the first to experiment with citizenship for Jews in the modern world. Although they were excluded from political life during the colonial era, the security bestowed by the tolerant milieu in this country encouraged Jews to participate in the American Revolution. Thereafter, they made the case for admission to civic equality, gradually gaining the right to vote and to serve in office—in most states before 1820. The history of this small group, therefore, is part of the larger story of the American experiment with egalitarianism. Jews provided an early test of the ability of the American polity to incorporate a people who differed in religion and who had borne the stigma of the undersirable outsider for so many centuries. The Jewish experience in early America verified that this was a land in which the outsider could become an insider, where the stranger in the land and the wanderer in history could find sanctuary and serenity.

NOTES

Introduction

1. Myer Moses, *An Oration, Delivered before the Hebrew Orphan Society, on the 15th Day of October, 1806* (Charleston: Apollo, 1807), 6–7, 15, 18.

2. Isidore S. Meyer, "The Hebrew Oration of Sampson Simson, 1800," *Publications of the American Jewish Historical Society* 46 (1956–57): 58; "Log Book of the Ship Sansom," *Publications of the American Jewish Historical Society* 27 (1920): 239.

Chapter One. Origins and Antecedents

1. The twenty-three arrivals included thirteen younger individuals, some of whom may have been born in Brazil. The group reached New Amsterdam by 7 September; Rosh Hashanah, the festival of the Jewish New Year, fell on 12 September in 1654. The account here follows Arnold Wiznitzer, "The Exodus from Brazil and Arrival in New Amsterdam of the Jewish Pilgrim Fathers, 1654," in *The Jewish Experience in Latin America: Selected Studies from the Publications of the American Jewish Historical Society,* ed. Martin A. Cohen (Waltham, Mass., and New York: American Jewish Historical Society and KTAV, 1971), 2:320–27. For a critique of Wiznitzer's identification of places and individuals, an account at odds with his, see Egon Wolff and Frieda Wolff, "The Problem of the First Jewish Settlers in New Amsterdam, 1654," *Studia Rosenthaliana* 15 (1981): 169–77. See also Leo Hershkowitz, "Asser Levy and the Inventories of Early New York Jews," *American Jewish History* 80 (1990–91): 25–27.

2. Ezra Stiles, *Literary Diary,* ed. F. B. Dexter (New York: Scribner's, 1901), 1:283; Joshua Trachtenberg, *Consider the Years: The Story of the Jewish Community of Easton, 1752–1942* (Easton, Pa.: Centennial Committee of Temple Beth Shalom, 1944), 2, 28–29. The estimate of twenty-five hundred is Jacob R. Marcus's,

in "The Jew and the American Revolution," *American Jewish Archives* 27 (1975): 103.

3. Abram Vossen Goodman, *American Overture: Jewish Rights in Colonial Times* (Philadelphia: Jewish Publication Society of America, 1947), 113, citing Peter Kalm, who visited North America in 1748; Stiles, *Literary Diary*, 1:6, 2:17, 19–20, 39–40, 91, 151–52, 254–56, 283, 370, 377, 422; Morris U. Schappes, *A Documentary History of the Jews of the United States, 1654–1875,* 3d ed. (New York: Schocken, 1971), 77–84.

4. Cecil Roth, *A History of the Marranos* (Philadelphia: Jewish Publication Society of America, 1932), 12–18.

5. For adherence to Jewish customs and rituals, see Haim Beinart, "The Converso Community in 15th Century Spain," in *The Sephardi Heritage: Essays on the History and Cultural Contributions of the Jews in Spain and Portugal,* ed. R. D. Barnett (London: Vallentine, Mitchell, 1971), 1:447–50. But for a more recent and contrary analysis of the Marranos, opposing the view that they secretly remained loyal to Judaism, see B. Netanyahu, *The Marranos of Spain from the Late XIVth to the Early XVIth Century, According to Contemporary Hebrew Sources* (New York: American Academy for Jewish Research, 1973).

6. Henry Kamen, *Inquisition and Society in Spain in the Sixteenth and Seventeenth Centuries* (Bloomington: Indiana University Press, 1985), 20–22; Roth, *History of the Marranos,* 31–32.

7. Beinart, "Converso Community," 428, 438–39; Kamen, *Inquisition and Society,* 41–42, 223–34; Richard E. Greenleaf, *The Mexican Inquisition of the Sixteenth Century* (Albuquerque: University of New Mexico Press, 1969); James C. Boyajian, "The New Christians Reconsidered: Evidence from Lisbon's Portuguese Bankers, 1497–1647," *Studia Rosenthaliana* 13 (1979): 132.

8. Boyajian, "New Christians Reconsidered," 132–33; Roth, *History of the Marranos,* 56–60.

9. Roth, *History of the Marranos,* 61–63; Kamen, *Inquisition and Society,* 219–22.

10. Roth, *History of the Marranos,* 66–73. For a detailed account of the origins of the Inquisition in Portugal, see Alexandre Herculano, *History of the Origin and Establishment of the Inquisition in Portugal,* trans. John C. Banner (New York: AMS Press, 1968).

11. Roth, *History of the Marranos,* 64–66, 74; C. R. Boxer, *The Portuguese Seaborne Empire, 1415–1825* (New York: Knopf, 1969), 281–82, 331–34. According to Boxer's account, the Portuguese engaged in racial labeling. *Limpeza de sangre* (purity of blood) was the test required for service to the Crown, and the taint of impure blood was passed by the converted Jews of 1497 to their descendants. For Boxer's account, in *Portuguese Seaborne Empire,* of Portuguese racism in the early modern era, directed against blacks, Moors, Jews, and mulattoes, as well as New Christians, see 249–72.

12. Roth, *History of the Marranos,* 196–97, 199–233; Boyajian, "New Christians Reconsidered," 133.

13. For the struggle between Spain and Holland, see C. R. Boxer, *The Dutch Seaborne Empire, 1600–1800* (New York: Knopf, 1965), 1–5, 18ff.

14. Simon Schama, *The Embarrassment of Riches: An Interpretation of Dutch Culture in the Golden Age* (New York: Knopf, 1987), 59–62, 590–93. For a discussion of religious pluralism in seventeenth-century Holland, see Paul Zumthor, *Daily Life in Rembrandt's Holland* (New York: Macmillan, 1963), 79–94. On the Calvinist ministry's views, see also Boxer, *Dutch Seaborne Empire,* 117–24, 129–32. The difficulties encountered by the first Jewish settlers in New Amsterdam are described in chapter 2.

15. Salo Wittmayer Baron, *A Social and Religious History of the Jews,* 2d ed., rev. (New York and Philadelphia: Columbia University Press and the Jewish Publication Society of America, 1973), 15:41–63. For their activities in commerce and finance, see Herbert I. Bloom, *The Economic Activities of the Jews of Amsterdam in the Seventeenth and Eighteenth Centuries* (Williamsport, Pa.: Bayard, 1937).

16. Arnold Wiznitzer, *Jews in Colonial Brazil* (New York: Columbia University Press, 1960), 51–54; C. R. Boxer, *The Dutch in Brazil, 1624–1654* (Oxford: Clarendon, 1957), 21–27; Boxer, *Dutch Seaborne Empire,* 24–27.

17. Boxer, *Dutch in Brazil,* 37–56, 121–23, 133–34; Wiznitzer, *Jews in Colonial Brazil,* 12–41, 46.

18. Boxer, *Dutch in Brazil,* 134; Wiznitzer, *Jews in Colonial Brazil,* 59, 65–66, 71–72, 74, 81, 86, 130–35.

19. The rebellion and war may be followed in Boxer, *Dutch in Brazil,* 159–245.

20. Wiznitzer, "Exodus from Brazil," 326–27.

21. Moses A. Shulvass, *From East to West: The Westward Migration of Jews from Eastern Europe during the Seventeenth and Eighteenth Centuries* (Detroit: Wayne State University Press, 1971), 22–23; Jonathan I. Israel, *European Jewry in the Age of Mercantilism* (Oxford: Clarendon, 1985), 104–5; Wiznitzer, *Jews in Colonial Brazil,* 84, 107.

22. Israel, *European Jewry in the Age of Mercantilism,* 144, 164.

23. Charles M. Andrews, *The Colonial Period of American History* (New Haven: Yale University Press, 1934–38), 3:50–63, 4:22ff.

24. Ibid., 3:21, 105; Samuel J. Hurwitz and Edith Hurwitz, "The New World Sets an Example for the Old: The Jews of Jamaica and Political Rights 1661–1831," *American Jewish Historical Quarterly* 55 (1965–66): 39–40.

25. Morris A. Gutstein, *The Story of the Jews of Newport: Two and a Half Centuries of Judaism, 1658–1908* (New York: Bloch, 1936), 36.

26. Todd Endelman, *The Jews of Georgian England 1714–1830: Tradition and Change in a Liberal Society* (Philadelphia: Jewish Publication Society of America, 1979), 20–24; Albert M. Hyamson, *The Sephardim of England: A History of the*

Spanish and Portuguese Community, 1492–1951 (London: Methuen, 1952), 14; Israel, *European Jewry in the Age of Mercantilism,* 64.

27. R. G. Fuks-Mansfield, "Problems of Overpopulation of Jewish Amsterdam in the Seventeenth Century," *Studia Rosenthaliana* 18 (1984): 142; Endelman, *Jews of Georgian England,* 15–17, 19, 31; V. D. Lipman, "Sephardi and other Jewish Immigrants in England in the Eighteenth Century," in *Migration and Settlement: Proceedings of the Anglo-American Jewish Historical Conference Held in London Jointly by the Jewish Historical Society of England and the American Jewish Historical Society, July 1970* (London: Jewish Historical Society of England, 1971), 38.

28. Endelman, *Jews of Georgian England,* 87–89, 97–100.

29. Ibid., 26–27, 32–47, 114–15.

30. R. D. Barnett, "The Correspondence of the Mahamad of the Spanish and Portuguese Congregation of London during the Seventeenth and Eighteenth Centuries," *Transactions of the Jewish Historical Society of England* 20 (1959–61): 10–11.

31. R. D. Barnett, "Dr. Samuel Nunes Ribeiro and the Settlement of Georgia," in *Migration and Settlement,* 87; Endelman, *Jews of Georgian England,* 110–11. Georgia's Jews during the 1730s did encounter stiff resistance to their settlement there among the colony's London-based trustees. Countering this attitude was the favorable one of James Oglethorpe, the colony's governor, and the assumption of the colony by the Crown in 1752; see Saul J. Rubin, *Third to None: The Saga of Savannah Jewry, 1733–1983* (Savannah: S. J. Rubin, 1983), 2, 10–13, 18; David T. Morgan, "Judaism in Eighteenth-Century Georgia," *Georgia Historical Quarterly* 58 (1974): 43.

32. Schappes, *Documentary History,* 26–30.

33. Endelman, *Jews of Georgian England,* 24–25.

34. Zosa Szajkowski, "Jewish Emigration from Bordeaux during the Eighteenth and Nineteenth Centuries," *Jewish Social Studies* 18 (1956): 118–23. For arrivals from Bordeaux earlier in the eighteenth century, see Joseph R. Rosenbloom, *A Biographical Dictionary of Early American Jews, Colonial Times through 1801* (Lexington: University of Kentucky Press, 1960), 45.

35. Rosenbloom, *Biographical Dictionary,* 45; Stanley F. Chyet, *Lopez of Newport: Colonial American Merchant Prince* (Detroit: Wayne State University Press, 1970), 18–19.

36. H. P. Salomon, "New Light on the Portuguese Inquisition: The Second Reply to the Archbishop of Cranganor," *Studia Rosenthaliana* 5 (1971): 182; Chyet, *Lopez of Newport,* 13–19, 22–23, 105–6; Barnett, "Ribeiro and the Settlement of Georgia," 66–77; "Items Relating to the Seixas Family," *Publications of the American Jewish Historical Society* 27 (1920): 161.

37. "Items Relating to Congregation Shearith Israel, New York," *Publications of the American Jewish Historical Society* 27 (1920): 15–16. Hazan Pinto feared he might once again be forced to move.

38. The discussion of Sephardic decline that follows is based on Israel, *Euro-*

pean Jewry in the Age of Mercantilism, 241; R. Cohen, "Patterns of Marriage and Remarriage among the Sephardi Jews of Surinam, 1788–1818," in *The Jewish Nation in Surinam: Historical Essays,* ed. R. Cohen (Amsterdam: S. Emmering, 1982), 91; Endelman, *Jews of Georgian England,* 31–32; Barnett, "Ribeiro and the Settlement of Georgia," 83–86; Barnett A. Elzas, *The Jews of South Carolina from the Earliest Times to the Present Day* (Philadelphia: Lippincott, 1905), 31–32; Rubin, *Third to None,* 1–4; and Barnett, "Correspondence of the Mahamad," 4, 16.

39. Israel, *European Jewry in the Age of Mercantilism,* 246–47; Endelman, *Jews of Georgian England,* 266.

40. For an explication built around this perspective, see Boyajian, "New Christians Reconsidered," passim.

41. For a case study of kinship among merchants in the Atlantic world, see Bernard Bailyn, *The New England Merchants in the Seventeenth Century* (Cambridge: Harvard University Press, 1955), 87–91.

42. J. William Frost, *The Quaker Family in Colonial America: A Portrait of the Society of Friends* (New York: St. Martin's, 1973), 204; Frederick B. Tolles, *Meetinghouse and Countinghouse: The Quaker Merchants of Colonial Philadelphia, 1682–1763* (Chapel Hill, University of North Carolina Press, 1948), 90–91; G. A. Rothrock, *The Huguenots: A Biography of a Minority* (Chicago: Nelson-Hall, 1979), 184–85.

43. Yosef Yerushalmi, "Between Amsterdam and New Amsterdam: The Place of Curaçao and the Caribbean in Early Modern Jewish History," *American Jewish History* 72 (1982–83): 177–78.

44. Israel, *European Jewry in the Age of Mercantilism,* 107–8, 111, 155, 162; Jonathan I. Israel, "The Changing Role of the Dutch Sephardim in International Trade, 1595–1715," in *Dutch Jewish History,* ed. Joseph Michman and Tirtsah Levie (Jerusalem: Daf-Chen Press, 1984), 45–48; D. M. Swetschinski, "Kinship and Commerce: The Foundations of Portuguese Jewish Life in Seventeenth-Century Holland," *Studia Rosenthaliana* 15 (1981): 65–67. For additional discussion of trade linking Sephardic and New Christian merchants, see Jonathan I. Israel, "Spain and the Dutch Sephardim, 1609–1660," *Studia Rosenthaliana* 12 (1978): 1–61; and his "Some Further Data on the Amsterdam Sephardim and the Trade with Spain during the 1650s," *Studia Rosenthaliana* 14 (1980): 7–19.

45. Isaac S. Emmanuel and Suzanne A. Emmanuel, *History of the Jews of the Netherland Antilles* (Cincinnati: American Jewish Archives, 1970), 1:68, 93, 109, 118, 206, 213, 234, 277.

46. Ibid., 70, 215.

47. For Jamaica, see Barnett, "Correspondence of the Mahamad," 10; for correspondence between the New York congregation and the ordained spiritual leader of Jamaica's Jews in 1758, see "The Earliest Extant Minute Books of the Spanish and Portuguese Congregation Shearith Israel in New York, 1728–1786," *Publications of the American Jewish Historical Society* 21 (1913): 77; and Bertram W. Korn, "The

Haham DeCordova of Jamaica," *American Jewish Archives* 18 (1966): 141–54. For Barbados, see E. M. Shilstone, *Monumental Inscriptions in the Burial Ground of the Jewish Synagogue at Bridgetown, Barbados* (New York: American Jewish Historical Society, 1956), vi–vii, xvi–xviii; and Richard S. Dunn, "The Barbados Census of 1680: Profile of the Richest Colony in English America," 3d ser., *William and Mary Quarterly* 26 (1969): 23. For Saint Eustatius, see John Hartog, "The Honen Dalim Congregation of St. Eustatius," *American Jewish Archives* 19 (1967): 60–64; and Emmanuel, *Jews of the Netherlands Antilles,* 518–27. For Surinam, see Cohen, *Jewish Nation in Surinam,* 11, 14, 19–20.

48. Shulvass, *From East to West,* passim.

49. Israel, *European Jewry in the Age of Mercantilism,* 145–50, 154–55; Endelman, *Jews of Georgian England,* 172–76.

50. Most of the Polish Jews who appeared in North America between 1750 and 1800 resided first in England or Holland; see Shulvass, *From East to West,* 93. Rosenbloom, *Biographical Dictionary,* passim, identifies the place of origin of many Ashkenazic Jews who immigrated to the English colonies, such as Moise Abrams, Isaac Adolphus, Chapman Ashers, Barnard Gratz, and Jacob Franks, all from Germany, Abraham Isaac Abrahams, of Lithuanian heritage, and Meyer Benjamin, from Hungary.

51. Benjamin W. De Vries, "A Corner of Jewish Economic History: Activities of Jews in the Dutch Textile Industry of the 19th Century," Michman and Levie, *Dutch Jewish History,* 294; Endelman, *Jews of Georgian England,* 31, 176, 186–91. For a description of a general decline in the position of European Jewry after 1713, see Israel, *European Jewry in the Age of Mercantilism,* 237–59.

52. Leo Hershkowitz and Isidore S. Meyer, eds., *The Lee Max Friedman Collection of American Jewish Colonial Correspondence: Letters of the Franks Family (1733–1748)* (Waltham, Mass.: American Jewish Historical Society, 1968), xvi, 124–25; Cecil Roth, *The Great Synagogue, London, 1690–1940* (London: Edward Goldstone and Son, 1950), 62–63; William Vincent Byars, *B. and M. Gratz, Merchants in Philadelphia, 1754–1798* (Jefferson City: Hugh Stephens Printing, 1916), 9–10, 37, 39, 41, 45, 51. The case of Uriah Hendricks is equally instructive. Hendricks showed so much commercial ability while working in his father's London countinghouse that his father advised him to immigrate to New York, where he established himself as a shopkeeper and trader. His father was his main supplier, but he also received merchandise from his brother, uncle, and mother-in-law, all of whom lived in London; Maxwell Whiteman, *Copper for America: The Hendricks Family and a National Industry, 1755–1939* (New Brunswick, N.J.: Rutgers University Press, 1971), 5, 7.

53. Bernard Bailyn, *The Peopling of British North America: An Introduction* (New York: Knopf, 1986), 20ff.

54. Ibid., 62–64.

55. For examples of artisanship, see Edwin Wolf and Maxwell Whiteman, *The History of the Jews of Philadelphia from Colonial Times to the Age of Jackson*

(Philadelphia: Jewish Publication Society of America, 1957), 50, 77; and Whiteman, *Copper for America,* 6. For the craftsmanship of Myer Myers, who may have been colonial America's most accomplished Jewish artisan, see Jeanette W. Rosenbaum, *Myer Myers, Goldsmith, 1723–1795* (Philadelphia: Jewish Publication Society of America, 1954).

Chapter Two. The Atlantic World of Colonial Jewry

1. For Jacob Henry's life and death, see his brother's letter to their parents in William Vincent Byars, *B. and M. Gratz, Merchants in Philadelphia, 1754–1798* (Jefferson City: Hugh Stephens Printing, 1916), 59–60. Conditions in Upper Silesia are described in Edwin Wolf and Maxwell Whiteman, *The History of the Jews of Philadelphia from Colonial Times to the Age of Jackson* (Philadelphia: Jewish Publication Society of America, 1957), 36; and Sidney M. Fish, "The Ancestral Heritage of the Gratz Family," in *Gratz College Anniversary Volume,* ed. Isidore D. Passow and Samuel T. Lachs (Philadelphia: Gratz College, 1971), 54–57.

2. Jerome H. Wood, Jr., *Conestoga Crossroads: Lancaster, Pennsylvania, 1730–1790* (Harrisburg: Pennsylvania Historical and Museum Commission, 1979), 97; Thomas J. Tobias, "Joseph Tobias of Charles Town: Linguister," *Publications of the American Jewish Historical Society* 49 (1959–60), 36; Charles Reznikoff and Uriah Z. Engelman, *The Jews of Charleston: A History of an American Jewish Community* (Philadelphia: Jewish Publication Society of America, 1950), 15.

3. Leo Hershkowitz, ed., *Wills of Early New York Jews (1704–1799)* (New York: American Jewish Historical Society, 1967), passim. Identifying themselves as merchants were Joseph Nunez, Isaac Rodriguez Marques, Joseph Bueno de Mesquita, Isaac Pinheiro, Samuel Levy, Abraham de Lucena, Moses Levy, Jacob Fonseca, Michael Michaels, Louis Moses Gomez, Samuel Myers–Cohen, Joshua Isaacs, Mordecai Gomez, Phillip Isaacs, Judah Hayes, David Gomez, Isaac Gomez, Benjamin Gomez, and Isaac Adolphus. The following provided no identification: Joseph Brown, Isaac Levy, and Sampson Simson. The chandler was Uriah Hyam. The wills of the following identified others as merchants: Joseph Nunez, Esther Brown, Joseph Bueno de Mesquita, Samuel Levy, Michael Michaels, Uriah Hyam, Phillip Isaacs, and Rachel Luis.

4. Morris U. Schappes, *A Documentary History of the Jews of the United States, 1654–1875,* 3d ed. (New York: Schocken, 1971), 1–2. For efforts by the clergy to support Stuyvesant, see Oliver A. Rink, *Holland on the Hudson: An Economic and Social History of Dutch New York* (Ithaca: Cornell University Press, 1986), 234.

5. In 1656, 4 percent of the investors in the Dutch West India Company were Jews, rising to 6.5 percent in 1658; Stephen A. Fortune, *Merchants and Jews: The Struggle for British West Indian Commerce, 1650–1750* (Gainesville: University Presses of Florida, 1984), 178.

6. Schappes, *Documentary History*, 2–4.

7. Ibid., 4–5.

8. Jonathan Israel, *European Jewry in the Age of Mercantilism* (Oxford: Clarendon, 1985), 63–64.

9. Schappes, *Documentary History*, 5–6; David De Sola Pool and Tamar De Sola Pool, *An Old Faith in the New World: Portrait of Shearith Israel, 1654–1954* (New York: Columbia University Press, 1955), 25.

10. Schappes, *Documentary History*, 7–8.

11. Ibid., 8–12.

12. Ibid., 12–13.

13. Isaac S. Emmanuel and Suzanne A. Emmanuel, *History of the Jews of the Netherlands Antilles* (Cincinnati: American Jewish Archives, 1970), 1:68. The four petitioners were Salvador Dandrada, Jacob Cohen Henricques, Abraham de Lucena, and Joseph D'Acosta; Schappes, *Documentary History*, 13. For the names of those who arrived in 1654, see Arnold Wiznitzer, "The Exodus from Brazil and Arrival in New Amsterdam of the Jewish Pilgrim Fathers, 1654," in *The Jewish Experience in Latin America: Selected Studies from the Publications of the American Jewish Historical Society*, ed. Martin A. Cohen (Waltham, Mass., and New York: American Jewish Historical Society and KTAV, 1971), 2:326.

14. Pool and Pool, *Old Faith in the New World*, 26, 31–32.

15. Hyman B. Grinstein, *The Rise of the Jewish Community of New York, 1654–1860* (Philadelphia: Jewish Publication Society of America, 1945), 469; Pool and Pool, *Old Faith in the New World*, 33–34; Doris Groshen Daniels, "Colonial Jewry: Religion, Domestic and Social Relations," *American Jewish Historical Quarterly* 66 (1976–77): 380.

16. Pool and Pool, *Old Faith in the New World*, 34–35, 40–42; "The Earliest Extant Minute Books of the Spanish and Portuguese Congregation Shearith Israel in New York, 1728–1786," *Publications of the American Jewish Historical Society* 21 (1913): 4, 9–13.

17. Pool and Pool, *Old Faith in the New World*, 44–45; "Earliest Extant Minute Books," 14.

18. The following is from Leo Hershkowitz, "Some Aspects of the New York Jewish Merchant and Community, 1654–1820," *American Jewish Historical Quarterly* 66 (1976–77): 11, 25–27.

19. "Gomez Ledger," *Publications of the American Jewish Historical Society* 27 (1920): 244–50; Leon Huhner, "Daniel Gomez, a Pioneer Merchant of Early New York," *Publications of the American Jewish Historical Society* 41 (1951–52): 107–25; Miriam K. Freund, *Jewish Merchants in Colonial America* (New York: Behrman's Jewish Book House, 1939), 34. Isaac Adolphus imported extensively from the West Indies, sending sugar, molasses, rum, coffee, and spices to the interior as part of the New York fur trade, while Hayman Levy was a major fur trader in the New York region. For both, see Byars, *B. and M. Gratz*, 67–68.

20. Cited in Virginia Harrington, *The New York Merchant on the Eve of the Revolution* (New York: Columbia University Press, 1935), 18.

21. Morris A. Gutstein, *The Story of the Jews of Newport: Two and a Half Centuries of Judaism, 1658–1908* (New York: Bloch, 1936), 340–42. Others, however, have traced the Newport settlers to Holland and Curaçao; Leon Huhner, *The Life of Judah Touro (1775–1854)* (Philadelphia: Jewish Publication Society of America, 1946), 10, 145 n. 5.

22. Carl Bridenbaugh, *Cities in the Wilderness: Urban Life in America, 1625–1742* (New York: Capricorn, 1964), 104–5.

23. Gutstein, *Jews of Newport,* 36–38, 40–43, 46, 81–82, 113–14; Emmanuel and Emmanuel, *Jews of Netherlands Antilles,* 1:90. Documents in the trade case of 1685 are in "Items Relating to the Jews of Newport," *Publications of the American Jewish Historical Society* 27 (1920): 175–76.

24. Gutstein, *Jews of Newport,* 86; Stanley F. Chyet, *Lopez of Newport: Colonial American Merchant Prince* (Detroit: Wayne State University Press, 1970), 22, 26–27, 42, 63–64, 66–71, 82–83, 85, 109, 119, 131; Virginia B. Platt, "Tar Staves and New England Rum: The Trade of Aaron Lopez of Newport, Rhode Island, with Colonial North Carolina," *North Carolina Historical Review* 48 (1971): 1–22.

25. Jacob Rader Marcus, ed., *American Jewry—Documents—Eighteenth Century* (Cincinnati: Hebrew Union College Press, 1959), 86–87; Gutstein, *Jews of Newport,* 82–98, 182; Ezra Stiles, *Literary Diary,* ed. F. B. Dexter (New York: Scribner's, 1901), 1:283.

26. Bridenbaugh, *Cities in the Wilderness,* 6, 143, 303, 334–35, 337.

27. Wolf and Whiteman, *Jews of Philadelphia,* 14–15, 23–27. For Jewish shipowners registered at Philadelphia, see Freund, *Jewish Merchants,* 74–76.

28. Wolf and Whiteman, *Jews of Philadelphia,* 30–31, 33, 36, 47, 53.

29. Ibid., 25, 32, 41–42, 53–55, 58, 117.

30. Ibid., 61, 78.

31. Wood, *Conestoga Crossroads,* 5, 71, 101–4, 113–17, 184; Byars, *B. and M. Gratz,* 47, 54–58; David Brener, *The Jews of Lancaster, Pennsylvania: A Story with Two Beginnings* (Lancaster: Congregation Shaarai Shomayim and the Lancaster County Historical Society, 1979), vii, ix, 1–7.

32. Barnett A. Elzas, *The Jews of South Carolina from the Earliest Times to the Present Day* (Philadelphia: Lippincott, 1905), 20, 277.

33. See Joseph R. Rosenbloom, *A Biographical Dictionary of Early American Jews, Colonial Times through 1801* (Lexington: University of Kentucky Press, 1960), for eight of the fifteen: Abraham Avila, Carvallo (no known first name), Aaron Gutteres, Solomon Isaacs, Samuel Levy, Moses De Mattos, Jacob Mendis, and Joseph Tobias. Simon Valentine is identified as a merchant by Elzas, *Jews of South Carolina,* 20. For the activities of Joseph Tobias, see Tobias, "Joseph Tobias of Charles Town," 33–38.

34. Elzas, *Jews of South Carolina,* 32, 50, 277–79; "Earliest Extant Minute

Books," 139; Soloman Breibart, "The Synagogues of Kahal Kadosh Beth Elohim, Charleston," *South Carolina Historical Magazine* 80 (1979): 215–20; "January 27, 1775. Fragment of MS. Minutes of Beth Elohim Congregation, Charleston, South Carolina," *Publications of the American Jewish Historical Society* 27 (1920): 226.

35. Saul J. Rubin, *Third to None: The Saga of Savannah Jewry, 1733–1983* (Savannah: S. J. Rubin, 1983), 17–18, 21; David T. Morgan, "Judaism in Eighteenth-Century Georgia," *Georgia Historical Quarterly* 58 (1974): 41, 47; Malcolm H. Stern, ed., "The Sheftall Diaries: Vital Records of Savannah Jewry (1733–1808)," *American Jewish Historical Quarterly* 54 (1964–65): 250–51.

36. Stern, "Sheftall Diaries," 248–51.

37. In 1743, David Franks in Philadelphia contemplated a voyage to India; Leo Hershkowitz and Isidore S. Meyer, eds., *The Lee Max Friedman Collection of American Jewish Colonial Correspondence: Letters of the Franks Family (1733–1748)* (Waltham, Mass.: American Jewish Historical Society, 1968), 113. Michael Gratz spent either one or two years in India before returning to London and subsequently immigrating to Philadelphia in 1759; Byars, *B. and M. Gratz,* 12. In 1753, an advocate in England of the Jewish naturalization bill pointed to the Jewish organization of the coral trade with India, with the exchange of diamonds in return, as evidence of the contributions of Jewish merchants to the economy; Edgar R. Samuel, "The Jews in English Foreign Trade—A Consideration of the 'Philo Patriae' Pamphlets of 1753," in *Remember the Days: Essays on Anglo-Jewish History Presented to Cecil Roth,* ed. John M. Shaftesley (London: Jewish Historical Society of England, 1966), 134.

38. The account here of Moses Lopez's trip is based on Thomas J. Tobias, "Charles Town in 1764," *South Carolina Historical Magazine* 67 (1966): 63–71, 73–74; Reznikoff and Engelman, *Jews of Charleston,* 13, 15; and Chyet, *Lopez of Newport,* 42–44, 80.

39. Samson Mears of New York journeyed to Saint Eustatius in 1763, Michael Gratz went to Saint Kitts and Curaçao in 1765, and Barnard Gratz went to London in 1769; see Byars, *B. and M. Gratz,* 65, 75, 77, 96. After emigrating from Germany, Jonas Phillips traveled from London to Charleston in 1756, to Albany by 1759, to Canada, New York City, and Philadelphia in 1762, again to New York in 1763, and finally again to Philadelphia in 1773, where he settled permanently; Wolf and Whiteman, *Jews of Philadelphia,* 62–63. Moses Michael Hays voyaged between New York, Jamaica, Newport, and Boston. Cullum Pollock traveled between the West Indies, North Carolina, and Newport; Freund, *Jewish Merchants,* 47, 61. For further elaboration on the phenomenon of wide travel by early America's Jews, see Jacob R. Marcus, *The Colonial American Jew, 1492–1776* (Detroit: Wayne State University Press, 1970), 2:575–82.

40. Hershkowitz, *Wills of Early New York Jews,* 8, 33, 44, 65.

41. Hershkowitz and Meyer, *Letters of the Franks Family,* 6, 37–38, 49, 55, 62, 72, 80, 83, 87, 106, 113, 126.

42. Ibid., xvi, 1, 7, 34, 77, 79, 83, 106, 112, 114, 123. Moses Franks maintained

commercial contact with his brother in Philadelphia throughout the American Revolution, more than three decades after his removal to London; Wolf and Whiteman, *Jews of Philadelphia*, 86.

43. Hershkowitz and Meyer, *Letters of the Franks Family*, 93.

44. "Earliest Extant Minute Books," 2–3, 32–33, 43, 57–58, 99, 109, 117, 121, 129, 131, 134; Marcus, *American Jewry*, 96–98.

45. Malcolm Stern, *Americans of Jewish Descent: A Compendium of Genealogy* (Cincinnati: Hebrew Union College Press, 1960), 133.

46. Ibid., 46, 63; "Gomez Ledger," 246; Wolf and Whiteman, *Jews of Philadelphia*, 21.

47. Stern, *Americans of Jewish Descent*, 63; Chyet, *Lopez of Newport*, 200; Cecil Roth, *Essays and Portraits in Anglo-Jewish History* (Philadelphia: Jewish Publication Society of America, 1962), 169–70.

48. Another example of a wide network is that of Isaac Mendes Seixas of New York, whose sons Moses and Abraham married women from Newport and Charleston, respectively, while a sister married in London and a niece wed a man in Kingston, Jamaica; "Items Relating to the Seixas Family," *Publications of the American Jewish Historical Society* 27 (1920): 161–62, 169. See also the four Savannah marriages described previously.

49. Wolf and Whiteman, *Jews of Philadelphia*, 40–41, 388; Hershkowitz, *Wills of Early New York Jews*, 65; Stern, *Americans of Jewish Descent*, 160, 194; Brener, *Jews of Lancaster*, 16; Byars, *B. and M. Gratz*, 13, 17, 83ff.

50. Chyet, *Lopez of Newport*, 97–103.

51. Reznikoff and Engelman, *Jews of Charleston*, 53–54.

52. "Earliest Extant Minute Books," 19–24, 37, 81; "Items Relating to Congregation Shearith Israel, New York," *Publications of the American Jewish Historical Society* 27 (1920): 2–3, 5, 20–21; Chyet, *Lopez of Newport*, 54–55, 60; Gutstein, *Jews of Newport*, 88, 95–97, 105–6; Wolf and Whiteman, *Jews of Philadelphia*, 41.

53. "Earliest Extant Minute Books," 73, 75, 92, 135.

54. Chyet, *Lopez of Newport*, 108, 134–35; Gutstein, *Jews of Newport*, 142–43; "Earliest Extant Minute Books," 67–68, 76–78; Wolf and Whiteman, *Jews of Philadelphia*, 48.

Chapter Three. Community

1. "The Earliest Extant Minute Books of the Spanish and Portuguese Congregation Shearith Israel in New York, 1728–1786," *Publications of the American Jewish Historical Society* 21 (1913): 74–75.

2. Ibid., 75–76.

3. Ibid., 104.

4. For example, Darrett Rutman, *Winthrop's Boston* (Chapel Hill: University

of North Carolina Press, 1965); and Kenneth A. Lockridge, *A New England Town: The First Hundred Years, Dedham, Massachusetts, 1636–1736* (New York: Norton, 1970).

5. Jonathan I. Israel, *European Jewry in the Age of Mercantilism, 1550–1750* (Oxford: Clarendon, 1985), 184–206.

6. For discussion of the only known records of the congregation prior to 1728, see Jacob R. Marcus, "The Oldest Known Synagogue Record Book of Continental North America, 1720–1721," in his *Studies in American Jewish History: Studies and Addresses* (Cincinnati: Hebrew Union College Press, 1969), 44–53.

7. "Earliest Extant Minute Books," 6–7; David De Sola Pool, *The Mill Street Synagogue (1730–1817) of the Congregation Shearith Israel* (New York: N.p., 1930), 18–21. For a description and illustration of the structure, see Rachel Wischnitzer, *Synagogue Architecture in the United States: History and Interpretation* (Philadelphia: Jewish Publication Society of America, 1955), 4, 11–12.

8. "Earliest Extant Minute Books," 1–5.

9. Arnold Wiznitzer, "The Minute Book of Congregations Zur Israel of Recife and Magen Abraham of Mauricia, Brazil," in *The Jewish Experience in Latin America: Selected Studies from the Publications of the American Jewish Historical Society,* ed. Martin A. Cohen (Waltham, Mass., and New York: American Jewish Historical Society and KTAV, 1971), 2:274; "Earliest Extant Minute Books," 97–98, 103–4.

10. Wiznitzer, "Minute Book of Congregations Zur Israel," 273; Jacob Neusner, "The Role of English Jews in the Development of American Jewish Life, 1775–1850," *YIVO Annual of Jewish Social Science* 12 (1958–59): 148; Israel, *European Jewry in the Age of Mercantilism,* 198. Curaçao's late-seventeenth-century regulations are in Isaac S. Emmanuel and Suzanne A. Emmanuel, *History of the Jews of the Netherlands Antilles* (Cincinnati: American Jewish Archives, 1970), 2:542–46.

11. Emmanuel and Emmanuel, *Jews of the Netherlands Antilles,* 2:549; Wiznitzer, "Minute Book of Congregations Zur Israel," 273.

12. H. P. Salomon, "Joseph Jesurun Pinto (1729–1782): A Dutch Hazzan in Colonial New York," *Studia Rosenthaliana* 13 (1979): 18–19, 23; Jacob Rader Marcus, ed. *American Jewry—Documents—Eighteenth Century* (Cincinnati: Hebrew Union College Press, 1959), 94, 177; Marcus, "Oldest Known Synagogue Record Book," 52.

13. Cecil Roth, *The Great Synagogue, London, 1690–1940* (London: Edward Goldstone and Son, 1950), 1.

14. Solomon B. Freehof, "Home Rituals and the Spanish Synagogue," in *Studies and Essays in Honor of Abraham A. Neuman,* ed. Meir Ben-Horin, Bernard Weinryb, and Solomon Zeitlin (Leiden: E. J. Brill, 1962), 215–27.

15. H. J. Zimmels, *Ashkenazim and Sephardim: Their Relations, Differences, and Problems as Reflected in Their Rabbinical Responsa* (London: Oxford University Press, 1958), 85–87, 99–102, 108, 110, 113–14, 165–66, 182.

16. Roth, *Great Synagogue,* 73; Zimmels, *Ashkenazim and Sephardim,* 188, 194, 241, 279–83.

17. R. D. Barnett, "Dr. Samuel Nunes Ribeiro and the Settlement of Georgia," in *Migration and Settlement: Proceedings of the Anglo-American Jewish Historical Conference Held in London Jointly by the Jewish Historical Society of England and the American Jewish Historical Society, July 1970* (London: Jewish Historical Society of England, 1971), 95.

18. Roth, *Great Synagogue,* 17, 59–60; D. M. Swetchinski, "Kinship and Commerce: The Foundations of Portuguese Jewish Life in Seventeenth-Century Holland," *Studia Rosenthaliana* 15 (1981): 67–70; Sigfried Stein, "Some Ashkenazi Charities in London at the End of the Eighteenth and the Beginning of the Nineteenth Centuries," *Transactions of the Jewish Historical Society of England* 20 (1959–61): 63–81.

19. Roth, *Great Synagogue,* 2–3, 7–8, 12–13, 16–17; Isidore Epstein, "The Story of Ascama I of the Spanish and Portuguese Jewish Congregation of London with Special Reference to Responsa Material," in Ben-Horin, Weinryb, and Zeitlin, *Studies and Essays in Honor of Abraham A. Neuman,* 175–76.

20. Israel, *European Jewry in the Age of Mercantilism,* 220; Salomon, "Joseph Jesurun Pinto," 24.

21. Albert M. Hyamson, *The Sephardim of England: A History of the Spanish and Portuguese Community, 1492–1951* (London: Methuen, 1952), 170–71.

22. John Hartog, "The Honen Dalim Cogregation of St. Eustatius," *American Jewish Archives* 19 (1967): 63; *The Jewish Nation in Surinam: Historical Essays,* ed. R. Cohen (Amsterdam: S. Emmering, 1982), 20; Lee M. Friedman, *Rabbi Haim Isaac Carigal: His Newport Sermon and His Yale Portrait* (Boston: Merrymount, 1940), 18.

23. Barnett, "Dr. Samuel Nunes Ribeiro," 87, 94.

24. Pool, *Mill Street Synagogue,* 49.

25. "Earliest Extant Minute Books," 3, 32; Marcus, "Oldest Known Synagogue Record Book," 47; Hyman B. Grinstein, *The Rise of the Jewish Community of New York, 1654–1860* (Philadelphia: Jewish Publication Society of America, 1945), 206.

26. The sixteen were Abraham Abrahams, Isaac Adolphus, Jacob Franks, Uriah Hendricks, Abraham Isaacs, Ralph (Raphael) Jacobs, Manuel Josephson, Hayman Levy, Nathan Levy, Michael Michaels, Asher Myers, Naphtaly Hart Myers, Isaac Polock, Issachar Polock, Joseph Simson, and Sampson Simson; for identification see, generally, Malcolm Stern, *Americans of Jewish Descent: A Compendium of Genealogy* (Cincinnati: Hebrew Union College Press, 1960); and Joseph R. Rosenbloom, *A Biographical Dictionary of Early American Jews, Colonial Times through 1801* (Lexington: University of Kentucky Press, 1960), as well as the following for the individuals indicated: for Hayman Levy, see Marcus, *American Jewry,* 14; for Manuel Josephson, who came from Germany, see Jacob R. Marcus, "Jews and the American

Revolution: A Bicentennial Documentary," *American Jewish Archives* 27 (1975): 220; for Uriah Hendricks, see Roth, *Great Synagogue,* 64, where Uriah's father, Aaron, is identified as a member of the Ashkenazic community of London; for Michael Michaels, see Leo Hershkowitz, ed., *Wills of Early New York Jews (1704–1799)* (New York: American Jewish Historical Society, 1967), 47, where he identified himself as the son of Moses Michaels. The latter is identified as an Ashkenazi in Marcus, "Oldest Known Synagogue Record Book," 50.

27. The fifteen were Benjamin Gomez, Daniel Gomez, David Gomez, Isaac Gomez, Jr., Isaac Gomez, Sr., Louis Moses Gomez, Mordecai Gomez, Moses Gomez, David Lopez, Isaac Pera Mendes, Benjamin Mendez Pacheco, Gabriel Pinedo, Isaac Mendes Seixas, Abraham Rodriguez Rivera, and Jacob Rodriguez Rivera. For identification as Sephardim, see the appropriate entries in Rosenbloom, *Biographical Dictionary;* and Stern, *Americans of Jewish Descent,* with the exception of Pinedo, identified as such because of his name.

28. These nine were Samuel Levy, Isaac Levy, Samuel Hart, David Hart, Myer Myers, Hyam Myers, Isaac Isaacs, Samuel Judah, and Hilyard Judah. Levy, Hart, Isaacs, and Myers recurred repeatedly as patronymics among the Ashkenazim; see Roth, *Great Synagogue,* 64–65, 299; and Marcus, "Oldest Known Synagogue Record Book," 50, where, in addition to Isaacs, Levy, and Myers, the patronymic Judah appears among the Ashkenazim of New York in 1720.

29. "Earliest Extant Minute Books," 11, 13, 53, 10–11, 50–51. A gauge of their wealth is the fact that Jacob Franks and Mordecai Gomez each paid fourteen pounds in the general congregational levy of 1747, while the next closest amount was ten pounds; see ibid., 53.

30. Leo Hershkowitz and Isidore S. Meyer, eds., *The Lee Max Friedman Collection of American Jewish Colonial Correspondence: Letters of the Franks Family (1733–1748)* (Waltham, Mass.: American Jewish Historical Society, 1968), 66–67, 76.

31. Ibid., 110; Stern, *Americans of Jewish Descent,* 63, 79. For Waage's Ashkenazic origins and his naive attempts to end the American Revolution, see Cecil Roth, *Essays and Portraits in Anglo-Jewish History* (Philadelphia: Jewish Publication Society of America, 1962), 168–82. For Uriah Hendricks, see also Roth, *Great Synagogue,* 64, where Uriah's father, Aaron, appears as a member of the Ashkenazic community of London.

32. Judah Hays married Rebecca Michaels, whose father came from Germany. Judah and Rebecca's son Michael married Rachel Myers, identifiable as Ashkenazic because of her family name. Their three daughters who wed Sephardim were Phila (married Daniel Nunez), Reyna (married Isaac Touro), and Josy (married Joseph Pinto). Daughter Rachel married Levy Michaels, an Ashkenazi, while Caty married first Abraham Sarzedas (Sephardic) and then Jacob Jacobs (Ashkenazic). For all, see Stern, *Americans of Jewish Descent,* 75.

33. Malcolm H. Stern, "The Function of Genealogy in American Jewish History," in *Essays in American Jewish History to Commemorate the Tenth Anniver-*

sary of the Founding of the American Jewish Archives under the Direction of Jacob Rader Marcus (Cincinnati: American Jewish Archives, 1958), 74–81.

34. Hershkowitz, *Wills of Early New York Jews,* 55–56, 65–71, 139–41, 146–48, 165–70. For Isaac Adolphus's origins see Roth, *Great Synagogue,* 64. For Sampson Simson, see Stern, *Americans of Jewish Descent,* 195. Samuel Myers-Cohen and Joshua Isaacs are identified here as Ashkenazim on the basis of their names. The discussion here of Sephardic and Ashkenazic cooperation focuses on the New York community; on the general pattern in North America, see Jacob R. Marcus, *The Colonial American Jew, 1492–1776* (Detroit: Wayne State University Press, 1970), 2:1003–6.

35. Roth, *Great Synagogue,* 68–69; Israel, *European Jewry in the Age of Mercantilism,* 198–202; Wiznitzer, "Minute Book of Congregations Zur Israel," 260–61, 273; Emmanuel and Emmanuel, *Jews of the Netherlands Antilles,* 2:544–45; Grinstein, *Jewish Community of New York,* 6. For the extremities of the herem in the Sephardic tradition, see Isaac S. Emmanuel, *Precious Stones of the Jews of Curaçao: Curaçaon Jewry, 1656–1957* (New York: Bloch, 1957), 95–96.

36. This section is based on "Earliest Extant Minute Books," 36, 52–53, 66–67, 71, 73, 84, 87, 89, 91, 94, 103–4, 113, 123–24.

37. This section is based on ibid., 4, 15, 29–30, 45–46, 60–61, 64, 68, 76, 90, 93–94, 106–7, 112–13, 123–28, 133–35.

38. Ibid., 14, 35–36, 72, 84–85; Bernard Bailyn, *Education in the Forming of American Society* (New York: Norton, 1972), 39–40.

39. "Earliest Extant Minute Books," 36, 54, 72, 81, 85; "Items Relating to Congregation Shearith Israel, New York," *Publications of the American Jewish Historical Society* 27 (1920): 17–18. In 1733, Phila Franks studied privately at the home of George Brownell, who taught, among other subjects, reading, writing, arithmetic, accounting, Latin, Greek, dancing, and embroidery. Moses Franks during the same year studied mathematics with Alexander Malcolm, though it is not clear whether he did so privately at Malcolm's home or at the school chartered by the New York Assembly late in 1732; Hershkowitz and Meyer, *Letters of the Franks Family,* 3–4, 12–13.

40. "Earliest Extant Minute Books," 2–3, 26–28, 32–33, 57–58, 69–73, 87–88, 91. For examples of actual accounts listing "Obras Pias," see 31–33, 38–41, 43.

41. For colonial attitudes toward strangers and poor relief for them, see David Rothman, *The Discovery of the Asylum: Social Order and Disorder in the New Republic* (Boston: Little, Brown, 1971), 5, 19; Carl Bridenbaugh, *Cities in Revolt: Urban Life in America, 1743–1776* (New York: Knopf, 1955), 122–24, 319–20, 323–24.

42. Marcus, *American Jewry,* 94–96.

43. The Sephardim were Jacob Rodriguez Rivera and Aaron Lopez, and the Ashkenazim were Moses Levy, Isaac Hart, Naphtali Hart, Isaac Elizer, Isaac Bar Moshe (Pollack), and Naphtali Hart Myers; Morris A. Gutstein, *The Story of the*

Jews of Newport: Two and a Half Centuries of Judaism, 1658–1908 (New York: Bloch, 1936), 83, 89, 92–95. For the comment by the Reverend Andrew Burnaby, see Carl Bridenbaugh, *Peter Harrison: First American Architect* (Chapel Hill: University of North Carolina Press, 1949), 110.

44. "Earliest Extant Minute Books," 14.

45. Hershkowitz and Meyer, *Letters of the Franks Family*, 28, 100.

46. "Earliest Extant Minute Books," 71, 81.

47. Ibid., 81–84, 87.

48. Ibid., 97–98, 103–5.

49. Ibid., 113; J. Solis-Cohen, Jr., "Barrak Hays: Controversial Loyalist," *Publications of the American Jewish Historical Society* 45 (1955–56), 56–57. The contentiousness of the members of the Hays family is evident also in Judah Hays's will, written in 1763, "having frequently taken very just offense at the Disobedience and General Conduct of [his] son MICHAEL." He then denounced his "daughter RACHEL to whom [he gave] only five shillings, as she married contrary to [his] will and desire." In Hershkowitz, *Wills of Early New York Jews*, 119. The widow Hetty Hays, described above as running afoul of the community for keeping an unkosher home, belonged to the same family.

50. "Earliest Extant Minute Books," 2, 49.

51. Ibid., 50–51. The rest of this section is based on ibid., 51–53, 57, 59, 65–66, 110–12, 115–18.

52. Roth, *Great Synagogue,* 67.

53. Wiznitzer, "Minute Book of Congregations Zur Israel," 274.

54. Emmanuel and Emmanuel, *Jews of Netherlands Antilles,* 2:544.

55. "Earliest Extant Minute Books," 36–37.

56. Ibid., 52, 66–67, 74–75.

57. For examples of individuals living in these localities, see Marcus, *American Jewry,* 89; *Publications of the American Jewish Historical Society* 21 (1913): 6; and Hershkowitz and Meyer, *Letters of the Franks Family,* 72. For others residing in Norwalk, Connecticut, Philipse's Manor and Bedford, New York, South Haven and Jamaica, Long Island, Spottswood, New Jersey, and Tiverton, Rhode Island, see "Registry of Circumcisions by Abm. I. Abrahams from June 1756 to January 1781 in New York, in Hebrew and English," *Publications of the American Jewish Historical Society* 27 (1920): 150–56.

58. Israel, *European Jewry in the Age of Mercantilism,* 248–51.

Chapter Four. Fitting In

1. Abram Vossen Goodman, "A German Mercenary Observes American Jews during the Revolution," *American Jewish Historical Quarterly* 59 (1969–70): 227.

2. Shearith Israel's Yom Kippur proclamation in 1757, discussed in chapter 3,

indicates that the consumption of unkosher meat did occur, but as described there, the organized community took steps to assure a ready supply of kosher meat and to enforce adherence to the dietary laws. More important, the mercenary observed New York and Newport Jewry under wartime conditions, when most Jews had fled the cities and communal institutions, including ritual slaughter, were largely if not entirely defunct. In 1779, Aaron Lopez informed one of his correspondents that the Jews still present in Newport had not had meat for two months because of the insufficient supply of kosher food; Stanley F. Chyet, *Lopez of Newport: Colonial American Merchant Prince* (Detroit: Wayne State University Press, 1970), 160.

3. Jacob Katz, *Out of the Ghetto: The Social Background of Jewish Emancipation, 1770–1870* (Cambridge: Harvard University Press, 1973), 1–27, 90, and passim.

4. Ibid., 34, 37; Todd Endelman, *The Jews of Georgian England 1714–1830: Tradition and Change in a Liberal Society* (Philadelphia: Jewish Publication Society of America, 1979), 120–22.

5. Leo Hershkowitz and Isidore S. Meyer, eds., *Letters of the Franks Family (1733–1748)* (Waltham, Mass.: American Jewish Historical Society, 1968), xxi, 4–5, 11–12, 24–26, 31, 34, 37, 40–41, 48, 52, 84–85, 103–6.

6. Of the nearly 100 names that appear in the Gomez account book, approximately 53 percent were Jewish merchants, roughly 37 percent were not, and the remainder, about 10 percent, cannot be determined; "Gomez Ledger," *Publications of the American Jewish Historical Society* 27 (1920): 244–50.

7. Ibid., 245; Chyet, *Lopez of Newport,* 46, 135, 144; Thomas J. Tobias, "Charles Town in 1764," *South Carolina Historical Magazine* 67 (1966): 69; Leon Huhner, "Daniel Gomez, a Pioneer Merchant of Early New York," *Publications of the American Jewish Historical Society* 41 (1951–52): 112–13; Miriam K. Freund, *Jewish Merchants in Colonial America* (New York: Behrman's Jewish Book House, 1939), 70; David Brener, *The Jews of Lancaster, Pennsylvania: A Story with Two Beginnings* (Lancaster: Congregation Shaarai Shomayim and the Lancaster County Historical Society, 1979), 10, 13; Jerome H. Wood, Jr., *Conestoga Crossroads: Lancaster, Pennsylvania 1730–1790* (Harrisburg: Pennsylvania Historical and Museum Commission, 1979), 99, 101–2, 133, and for other Simon partnerships with non-Jews, 119; Edwin Wolf and Maxwell Whiteman, *The History of the Jews of Philadelphia from Colonial Times to the Age of Jackson* (Philadelphia: Jewish Publication Society of America, 1957), 66–75; William V. Byars, *B. and M. Gratz, Merchants in Philadelphia, 1754–1798* (Jefferson City: Hugh Stephens Printing, 1916) 14, 83ff, 131–32, 134, 155–56.

8. Hannah R. London, *Portraits of Jews by Gilbert Stuart and Other Early American Artists* (New York: William Edwin Rudge, 1927), passim; Hannah R. London, *Miniatures of Early American Jews* (Springfield: Pond-Ekberg, 1953), passim. For comparison with portraits of non-Jewish contemporaries in the colonies, see James Thomas Flexner, *First Flowers of Our Wilderness: American Painting in the Colonial Period* (New York: Dover, 1969), passim, and 70 and 88, where the

portraits of Moses Levy and the young David and Phila Franks are reproduced. For a particularly fine reproduction in full color of the portrait of Abigail Franks, see the plate facing the title page in Hershkowitz and Meyer, *Letters of the Franks Family.*

9. For Carigal's appearance, see London, *Portraits of Jews,* 95. An especially clear reproduction of his portrait is in Jacob R. Marcus, "Jews and the American Revolution: A Bicentennial Documentary," *American Jewish Archives* 27 (1975): facing 144. For the career and travels of the remarkable Rabbi Carigal, see Lee M. Friedman, *Rabbi Haim Isaac Carigal: His Newport Sermon and His Yale Portrait* (Boston: Merrymount, 1940), passim, where the portrait is reproduced opposite the title page; and Arthur A. Chiel, "The Rabbis and Ezra Stiles," *American Jewish Historical Quarterly* 61 (1971–72): 299–304. For the description of Seixas, see David De Sola Pool, "Descriptions of the Synagogues in New York in 1776 and 1828," *Publications of the American Jewish Historical Society* 40 (1950–51): 187–88. Seixas, it should be noted, did not hold a bachelor of arts degree.

10. Byars, *B. and M. Gratz,* 52. For the synagogues of Prague and Poland, with illustrations of ones that Jacob Henry might have viewed, see Rachel Wischnitzer, *The Architecture of the European Synagogue* (Philadelphia: Jewish Publication Society of America, 1964), 52–56, 78–81, 107–47. For the interior of London's Hambro Synagogue, see Cecil Roth, *The Great Synagogue, London, 1690–1940* (London: Edward Goldstone and Sons, 1950), plate 20, facing 120.

11. Byars, *B. and M. Gratz,* 49, 60; Carl Bridenbaugh, *Peter Harrison, First American Architect* (Chapel Hill: University of North Carolina Press, 1949), 1–2, 38–53, 98–104, and, following 182, figures 27–29. For Curacao's synagogue, see the illustration in Rachel Wischnitzer, *Synagogue Architecture in the United States: History and Interpretation* (Philadelphia: Jewish Publication Society of America, 1955), 3–4.

12. Hershkowitz and Meyer, *Letters of the Franks Family,* 7–8, 69.

13. Ibid., 116–119, 124–25, 129.

14. "Items Relating to the Jews of Newport," *Publications of the American Jewish Historical Society* 27 (1920): 185–90; Jacob Rader Marcus, ed., *American Jewry—Documents—Eighteenth Century* (Cincinnati: Hebrew Union College Press, 1959), 134–36. For Josephson's portrait, see Wolf and Whiteman, *Jews of Philadelphia,* plate 12, following 240.

15. Bridenbaugh, *Peter Harrison,* 101, 110, and following 182, figure 27.

16. Nancy Halverson Schless, "Peter Harrison, the Touro Synagogue, and the Wren City Church," *Winterthur Portfolio* 8 (Charlottesville: University of Virginia Press, 1973), 187–92, 195–200.

17. Byars, *B. and M. Gratz,* 154; Wolf and Whiteman, *Jews of Philadelphia,* 64, 74.

18. Brener, *Jews of Lancaster,* 6–7, 10–11; Joshua N. Neumann, "Some Eighteenth Century American Jewish Letters," *Publications of the American Jewish Historical Society* 34 (1937): 85–86.

19. Tobias, "Charles Town in 1764," 64–65; Chyet, *Lopez of Newport,* 188–89.

20. Doris Groshen Daniels, "Colonial Jewry: Religion, Domestic and Social Relations," *American Jewish Historical Quarterly* 66 (1976–77): 396; Tobias, "Charles Town in 1764," 72; Malcolm H. Stern, "The Sheftall Diaries: Vital Records of Savannah Jewry (1733–1808)," *American Jewish Historical Quarterly* 54 (1964–65): 251.

21. Morris A. Gutstein, *The Story of the Jews of Newport: Two and a Half Centuries of Judaism, 1658–1908* (New York: Bloch, 1936), 132.

22. Cited in Hyman B. Grinstein, *The Rise of the Jewish Community of New York, 1654–1860* (Philadelphia: Jewish Publication Society of America, 1945), 333.

23. *Evening Service of Roshashanah, and Kippur. Or the Beginning of the Year, and the Day of Atonement* (New York: W. Weyman, 1761); Isaac Pinto, trans., *Prayers for Shabbath, Rosh-Hashana, and Kippur, or the Sabbath, the Beginning of the Year, and the Day of Atonements; With the Amidah and Musaph of the Moadim or Solemn Seasons. According to the Order of the Spanish and Portuguese Jews* (New York: John Holt, 5526 [1765–66]), iii. For attribution of the first volume to Isaac Pinto, see Abraham J. Karp, *Beginnings: Early American Judaica* (Philadelphia: Jewish Publication Society of America, 1975), 1–10.

24. Jacob Rader Marcus, "The Handsome Young Priest in the Black Gown: The Personal World of Gershom Seixas," *Hebrew Union College Annual* 40–41 (1969–70): 441–44.

25. Cited in Wolf and Whiteman, *Jews of Philadelphia,* 64.

26. Malcolm H. Stern, "The Function of Genealogy in American Jewish History," in *Essays in American Jewish History to Commemorate the Tenth Anniversary of the Founding of the American Jewish Archives under the Direction of Jacob Rader Marcus* (Cincinnati: American Jewish Archives, 1958), 83–86, 94, 97. For Shinah Simon's conversion to Christianity, see Wolf and Whiteman, *Jews of Philadelphia,* 239–40.

27. Richard Barnett, "The Travels of Moses Cassuto," in *Remember the Days: Essays on Anglo-Jewish History Presented to Cecil Roth,* ed. John M. Shaftesley (London: Jewish Historical Society of England, 1966), 103–5.

28. For conversionist ideas in England, see Endelman, *Jews of Georgian England,* 50–65.

29. Wolf and Whiteman, *Jews of Philadelphia,* 43.

30. Ibid., 30; Marcus, "Jews and the American Revolution," 205.

31. Wolf and Whiteman, *Jews of Philadelphia,* 34; Byars, *B. and M. Gratz,* 81; Chyet, *Lopez of Newport,* 190, 195; Marcus, "Jews and the American Revolution," 205.

32. Endelman, *Jews of Georgian England,* 28–30, 96–101, 105–6.

33. Brener, *Jews of Lancaster,* 10–11; Byars, *B. and M. Gratz,* 127.

34. Marcus, "Jews and the American Revolution," 149–50.

35. Endelman, *Jews of Georgian England,* 21–25; Stephen Alexander Fortune,

Merchants and Jews: The Struggle for British West Indian Commerce, 1650–1750 (Gainesville: University of Florida Presses, 1984), 1, 9–13, 45–46, 62–63, 66–68; Malcolm H. Stern, "A Successful Caribbean Restoration: The Nevis Story," *American Jewish Historical Quarterly* 61 (1971–72): 23; and, for Jamaica, R. D. Barnett, "The Correspondence of the Mahamad of the Spanish and Portuguese Congregation of London during the Seventeenth and Eighteenth Centuries," *Transactions of the Jewish Historical Society of England* 20 (1959–61): 10–11.

36. Abram Vossen Goodman, *American Overture: Jewish Rights in Colonial Times* (Philadelphia: Jewish Publication Society of America, 1947), 51; Charles Reznikoff and Uriah Z. Engelman, *The Jews of Charleston: A History of an American Jewish Community* (Philadelphia: Jewish Publication Society of America, 1950), 23–33.

37. Chyet, *Lopez of Newport,* 34–40.

38. Morris U. Schappes, *A Documentary History of the Jews of the United States, 1654–1875,* 3d ed. (New York: Schocken, 1971), 35–37.

39. For the importance of club life, see Carl Bridenbaugh, *Cities in the Wilderness: The First Century of Urban Life in America, 1625–1742* (New York: Capricorn, 1964), 436–37, 440–41; Carl Bridenbaugh, *Cities in Revolt: Urban Life in America, 1743–1776* (New York: Knopf, 1968), 162–63, 363. For Jewish participation in Masonry, see Samuel Oppenheim, "The Jews and Masonry in the United States before 1810," *Publications of the American Jewish Historical Society* 19 (1910): 2–7, 18, 20–23, 28, 76; Goodman, *American Overture,* 148–49, 164; Wolf and Whiteman, *Jews of Philadelphia,* 50; Reznikoff and Engelman, *Jews of Charleston,* 93–94; and Herbert T. Ezekiel and Gaston Lichtenstein, *The History of the Jews of Richmond from 1769 to 1917* (Richmond: Herbert T. Ezekiel, 1917), 35–36.

40. Jacob R. Marcus, *The Colonial American Jew, 1492–1776* (Detroit: Wayne State University Press, 1970), 3:1130.

41. Lopez's biographer dismisses the possibility of anti-Semitism in the matter, suggesting instead that the denial of naturalization had its origins in contemporary political conflict that divided the colony sectionally and economically; Chyet, *Lopez of Newport,* 38–39.

42. Marcus, *Colonial American Jew,* 3:1127; Saul J. Rubin, *Third to None: The Saga of Savannah Jewry, 1783–1983* (Savannah: S. J. Rubin, 1983), 23–24; Goodman, *American Overture,* 112.

43. Rubin, *Third to None,* 23–24; Wood, *Conestoga Crossroads,* 205, 212, 215; Wolf and Whiteman, *Jews of Philadelphia,* 44–45; Bridenbaugh, *Cities in the Wilderness,* 250, 391, 410; Bridenbaugh, *Cities in Revolt,* 135, 333–34; John T. Ellis, *Catholics in Colonial America* (Baltimore: Helicon, 1965), 365, 369–70, 376–80, 387.

44. Marcus, *Colonial American Jew,* 3:1117–34.

45. Goodman, *American Overture,* 43–45, Charles M. Andrews, *The Colonial Period of American History,* (New Haven: Yale University Press, 1934–38), 2:61.

46. Goodman, *American Overture,* 122–24, 155–56, 159, 162.

47. In the gathering storm of the American Revolution, Francis Salvador was elected to the first and second South Carolina provincial congresses, while in Georgia, Mordecai Sheftall served as chairman of the Committee of Christ Church Parish, which functioned to implement policies approved by the American patriots. Daniel and Moses Nunez served as port officials in Georgia in the 1760s. Goodman, *American Overture*, 165–66, 199; Marcus, "Jews and the American Revolution," 116–18.

48. Leo Hershkowitz, "Some Aspects of the New York Jewish Merchant and Community, 1654–1820," *American Jewish Historical Quarterly* 66 (1976–77): 13, 16–18; Beverly McAnear, "The Place of the Freeman in Old New York," *New York History* 21 (1940): 419, 425. At least one Jew is known to have been admitted to freemanship in Albany; see "Facsimile of Jonas Phillips' Certificate of Freemanship and Citizenship in the Colony of New York Signed by Sybrant G. Van Schaick, Mayor," *Publications of the American Jewish Historical Society* 27 (1920): 156–57.

49. Goodman, *American Overture*, 111–12.

50. Ibid., 114; Hershkowitz, "Aspects of the New York Jewish Merchant," 13.

51. For the duties and dangers of the office, see Bridenbaugh, *Cities in the Wilderness*, 63–64, 215–16, 374–75. For Jews who served as constables or declined to do so after election, see Leo Hershkowitz, ed., *Wills of Early New York Jews (1704–1799)* (New York: American Jewish Historical Society, 1967), 36, 56, 65, 75, 99, 118, 140; and Hershkowitz, "Aspects of the New York Jewish Merchant," 13.

52. The only exception of note was Rodrigo Pacheco, who was appointed to serve as New York's colonial agent to Parliament in 1731 and one of five merchants designated by the Assembly to protest the Molasses Act of 1733 to the Crown; Hershkowitz, "Aspects of the New York Jewish Merchant," 13; Lee M. Friedman, "A Great Colonial Case and a Great Colonial Lawyer," *Publications of the American Jewish Historical Society* 42 (1952–53): 74–75.

53. Freund, *Jewish Merchants*, 40; Byars, *B. and M. Gratz*, 14.

54. Marcus, "Jews and the American Revolution," 116–19.

55. Samuel Rezneck, *Unrecognized Patriots: The Jews in the American Revolution* (Westport, Conn.: Greenwood, 1975), 23–24; Marcus, "Jews and the American Revolution," 124–25, 128–29.

56. Rezneck, *Unrecognized Patriots*, 21–66.

57. "Items Relating to Congregation Shearith Israel, New York," *Publications of the American Jewish Historical Society* 27 (1920): 31.

58. Chyet, *Lopez of Newport*, 156–62; Byars, *B. and M. Gratz*, 20, 158; Wolf and Whiteman, *Jews of Philadelphia*, 84; David De Sola Pool, *The Mill Street Synagogue (1730–1817) of the Congregation Shearith Israel* (New York: n.p., 1930), 56; Gutstein, *Jews of Newport*, 182; Reznikoff and Engelman, *Jews of Charleston*, 50.

59. Wolf and Whiteman, *Jews of Philadelphia*, 92, 96, 114–21; Marcus, *American Jewry*, 116–19.

60. Marcus, "Jews and the American Revolution," 208–9; Wolf and Whiteman,

Jews of Philadelphia, 101–9; Rezneck, *Unrecognized Patriots,* 15–16, 81–97, and for a summary of the controversy regarding the extent of Salomon's importance, 214–17, 229–35. For Salomon's commercial activities, see Nathan M. Kaganoff, "The Business Career of Hyam Salomon as Reflected in His Newspaper Advertisements," *American Jewish Historical Quarterly* 66 (1976–77): 35–49.

61. Ezra Stiles, *Literary Diary,* ed. F. B. Dexter (New York: Scribner's, 1901), 2:29, 151.

62. Rezneck, *Unrecognized Patriots,* 23, 61, 135–53.

63. Cited in Chyet, *Lopez of Newport,* 37–38.

Chapter Five. The Jewish Communities of the Early Republic

1. Jacob R. Marcus, "Jews and the American Revolution: A Bicentennial Documentary," *American Jewish Archives* 27 (1975): 151–55, 159–62, 174–75, 209–10.

2. Ira Rosenswaike, "An Estimate and Analysis of the Jewish Population of the United States in 1790," in *The Jewish Experience in America: Selected Studies from the Publications of the American Jewish Historical Society,* ed. Abraham J. Karp (Waltham and New York: American Jewish Historical Society and KTAV, 1969), 1:401–2. For further refinements, see Malcolm Stern, "Some Additions and Corrections to Rosenswaike's 'An Estimate and Analysis of the Jewish Population of the United States in 1790,'" *American Jewish Historical Quarterly* 53 (1963–64): 285–88; and Ira Rosenswaike, "Comments on Dr. Stern's Additions and Correction," *American Jewish Historical Quarterly* 53 (1963–64): 289–92.

3. Ira Rosenswaike, "The Jewish Population of the United States as Estimated from the Census of 1820," *American Jewish Historical Quarterly* 53 (1963–64): 136–45, 148, 159–75.

4. Zosa Szajkowski, "Jewish Emigration from Bordeaux during the Eighteenth and Nineteenth Centuries," *Jewish Social Studies* 18 (1956): 121–22. For the arrival of an immigrant from France or one of her possessions as early as 1782, see Jacob Rader Marcus, ed., *American Jewry—Documents—Eighteenth Century* (Cincinnati: Hebrew Union College Press, 1959), 121, recording the discussion in Philadelphia's congregation of an impoverished "French boy," of whom it was "Resolved: That he be relieved by subscription."

5. "Items Relating to Congregation Shearith Israel, New York," *Publications of the American Jewish Historical Society* 27 (1920): 73–78; Ira Rosenswaike, "The Jews of Baltimore to 1810," *American Jewish Historical Quarterly* 64 (1974–75): 315–18; Ira Rosenswaike, "The Jews of Baltimore: 1810 to 1820," *American Jewish Historical Quarterly* 67 (1977–78): 104, 108, 114–17.

6. Malcolm H. Stern, "The Sheftall Diaries: Vital Records of Savannah Jewry (1733–1808)," *American Jewish Historical Quarterly* 54 (1964–65): 252–53, 255, 268,

270; "Items Relating to Congregation Shearith Israel," 73–78. Seixas also officiated at the wedding of a couple from Surinam.

7. Edwin Wolf and Maxwell Whiteman, *The History of the Jews of Philadelphia from Colonial Times to the Age of Jackson* (Philadelphia: Jewish Publication Society of America, 1957), 121–22, 138–45.

8. Morris A. Gutstein, *The Story of the Jews of Newport: Two and a Half Centuries of Judaism, 1658–1908* (New York: Bloch, 1936), 191, 198–99, 216–17; Rosenswaike, "Jewish Population in 1790," 393–94; Rosenswaike, "Jewish Population of 1820," 141.

9. Rosenswaike, "Jews of Baltimore to 1810," 292–93; Malcolm H. Stern, "Two Jewish Functionaries in Colonial Pennsylvania," *American Jewish Historical Quarterly* 57 (1967–68): 33; David Brener, *The Jews of Lancaster, Pennsylvania: A Story with Two Beginnings* (Lancaster: Congregation Shaarai Shomayim and the Lancaster County Historical Society, 1979), vii–ix, 7, 19; Jerome H. Wood, Jr., *Conestoga Crossroads: Lancaster, Pennsylvania, 1730–1790* (Harrisburg: Pennsylvania Historical and Museum Commission, 1979), 154–56, 254.

10. Rosenswaike, "Jews of Baltimore to 1810," 295, 302, 302–8, 310, 312–14, 318–19; Rosenswaike, "Jews of Baltimore: 1810 to 1820," 101–3. The fact that Maryland did not extend religious toleration to Jews in its constitution, restricting it explicitly to Christians, may have also made the Jewish inhabitants dubious about remaining there long or building a synagogue. For the absence of civic equality for Jews in Maryland, see Stanley F. Chyet, "The Political Rights of the Jews in the United States: 1776–1840," in *Critical Studies in American Jewish History: Selected Articles from American Jewish Archives* (Cincinnati and New York: American Jewish Archives and KTAV, 1971), 2:41–42, 59–60.

11. Marcus, *American Jewry,* 144–46; Rosenswaike, "Jewish Population in 1790," 398; Rosenswaike, "Jewish Population of 1820," 138–39; Herbert T. Ezekiel and Gaston Lichtenstein, *The History of the Jews of Richmond from 1769 to 1917* (Richmond: Herbert T. Ezekiel, 1917), 29, 32; Myron Berman, *Richmond's Jewry, 1769–1976* (Charlottesville: University Press of Virginia, 1979), 38–40.

12. Stern, "Sheftall Diaries," 251–55, 265–68, 280–72, 275.

13. Marcus, *American Jewry* 172–80; Rosenswaike, "Jewish Population in 1790," 401; Rosenswaike, "Jewish Population of 1820," 140–41; Saul J. Rubin, *Third to None: The Saga of Savannah Jewry; 1733–1983* (Savannah: S. J. Rubin, 1983), 43, 45, 63–64.

14. Stern, "Sheftall Diaries," 253, 266–67, 270–72; Rosenswaike, "Jewish Population in 1790," 395, 400; Rosenswaike, "Jewish Population of 1820," 152; for immigrants from Amsterdam between 1807 and 1819, see Malcolm H. Stern, "South Carolina Jewish Marriage Settlements, 1785–1839," *National Genealogical Society Quarterly* 66 (1978): 110.

15. Charles Reznikoff and Uriah Engelman, *The Jews of Charleston: A History of an American Jewish Community* (Philadelphia: Jewish Publication Society

of America, 1950), 54–55; Samuel Rezneck, *Unrecognized Patriots: The Jews in the American Revolution* (Westport, Conn.: Greenwood, 1975), 47–49, 150–51, 154–55.

16. Leo Hershkowitz, "Some Aspects of the New York Jewish Merchant and Community, 1654–1820," *American Jewish Historical Quarterly* 66 (1976–77): 30, 32–34.

17. Rosenswaike, "Jews of Baltimore to 1810," 312, 320.

18. For an account of the mercantile career of Harmon Hendricks during the first two decades of the nineteenth century and the vicissitudes he encountered because of war, see Maxwell Whiteman, *Copper for America: The Hendricks Family and a National Industry, 1755–1939* (New Brunswick: Rutgers University Press, 1971), 46–69, 75–92. Hendricks was a member of the New York Jewish community.

19. John Hartog, "The Honen Dalim Congregation of St. Eustatius," *American Jewish Archives* 19 (1967): 65; Isaac S. Emmanuel and Suzanne A. Emmanuel, *History of the Jews of the Netherlands Antilles* (Cincinnati: American Jewish Archives, 1970), 1:301–2.

20. Marcus, *American Jewry*, 114–15, 128–30; Wolf and Whiteman, *Jews of Philadelphia*, 141.

21. Hyman B. Grinstein, *The Rise of the Jewish Community of New York, 1654–1860* (Philadelphia: Jewish Publication Society of America, 1945), 88, 105, 144, 338; David De Sola Pool, *The Mill Street Synagogue (1730–1817) of the Congregation Shearith Israel* (New York: n.p., 1930), 60–62. For the constitution and bylaws of 1790, see Marcus, *American Jewry*, 149–67. The constitution of 1805 is in Joseph L. Blau and Salo W. Baron, eds., *The Jews of the United States, 1790–1840: A Documentary History* (New York: Columbia University Press, 1963), 2:517–21.

22. Marcus, *American Jewry*, 153.

23. Ibid., 121–22; Wolf and Whiteman, *Jews of Philadelphia*, 120–21.

24. See Rubin, *Third to None*, 68, for identification of the organ's player; for the complete description of the ceremony, see Blau and Baron, *Jews of the United States*, 3:686–87.

25. Blau and Baron, *Jews of the United States*, 3:687–90.

26. Rachel Wischnitzer, *Synagogue Architecture in the United States: History and Interpretation* (Philadelphia: Jewish Publication Society of America, 1955), 20–22.

27. On this point generally, see Jonathan D. Sarna, "The Impact of the American Revolution on American Jews," in *The American Jewish Experience,* ed. Jonathan D. Sarna (New York: Holmes and Meier, 1986), 25–26.

28. Marcus, *American Jewry*, 116, 118, 128, 130.

29. Ibid., 149–50, 154–55.

30. Wischnitzer, *Synagogue Architecture*, 12; Marcus, *American Jewry*, 194–95.

31. Marcus, *American Jewry*, 128, 146, 177.

32. Ibid., 151, 157.

33. Ibid., 130, 146, 152, 180. In response to a new law of incorporation for

religious societies enacted by the New York State legislature in 1801, New York's congregation adopted a new constitution in 1805; for the procedures to amend it, see Blau and Baron, *Jews of the United States,* 2:519–20.

34. Wolf and Whiteman, *Jews of Philadelphia,* 150.

35. Jacob Rader Marcus, "The Handsome Young Priest in the Black Gown: The Personal World of Gershom Seixas," *Hebrew Union College Annual* 40–41 (1969–70): 427–30; "Items Relating to Gershom M. Seixas," *Publications of the American Jewish Historical Society* 27 (1920): 132, 137–38; Thomas Kessner, "Gershom Mendes Seixas: His Religious 'Calling,' Outlook and Competence," *American Jewish Historical Quarterly* 58 (1968–69): 455.

36. For the title *Reverend,* see, for example, the title page of his *Discourse Delivered in the Synagogue in New-York, on the Ninth of May, 1798, Observed as a Day of Humiliation, etc. etc. Conformably to a Recommendation of the President of the United States of America* (New York: Naphtali Judah, 1797 [sic]), where, as author, he is referred to as "Rev. G. Seixas."

37. Grinstein, *Jewish Community of New York,* 86.

38. Marcus, "Handsome Young Priest," 438, 445; Kessner, "Gershom Mendes Seixas," 468; Leon A. Jick, *The Americanization of the Synagogue, 1820–1870* (Hanover: University Press of New England, 1976), 10.

39. Marcus, *American Jewry,* 128–29, 162, 192–94. For regulation of the slaughterer in New York and his practices certifying meat as kosher, see "Items Relating to Congregation Shearith Israel," 84, 91.

40. "Items Relating to Congregation Shearith Israel," 51–55; Marcus, *American Jewry,* 162; Jacob I. Hartstein, "The Polonies Talmud Torah of New York," in Karp, *Jewish Experience in America,* 2:45.

41. Marcus, *American Jewry,* 121, 123–24, 126.

42. Ibid., 166, 179, 181; Blau and Baron, *Jews of the United States,* 2:552.

43. It should be noted, however, that a Shearith Israel rule in 1763 prohibited marriage with a convert; Marcus, *American Jewry,* 187.

44. Ibid., 129, 150, 158, 160–61; Blau and Baron, *Jews of the United States,* 2:551.

45. Hartstein, "Polonies Talmud Torah," 46–47; "Items Relating to Congregation Shearith Israel," 81–83.

46. Uriah Z. Engelman, "Jewish Education in Charleston, South Carolina, during the Eighteenth and Nineteenth Centuries," *Publications of the American Jewish Historical Society* 42 (1952–53): 52–53.

47. Marcus, *American Jewry,* 129; Grinstein, *Jewish Community of New York,* 335–38; Berman, *Richmond's Jewry,* 6–7.

48. Marcus, *American Jewry,* 179; "Items Relating to Congregation Shearith Israel," 54.

49. Grinstein, *Jewish Community of New York,* 104–5, 144; Myer Moses, *An Oration, Delivered before the Hebrew Orphan Society, on the 15th Day of October, 1806* (Charleston: Apollo, 1807), 23–26.

50. Solomon Breibart, "Two Jewish Congregations in Charleston, S.C., before 1791: A New Conclusion," *American Jewish History* 69 (1979–80): 360–63.

51. Jeanette W. Rosenbaum, "Hebrew German Society Rodeph Shalom in the City and County of Philadelphia (1800–1950)," *Publications of the American Jewish Historical Society* 41 (1951–52): 84–86; Edward Davis, *The History of Rodeph Shalom Congregation Philadelphia, 1802–1926* (Philadelphia: Edward Stein, 1926), 11–32.

52. Grinstein, *Jewish Community of New York,* 41–49.

53. Rosenswaike, "Jews of Baltimore: 1810 to 1820," 121–23.

Chapter Six. A Second Jerusalem?

1. Rev. G. Seixas, *Discourse, Delivered in the Synagogue in New-York, on the Ninth of May, 1798, Observed as a Day of Humiliation, etc. etc. Conformably to a Recommendation of the President of the United States of America* (New York: Naphtali Judah, 1797 [sic]), 23.

2. Myer Moses, *An Oration, Delivered before the Hebrew Orphan Society, on the 15th Day of October, 1806* (Charleston: Apollo, 1807), 6–7, 15, 18.

3. Morris U. Schappes, *A Documentary History of the Jews in the United States, 1654–1875,* 3d ed. (New York: Schocken, 1971), 154–55.

4. Jacob Neusner, "The Role of English Jews in the Development of American Jewish Life, 1775–1850," *YIVO Annual of Jewish Social Science* 12 (1958–59): 137.

5. Joseph L. Blau and Salo W. Baron, eds., *The Jews of the United States, 1790–1840: A Documentary History* (New York: Columbia University Press, 1963), 1:82. For Noah, see Jonathan D. Sarna, *Jacksonian Jew: The Two Worlds of Mordecai Noah* (New York: Holmes and Meier, 1981).

6. Jacob R. Marcus, "Jews and the American Revolution: A Bicentennial Documentary," *American Jewish Archives* 27 (1975): 124; Schappes, *Documentary History,* 67; *The Constitution of the State of New York* (Fishkill, 1777), 17, 18, 21–22.

7. Stanley F. Chyet, "The Political Rights of the Jews in the United States: 1776–1840," in *Critical Studies in American Jewish History: Selected Articles from American Jewish Archives* (Cincinnati and New York: American Jewish Archives and KTAV, 1971), 2:35–62. Delaware's elimination of its religious test for officeholding in 1792 indicates that it too embraced liberal principles regarding the place of religion in the civic order; ibid., 59.

8. Schappes, *Documentary History,* 77–84; Paul F. Boller, Jr., "George Washington and Religious Liberty," 3rd ser., *William and Mary Quarterly* 17 (1960): 503.

9. Blau and Baron, *Jews of the United States,* 1:60; Sarna, *Jacksonian Jew,* 9, 13, 27. Noah never did go to Riga.

10. Blau and Baron, *Jews of the United States,* 1:60; Saul J. Rubin, *Third to None: The Saga of Savannah Jewry, 1733–1983* (Savannah: S. J. Rubin, 1983), 88–91. For others who served in local offices, see Herbert T. Ezekiel and Gaston

Lichtenstein, *The History of the Jews of Richmond from 1769 to 1917* (Richmond: Herbert T. Ezekiel, 1917), 41–42, 63–66.

11. For the activities of Naphtali Phillips, Mordecai Noah, and Isaac Harby as political journalists in New York and Charleston, see Sarna, *Jacksonian Jew*, 4–5, 11, 35ff; and Blau and Baron, *Jews of the United States*, 2:315, 318–22. For others as members of political parties, see Morris U. Schappes, "Anti-Semitism and Reaction, 1795–1800," in *The Jewish Experience in America: Selected Studies from the Publications of the American Jewish Historical Society*, ed. Abraham J. Karp (Waltham, Mass., and New York: American Jewish Historical Society and KTAV, 1969), 1:368–69, 377.

12. "Items Relating to Congregation Shearith Israel, New York," *Publications of the American Jewish Historical Society* 27 (1920): 37–39; Blau and Baron, *Jews of the United States*, 2:517; Jacob Rader Marcus, ed., *American Jewry—Documents—Eighteenth Century* (Cincinnati: Hebrew Union College Press, 1959), 172–75; Neusner, "Role of English Jews," 137.

13. For examples, see Schappes, *Documentary History*, 151; Sarna, *Jacksonian Jew*, 55; and Moses, *Oration*, 18.

14. Moses, *Oration*, 18, 32.

15. Isaac M. Fein, "Niles Weekly Register on the Jews," *Publications of the American Jewish Historical Society* 50 (1960–61): 10.

16. Sarna, *Jacksonian Jew*, 63.

17. Schappes, *Documentary History*, 66.

18. Marcus, "Jews and the American Revolution," 241.

19. Blau and Baron, *Jews of the United States*, 1:91, 257.

20. George L. Berlin, "Solomon Jackson's *The Jew:* An Early American Jewish Response to the Missionaries," *American Jewish History* 71 (1981–82): 11, 16.

21. Schappes, *Documentary History*, 66, 583.

22. Ibid., 146, 156–57; Charles Reznikoff and Uriah Z. Engelman, *The Jews of Charleston: A History of an American Jewish Community* (Philadelphia: American Jewish Historical Society, 1950), 56; Blau and Baron, *Jews of the United States*, 1:12.

23. Marcus, "Jews and the American Revolution," 207; Reznikoff and Engelman, *Jews of Charleston*, 56.

24. David De Sola Pool, *The Mill Street Synagogue (1730–1817) of the Congregation Shearith Israel* (New York: N.p., 1930), 62; Schappes, *Documentary History*, 156–57; Blau and Baron, *Jews of the United States*, 1:12; Myron Berman, *Richmond's Jewry, 1769–1976* (Charlottesville: University Press of Virginia, 1979), 36.

25. Nathan M. Kaganoff, "An Early American Synagogue Desecration," *American Jewish Historical Quarterly* 58 (1968–69): 136; Isaac Kramnick, "The 'Great National Discussion': The Discourse of Politics in 1787," 3d ser., *William and Mary Quarterly* 45 (1988): 10–11.

26. Rubin, *Third to None*, 96–97; Jacob Rader Marcus, ed., *Memoirs of American Jews, 1775–1865* (Philadelphia: Jewish Publication Society of America, 1955–56), 1:85–86.

27. Edwin Wolf and Maxwell Whiteman, *The History of the Jews of Philadelphia from Colonial Times to the Age of Jackson* (Philadelphia: Jewish Publication Society of America, 1957), 110–13.

28. Fein, "Niles Weekly Register on the Jews," 8–9.

29. Wolf and Whiteman, *Jews of Philadelphia,* 111–12.

30. Schappes, *Documentary History,* 92–96.

31. Schappes, "Anti-Semitism and Reaction," 367–68, 382–84.

32. Schappes, *Documentary History,* 94–95.

33. For the episode described here, see Blau and Baron, *Jews of the United States,* 2:318–23; Sarna, *Jacksonian Jew,* 27–28. For Harby, see L. C. Moise, *Biography of Isaac Harby* (N.p.: Central Conference of American Rabbis, 1931).

34. The colonial charters of Connecticut and Rhode Island remained in effect until 1818 and 1842, respectively; Chyet, "Political Rights," 52, 54.

35. Marcus, "Jews and the American Revolution," 121–22; Schappes, *Documentary History,* 68–69, 79, 122–25.

36. Schappes, *Documentary History,* 65.

37. Ibid., 69.

38. Chyet, "Political Rights," 37–59, 62, 80.

39. Ibid., 53–62. For the struggle in Maryland, see, for example, Edward Eitches, "Maryland's 'Jew Bill,'" *American Jewish Historical Quarterly* 60 (1970–71): 258–79; and Blau and Baron, *Jews of the United States,* 1:33–55. For a general discussion of freedom of religion and civil disabilities in the immediate aftermath of the Revolution, see Allan Nevins, *The American States During and After the Revolution, 1755–1789* (New York: Macmillan, 1924), 420–41.

BIBLIOGRAPHICAL ESSAY

Primary Sources

Primary sources for the study of the Jewish people in America during the seventeenth and eighteenth centuries have been assembled and edited by Morris U. Schappes, *A Documentary History of the Jews of the United States, 1654–1875,* 3d ed. (New York: Schocken, 1971); and by Jacob Rader Marcus, *American Jewry—Documents—Eighteenth Century* (Cincinnati: Hebrew Union College Press, 1959). The records of the country's first congregation are published in *Publications of the American Jewish Historical Society* 21 (1913): 1–171 as "The Earliest Extant Minute Books of the Spanish and Portuguese Congregation Shearith Israel in New York, 1728–1786." Other Shearith Israel materials are published in the society's *Publications* 27 (1920), as are original records relevant to the Jews of Newport, records pertaining to Hazan Gershom Mendes Seixas and the Seixas family, and the illuminating commercial ledger attributed to Daniel Gomez. The personal correspondence of members of two of America's leading colonial Jewish families—a rich source of information on their lives, activities, and beliefs—may be read in Leo Hershkowitz and Isidore S. Meyer, eds., *The Lee Max Friedman Collection of American Jewish Colonial Correspondence: Letters of the Franks Family (1733–1748)* (Waltham, Mass.: American Jewish Historical Society (1968); and in William Vincent Byars, *B. and M. Gratz, Merchants in Philadelphia, 1754–1798* (Jefferson City: Hugh Stephens Printing, 1916). Personal statements of a different nature have been transcribed in Leo Hershkowitz, ed., *Wills of Early New York Jews (1704–1799)* (New York: American Jewish Historical Society, 1967). Malcolm Stern, ed., "The Sheftall Diaries: Vital Records of Savannah Jewry (1733–1808)," *American Jewish Historical Quarterly* 54 (1964-65): 243–77, is a rich source of information not only for the Jews of Savannah but for the Jewish inhabitants of eighteenth-century America generally.

For the late-eighteenth and early-nineteenth centuries, Jacob Rader Marcus, "The Jew and the American Revolution: A Bicentennial Documentary," *American Jewish Archives* 27 (1975): 103–257; and Jacob Rader Marcus, *Memoirs of American Jews 1775–1865,* vol. 1 (Philadelphia: Jewish Publication Society of America, 1955), are available. The collection of documents gathered by Joseph L. Blau and Salo W. Baron, *The Jews of the United States, 1790–1840: A Documentary History,* 3 vols. (New York: Columbia University Press, 1963), is particularly useful because of its extensive, well-written introductory notes and rich editorial apparatus.

Physical Artifacts

Physical artifacts are in their own right original sources. Rachel Wischnitzer, *Synagogue Architecture in the United States: History and Interpretation* (Philadelphia: Jewish Publication Society of America, 1955) contains excellent reproductions of early America's synagogues. For the important Newport synagogue, the illustrations (and discussions) in Carl Bridenbaugh, *Peter Harrison, First American Architect* (Chapel Hill: University of North Carolina Press, 1949); and in Nancy Halverson Schless, "Peter Harrison, the Touro Synagogue, and the Wren City Church," *Winterthur Portfolio 8* (Charlottesville: University of Virginia Press, 1973), 187–200, bear examination. For portraiture, see Hannah R. London, *Portraits of Jews by Gilbert Stuart and Other Early American Artists* (New York: William Edwin Rudge, 1927); and, assembled by the same author, *Miniatures of Early American Jews* (Springfield: Pond-Ekberg, 1953).

Secondary Sources

Among the secondary sources devoted to early American Jewry, the works of Jacob Rader Marcus are preeminent, providing the fullest coverage and deeply influencing all subsequent works on the subject, including the present one. In *Early American Jewry,* 2 vols. (Philadelphia: Jewish Publication Society of America, 1951–53), and *The Colonial American Jew, 1492–1776,* 3 vols. (Detroit: Wayne State University Press, 1970), Marcus explores virtually every aspect of the subject with richness in detail, texture, and context. In volume 1 of *United States Jewry 1776–1985* (Detroit: Wayne State University Press, 1989), a projected three-volume work, he extends his description and analysis to the period between 1776 and 1840.

Histories of Local Communities

For the histories of local communities, though they are of widely varying quality and must often be used with caution, see Morris A. Gutstein,

The Story of the Jews of Newport: Two and a Half Centuries of Judaism, 1658–1908 (New York: Bloch, 1936); Edwin Wolf and Maxwell Whiteman, *The History of the Jews of Philadelphia from Colonial Times to the Age of Jackson* (Philadelphia: Jewish Publication Society of America, 1957); David Brener, *The Jews of Lancaster, Pennsylvania: A Story with Two Beginnings* (Lancaster: Congregation Shaarai Shomayim and the Lancaster County Historical Society, 1979); Herbert T. Ezekiel and Gaston Lichtenstein, *The History of the Jews of Richmond from 1769 to 1917* (Richmond: Herbert T. Ezekiel, 1917); Myron Berman, *Richmond's Jewry, 1769–1976* (Charlottesville: University Press of Virginia, 1979); Barnett A. Elzas, *The Jews of South Carolina, from the Earliest Times to the Present Day* (Philadelphia: Lippincott, 1905); Charles Reznikoff and Uriah Z. Engelman, *The Jews of Charleston: A History of an American Jewish Community* (Philadelphia: Jewish Publication Society of America, 1950); Solomon Breibart, "The Synagogues of Kahal Kadosh Beth Elohim, Charleston," *South Carolina Historical Magazine* 80 (1979): 215–35; Saul J. Rubin, *Third to None: The Saga of Savannah Jewry, 1733–1983* (Savannah: S. J. Rubin, 1983); and David T. Morgan, "Judaism in Eighteenth-Century Georgia," *Georgia Historical Quarterly* 58 (1972–73): 41–54.

Although not a history of the Jewish community, Jerome H. Wood, Jr., *Conestoga Crossroads: Lancaster, Pennsylvania, 1730–1790* (Harrisburg: Pennsylvania Historical and Museum Commission, 1979), is a first-rate local history and is highly informative regarding the Jews who settled there. For Baltimore, Ira Rosenswaike's "The Jews of Baltimore to 1810," *American Jewish Historical Quarterly* 64 (1974–75): 291–320, and his "The Jews of Baltimore, 1810 to 1820," *American Jewish Historical Quarterly* 67 (1977–78): 101–24, must be consulted. For the all-important New York Jewish community, see Hyman B. Grinstein, *The Rise of the Jewish Community of New York, 1654–1860* (Philadelphia: Jewish Publication Society of America, 1945); David De Sola Pool, *The Mill Street Synagogue (1730–1817) of the Congregation Shearith Israel* (New York: N.p., 1930); and Pool's much larger history, *An Old Faith in the New World: Portrait of Shearith Israel, 1654–1954* (New York: Columbia University Press, 1955).

Biographies

For the biographies of individual Jewish residents of early America, see Stanley F. Chyet, *Lopez of Newport: Colonial American Merchant Prince* (Detroit: Wayne State University Press, 1970); Leon Huhner, *The Life of Judah Touro (1775–1854)* (Philadelphia: Jewish Publication Society of America, 1946); Jonathan D. Sarna, *Jacksonian Jew: The Two Worlds of Mordecai Noah* (New York: Holmes and Meier, 1981); and Maxwell Whiteman, *Copper for America: The Hendricks Family and a National Industry, 1755–1939* (New Brunswick: Rutgers University Press, 1971). The biography of Gershom Mendes Seixas has as yet not been written, but for aspects of the life and activities of America's first native-born hazan, see Jacob Rader Marcus, "The Handsome Young Priest in the Black Gown: The Personal World of Gershom Seixas," *Hebrew Union College Annual* 40-41 (1969–70): 409–67, and Thomas Kessner, "Gershom Mendes Seixas: His Religious 'Calling,' Outlook and Competence," *American Jewish Historical Quarterly* 58 (1968–69): 445–71. Seixas's life is sketched as well in David De Sola Pool, *Portraits Etched in Stone: Early Jewish Settlers, 1682–1831* (New York: Columbia University Press, 1952), which has the virtue of describing not only the prominent but also the lesser-known individuals who lie buried in New York's oldest Jewish cemetery. An adequate biography of Isaac Harby also remains to be written, but L. C. Moise, *Biography of Isaac Harby* (N.p.: Central Conference of American Rabbis, 1931), provides a starting point.

Genealogies

Genealogies, indispensable for the study of demography, marriage patterns, and other issues related to family history, have been compiled and synthesized from many sources in Malcolm Stern, *Americans of Jewish Descent: A Compendium of Genealogy* (Cincinnati: Hebrew Union College Press, 1960). Stern's essay, "The Function of Genealogy in American Jewish History," in *Essays in American Jewish History to Commemorate the Tenth Anniversary of the Founding of the American Jewish Archives under the Direction of Jacob Rader Marcus* (Cincinnati: American Jewish Archives, 1958), 69–97, summarizes his conclusions about marriages based upon the genealogical records, while his "South Carolina Jewish Marriage Settlements, 1785–1839," *National Genealogical Society Quarterly* 66 (1978): 105–11, provides helpful supplementary data. For a quick genealogical guide, Joseph R. Rosenbloom, *A Biographical Dictionary of Early American Jews, Colonial Times through 1801* (Lexington: University of Kentucky Press, 1960) may be consulted.

Specialized Studies

Specialized studies of many aspects of early American Jewish history include, for demography, Uriah Z. Engelman, "The Jewish Population of Charleston: What Stunted Its Growth and Retarded Its Decline?" *Jewish Social Studies* 13 (1951): 195–210; Ira Rosenswaike, "An Estimate and Analysis of the Jewish Population of the United States in 1790," in *The Jewish*

Experience in America: Selected Studies from the Publications of the American Jewish Historical Society, ed. Abraham J. Karp (Waltham, Mass., and New York: American Jewish Historical Society and KTAV, 1969), 1:391–403; and Ira Rosenswaike, "The Jewish Population of the United States as Estimated from the Census of 1820," *American Jewish Historical Quarterly* 53 (1963–64): 131–78.

For the commercial activities of the Jewish settlers, the following, in addition to the biographies cited above, provide insights: Miriam K. Freund, *Jewish Merchants in Colonial America* (New York: Behrman's Jewish Book House, 1939); Virginia B. Platt, "Tar Staves and New England Rum: The Trade of Aaron Lopez of Newport, Rhode Island with Colonial North Carolina," *North Carolina Historical Review* 48 (1971): 1–22; Leo Hershkowitz, "Some Aspects of the New York Jewish Merchant and Community, 1654–1820," *American Jewish Historical Quarterly* 66 (1976–77): 10–34; Leon Huhner, "Daniel Gomez, A Pioneer Merchant of Early New York," *Publications of the American Jewish Historical Society* 41 (1951–52): 107–25; Thomas J. Tobias, "Charles Town in 1764," *South Carolina Historical Magazine* 67 (1966): 63–74; Thomas J. Tobias, "Joseph Tobias of Charles Town: Linguister," *Publications of the American Jewish Historical Society* 49 (1959–60): 33–38; and Nathan M. Kaganoff, "The Business Career of Hyam Salomon as Reflected in his Newspaper Advertisements," *American Jewish Historical Quarterly* 66 (1976–77): 35–49.

The Larger Community

Studies that illuminate the relationship between the early American Jewish population and the larger community include Robert M. Healey, "Jefferson on Judaism and the Jews: 'Divided We Stand, United We Fall!'" *American Jewish History* 73 (1983–84): 359–74; Louis Harap, *The Image of the Jew in American Literature: From Early Republic to Mass Immigration* (Philadelphia: Jewish Publication Society of America, 1974); and Louis Harap, "Image of the Jew in American Drama, 1794 to 1823," *American Jewish Historical Quarterly* 60 (1970–71): 242–57. Samuel Rezneck, *Unrecognized Patriots: The Jews in the American Revolution* (Westport, Conn.: Greenwood, 1975), successfully synthesizes an accumulation of material regarding Jewish participation on both sides of the struggle and provides an excellent summary of the arguments about the place of Hyam Salomon in the Revolution's history. For their political position, see Stanley F. Chyet, "The Political Rights of the Jews in the United States: 1776–1840," in *Critical Studies in American Jewish History: Selected Articles from American Jewish Archives* (Cincinnati and New York: American Jewish Archives and KTAV, 1971),

2:27–88; Edward Eitches, "Maryland's Jew Bill," *American Jewish Historical Quarterly* 60 (1970–71): 258–79; and Richard B. Morris, "Civil Liberties and the Jewish Tradition in Early America, in *The Jewish Experience in America: Selected Studies from the Publications of the American Jewish Historical Society,* ed. Abraham J. Karp, 1:404–23. For developments after the Revolution, see Jonathan D. Sarna, "The Impact of the American Revolution on American Jews," in *The American Jewish Experience,* ed. Jonathan D. Sarna (New York: Holmes and Meier, 1986); and Morris U. Schappes, "Anti-Semitism and Reaction, 1785–1800," in Karp, *Jewish Experience in America,* 1:362–90.

General

Finally, the journal published by the American Jewish Historical Society during its first century of existence contains a wealth of relevant articles, many of them cited in the present work. Volumes 1–50 (1893–1961) are entitled *Publications of the American Jewish Historical Society,* while volumes 51–67 (1961–78) are called *American Jewish Historical Quarterly.* Issues from 1978 to the present (volumes 68–80) are published under the title *American Jewish History.* Articles of particular importance have been republished in *The Jewish Experience in America: Selected Studies from the Publications of the American Jewish Historical Society,* ed. Abraham J. Karp, 5 vols. (Waltham, Mass., and New York: American Jewish Historical Society and KTAV, 1969); and in *The Jewish Experience in Latin America: Selected Studies from the Publications of the American Jewish Historical Society,* ed. Martin A. Cohen, 2 vols. (Waltham, Mass., and New York: American Jewish Historical Society and KTAV, 1971). The first two volumes of the former and the second volume of the latter republish articles relevant to the period covered in the present work.

INDEX

ABOUT THE AMERICAN
JEWISH HISTORICAL SOCIETY

THE TWENTIETH CENTURY has been a period of change for the American Jewish community, bringing growth in numbers and in status and, most important, a new perception of itself as part of the history of the United States. The American Jewish Historical Society has also grown over the century, emerging as a professional historical association with a depth of scholarship that enables it to redefine what is *American* and what is *Jewish* in the American saga. To record and examine this saga and to honor its own centennial, the society has published this five-volume series, *The Jewish People in America.*

The society was founded on 7 June 1892 in New York City, where it was housed in two crowded rooms in the Jewish Theological Seminary. At the first meeting, its president Cyrus Adler declared that it was the patriotic duty of every ethnic group in America to record its contributions to the country. Another founding father emphasized the need to popularize such studies "in order to stem the growing anti-Semitism in this country." As late as the 1950s, the society was encouraging young doctoral students in history to research and publish material of Jewish interest, even though such research, according to Rabbi Isidore Meyer, then the society's librarian, would impede the writers' advancement in academia. In this climate, the early writings in the society's journal, *Publications of the American Jewish Historical Society,* were primarily the work of amateurs; they were narrowly focused, often simply a re-counting of the deeds of the writers' ancestors. However, these studies did bring to light original data of great importance to subsequent historians and constitute an invaluable corpus of American Jewish historiography.

The situation has changed materially. One hundred years later, the society has its own building on the campus of Brandeis University; the building houses the society's office space, exhibit area, and library. The Academic Council of the society includes sixty-three professors of American history whose primary interest is American Jewish history. Articles in the society's publication, now called *American Jewish History,* meet the highest professional standards and are often presented at the annual meeting of the American Historical Association. The society has also published an extensive series of monographs, which culminates in the publication of these volumes. The purpose of *The Jewish People in America* series is to provide a comprehensive historical study of the American Jewish experience from the age of discovery to the present time that both satisfies the standards of the historical profession and holds the interest of the intelligent lay reader.

Dr. Abraham Kanof
Past President
American Jewish Historical Society
and Chairman
The Jewish People in America Project